Redefining Irishness in a Maine City, 1770–1870

Redefining Irishness in a Coastal Maine City, 1770–1870: Bridget's Belfast examines how Irish immigrants shaped and reshaped their identity in a rural New England community. Forty percent of Irish immigrants to the United States settled in rural areas. Achieving success beyond large urban centers required distinctive ways of performing Irishness. Class, status, and gender were more significant than ethnicity. Close reading of diaries, newspapers, local histories, and public papers allows for a nuanced understanding of immigrant lives amid stereotype and the nineteenth-century evolution of a Scotch-Irish identity.

Kay Retzlaff is Professor of English at the University of Maine at Augusta.

Routledge Advances in American History

For more information about this series, please visit: https://www.routledge.com/
Routledge-Advances-in-American-History/book-series/RAAH

Redefining Irishness in a Coastal Maine City, 1770–1870

Bridget's Belfast

Kay Retzlaff

Routledge
Taylor & Francis Group

NEW YORK AND LONDON

First published 2022
by Routledge
605 Third Avenue, New York, NY 10158

and by Routledge
2 Park Square, Milton Park, Abingdon, Oxon, OX14 4RN

*Routledge is an imprint of the Taylor & Francis Group, an
informa business*

© 2022 Kay Retzlaff

Library of Congress Cataloging-in-Publication Data
Names: Retzlaff, Kay, author.
Title: Redefining Irishness in a coastal Maine city, 1770-1870 :
Bridget's Belfast / Kay Retzlaff.
Description: New York, NY : Routledge Taylor & Francis Group,
2022. |
Series: Routledge advances in American History; vol 20 | Includes
bibliographical references and index.
Subjects: LCSH: Belfast (Me.)--History--19th century. |
Irish--Maine--Belfast--Ethnic identity. |
Irish--Maine--Belfast--History--19th century. |
Irish Americans--Maine--Belfast--History--19th century. |
Maine–History--1775-1865. | Belfast (Me.)--Social life and
customs. | Belfast (Me.)--Ethnic relations.
Classification: LCC F29.B5 R48 2022 (print) |
LCC F29.B5 (ebook) | DDC 305.8916/2074152--dc23
LC record available at https://lccn.loc.gov/2021034114
LC ebook record available at https://lccn.loc.gov/2021034115

ISBN: 978-1-032-03506-2 (hbk)
ISBN: 978-1-032-03507-9 (pbk)
ISBN: 978-1-003-18766-0 (ebk)

DOI: 10.4324/9781003187660

Typeset in Sabon
by MPS Limited, Dehradun

View from Primrose Hill of Belfast, Maine, Harbor, 1868. Courtesy of the Belfast Historical Society and Museum.

Contents

Figures

Acknowledgments

Many people have helped on this project. The following two people deserve special thanks: Megan Pinette, president of the Belfast Historical Society and Museum, and Betsy Paradis, former Reference and Special Collections librarian at the Belfast Free Library (now the Local History and Special Collections librarian at Bangor Public Library). Thanks, too, to Cipperly Good, Richard Saltonstall Jr. Curator of Maritime History at the Penobscot Marine Museum; Cheryl Coats, nineteenth-century archivist at the Waldo County Courthouse; Father Mark Reinhardt and Kathleen Gross and Kathleen Benedict, St. Brendan the Navigator Parish staff, who provided a quiet room, a clean table, and boxes of wonderful old parish documents to study; the librarians at Special Collections at the University of Maine Fogler Library; and University of Maine at Augusta library staff, especially Lisa Feldman, Andrea Thorne, and Cynthia Young, who tracked down hard-to-find resources. The Maine Historical Society in Portland and the Massachusetts Historical Society in Boston collections, with their lovely reading rooms, have been a researcher's dream. Thanks, one and all.

Go raibh maith agat, Dr. Nollaig MacCongáil, friend and colleague, who provided me library privileges at James Hardiman Library, National University Ireland–Galway, and who introduced me to Margaret Hughes, library assistant in Special Collections, who allowed me access to the nineteenth-century newspaper collection. Dr. Alan Taylor graciously allowed me to quote extensively from his edited *Early Histories of Belfast, Maine*. First Church Congregational has allowed me to quote from their parish records housed at the Belfast Free Library. Thank you, to the Reverend Joel Krueger, for his help in securing permission to use church documents, and to Dr. Thomas Maycock, M.D., who translated nineteenth-century medical jargon into modern terminology. My anonymous readers provided valuable insights and advice. Thank you, one and all. Portions of this work were previously published in *Maine History* 51, no. 1 (Winter 2016–17): 109–130.

The University of Maine at Augusta (UMA) has supported my research, helping defray cost as I traveled to American Conference for Irish Studies (ACIS) conferences. Special thanks to colleagues who have commented on my papers at ACIS. UMA awarded me a Trustees Fellowship Summer 2009, which allowed me to hire a research assistant. Justin Fowler went through real estate transaction files and probate records. UMA also awarded me a sabbatical in 2010/11, so I could do more thorough research. Then-Provost Josh Nadel and then-Dean Peggy Danielson were most supportive of my endeavors. Thanks, too, to colleagues who supported the work by taking over my responsibilities: The late Nancy Schneider drove to Bangor weekly to take over my professional writing class while I was on sabbatical; Sarah Hentges covered my women's studies courses; Marcia Mower covered my advising obligations; Harry Batty, Christopher Bates, and Barbara Pincus covered my committee responsibilities. Bless you. Thank you, too, to the great staff at Routledge for their guidance and good cheer: Max Novick, Senior Editor, Jennifer Morrow, Senior Editorial Assistant, Anjali Kukreti, Project Manager, Sunila M., Copyeditor and team.

Thanks, too, go to my mother Jeanne Carrick Retzlaff, who instilled in me a love of all things Irish when she handed down the stories of my great-grandmother Cate and my great-great-grandmother Bridget. Thank you, Thomas Ross McCord, sounding board and editor. I love your love of words.

Any defects, however, are my responsibility alone.

Prologue

Why study the history of the Irish in a small city on Penobscot Bay in the rural state of Maine? How can a micro-historical study prove useful? The answer at first is simple: A micro approach has maneuverability in ways larger studies do not. In addition, Belfast, Maine, has extensive records. Those materials provide migration routes once immigrants took up residence, for example, or discuss in detail the local gender norms and so forth. In other words, the micro-historical view gives a close-up on individual Irish immigrant lives in ways that "big screen" studies cannot. This is a way to look at immigration on an individual basis rather than as part of a bloc movement and to look at ethnicity (and culture) from a household perspective rather than from a political, congregational, or nationalist stance.

The more extensive answer is that global Irish migration affected America, especially New England and the Maritimes early. Seasonal migratory work brought Irish workers to cod fisheries annually. These trans-Atlantic business networks were long established before the economics of the eighteenth and nineteenth centuries made permanent immigration desirable. Yet those who settled in Belfast, Maine, in 1770 came as family groups via New Hampshire's Londonderry, Derry, Windham, and environs, with a handful of single men in the advance guard. Roughly four dozen shareholders purchased the site of Belfast from the heirs of the late General Samuel Waldo of Massachusetts, who held the patent. Some of the investors viewed the purchase of shares as an investment; others saw it as a new start. Immigrants from Ireland in the nineteenth century also came as families. Unlike those who settled in urban enclaves, which allowed them to retain old-world cultural norms in multigenerational groupings, those who came to Belfast spread out—the area was theirs to create. (The British seized Native Penobscot rights to the area at the end of the French and Indian War in 1763.) A second migration of American-born Irish merchants and lawyers occurred in Belfast after the American Revolution and before the War of 1812, looking for wealth, position, and power. These migrants were educated in the professions or adept at commerce. Individuals in the

DOI: 10.4324/9781003187660-101

third migration, which took place in the early to mid-nineteenth century, sometimes made stops in other places in America before coming to Belfast. William Brannagan, from Ashbourne, County Meath, for example, sailed to Philadelphia from Ireland. From Philadelphia, he moved to Boston, thence to Belfast (because of mercantile networks). He spent the rest of his long life in Belfast and was buried there.

Some members of the settlement group of 1770 traced their heritage to Ulster. The migration to the mid-coast area of Maine by descendants of this group, however, was a secondary (if not tertiary) migration, as families had been in New Hampshire fifty years by 1770. Only two of the people who formed the Belfast settlement were born in Ireland, for example: John Mitchell and James Miller, both of whom left Ulster when they were small children. The remainder of the group were first-, second-, and third-generation American-born people of Irish extraction. Perhaps the easiest way to envision the migrants to the Belfast area is to think in terms of a modern metaphor. The migrants head out from a "sending" community and arrive in "receiving" communities. The migrants, like software, come with cultural codes; however, their children rewrite those codes. Therefore, if parents are generation 1, children born in the sending community but raised in the receiving community are generation 1.5, and children born in the receiving community are generation 2.[1] At any one time all three versions could have occupied the same dwelling, and like a number of computer programs, sometimes the hardware might not have recognized the newest software. When the second generation acculturated more rapidly than its parents, it could create dissonance; however, there were instances of consonant acculturation—times when second-generation children and their parents moved at the same rate. This might have happened only in gateway city enclaves where the "old culture" from the sending culture could have been maintained more readily. Smaller and more rural communities might not have provided such a luxury. Perhaps immigrants could adapt to the receiving culture more readily in such an environment. The questions are how and to what extent? What form of Americanism did these immigrants to Belfast, Maine, create? How did their economic realities affect their creation? Only wealthy immigrants could afford to keep transnational ties vibrant.[2] Gateway cities, such as Boston, always led to concentrations of immigrants. Did the "middling" types really tend to stay home?[3] The migratory record of Belfast disproves this adage—it was precisely the middling types who continued to migrate.

Belfast, then, offers a chance to look at three waves of Irish immigration closely over the course of a century. The language used to set up categories, define terms, and apply labels must be carefully refined, including precisely what *Irish* and *Irishness* mean. For example, what similarities and/or contrasts existed among the three waves of Belfast's immigrants or migrants? The smaller canvas also allows a discussion of how we ascertain who is and is not Irish or how they perform Irishness—or not. The tools used to date have been inadequate.

Surnames, for instance, are supposed to provide vital clues about who is Irish. If only things could be so easily defined! Consider that John Kennedy (the name Americans recognize as the first Irish American Catholic U.S. president) was also the name of an eighteenth-century Presbyterian minister in Ulster.[4] On the other hand, the Reverend William McDonald, whose name seems quintessentially Scottish, was a pioneer Catholic priest in Manchester, New Hampshire, in the 1840s, who exhibited stereotypical Irish behavior, including "the Irishman's love for bright repartee or good story.... And all in the sweetest of English; that is, slightly tinctured with the Irish brogue."[5] Names, ultimately, tell us nothing about religious affiliation, and religious affiliation tells us very little about ethnicity.

Using surnames as indices of ethnic origins, then, is rife with difficulties.[6] Ireland, like all nations, is the sum of many *races,* although the supposed Celtic had widespread influence.[7] Mac and Mc don't really designate ethnic difference.[8] Mac is Gaelic for "son of," whether the name is found in Ireland or Scotland. Mc is merely an abbreviation of Mac. English settlers took Irish names, and Irish families were compelled to adopt English surnames during Ireland's turbulent history. Families of Scandinavian origin also took Irish surnames, prefixing O and Mac, so that it is next to impossible to pick out their names. (In my own family there are McKeevers, for example, from Mac Ivor/Ibhor.) There are Anglo-Norman names, such as Fitzgerald, FitzMaurice, and FitzSimmons, and Welsh, Cornish, Scottish, Huguenot, German Palatinate, and Jewish names in Ireland.[9] Surname, then, is not an adequate signifier of ethnicity.[10] Thus, making assumptions about religious affiliation, nationalist tendencies, and cultural and ethnic affiliations based on names and area of origin leads to utter confusion.[11] Even city names should be taken with the traditional modicum of salt. In Maine, for example, naming a city for some exotic place was popular: China, Maine, was not so named by an Asian community. Cities such as Londonderry, New Hampshire, and Belfast, Maine, also deserve closer inspection. This book provides that inspection by examining private performances of Irishness, which encompasses a range of people and evolving identities from settlement beginnings in the eighteenth through the nineteenth centuries. It looks at how Irish identity was negotiated in rural areas differently from America's city landscapes. Individuals' stories take precedence in answering some important questions: How did gender, class, and status affect or influence newcomers' reception by old-timers? How secure was the Presbyterian–Catholic divide in establishing ethnic identity? How did stereotype—and the reaction of the newcomers to those stereotypes—help create an Irish American identity? How did Ulster Presbyterians—and their descendants—establish the American Scotch-Irish origin mythology? How was migration or movement tied to acculturation?

Irish immigration to America was of biblical proportions—at least a number of writers have so proclaimed. Kerby Miller drew attention to this tendency of using mythological language in *Emigrants and Exiles: Ireland and the Irish Exodus to North America* (1985). The plight of the Irish has been compared to Moses leading the Hebrews out of Egypt in an *exodus* or as being akin to the destruction of the Temple at Jerusalem and the *exile* of the tribes of Israel into the Babylonian Captivity. Even the term *diaspora*, taken from the Jewish dispersal across the globe because of a loss of homeland and centuries of prejudice among receiving cultures, has been co-opted to discuss Irish (and others') immigration worldwide.[12] For example, Wilkins Updike's *A History of the Episcopal Church in Narragansett, Rhode Island: Including a History of Other Episcopal Churches in the State*, published in 1907, offers a prevalent thought of his day—that all nations were somehow connected to the Jewish nation because of the Tribes of the Dispersion. This, too, was a theme throughout Europe in the Middle Ages.[13] This freighted language continues to be used, especially in comparative studies of Irish immigration worldwide.[14]

There has long been a presumption that the immigrant Irish in America were urbanites, shunning farming and/or rural places; however, looking at the Irish diaspora worldwide challenges that notion. Vast numbers of studies on the Irish in urban settings are available, and, given that 60 percent of Irish immigrants settled in cities, such studies are appropriate. Yet 40 percent of Irish immigrants settled in rural areas. It behooves students of the Irish in America to consider the lives of those who settled in places away from those sometimes comforting confines of "Irish" neighborhoods in large urban areas. A study of a small city in a rural area helps explain how the reality of immigration was distinctive. A number of studies of urban Irish immigrants have focused upon the Irish as a group, as a bloc, working together on a project that declaimed in a very public way—"We made it!" Scholars have looked at the political Irish, especially how nationalism traveled back and forth across the Atlantic and around the world with former political prisoners. Such works discuss how the American Irish were "mined," for example, to provide money for the nationalist cause in Ireland. The paperwork surrounding this public performance of Irish identity is massive—and scholars have dug into troves of Irish political newspapers and/or Catholic newspapers. A major problem with any one of these approaches is that they privilege urban life. Mid-twentieth-century sociological studies of immigration also critiqued this approach, positing that ethnic communities were American creations, something new, "not an old world survival." Over the course of the twentieth century, research projects have

> tended to take ethnic communities—places—as opposed to indivi-
> dually experienced adaptation—immigrant lifecourses [*sic*]—as

[their] object of inquiry, and that has tended to focus precisely on those kinds of places—areas of concentrated first-generation settlement—where the odds of finding evidence for ethnic maintenance are greatest.[15]

One such study—a landmark—is Oscar Handlin's *Boston's Immigrants: A Study in Acculturation*, published just at the outset of World War II, which focused on the relationships among Boston Irish neighborhoods, the Catholic Church, and politics.[16] His approach linked ethnic with religious identities. He looked at how quickly (or not) Irish Catholic immigrants and their progeny achieved success in American society. His book was reprinted in 1959, just as John Fitzgerald Kennedy was poised to become the thirty-fifth president of the United States. President Kennedy became the prime example of Catholic Irish accomplishment in America, yet Handlin's study of class surmised that as immigrants were acculturated into the new society, they ceased to be Irish.

In Handlin's view, the Irish in Boston were "doomed to failure from the start."[17] The sign of that failure was servant-class status—taking care of horses; serving as grocers, butchers, fruiterers, peddlers, saloonkeepers, restaurateurs; or running boarding houses and/or hotels.[18] This class-based approach privileged white-collar (or middling class) status; the fact is that people with little to no education *were able to find work* in the service industry. Handlin argued that the immigrants from Ireland "brought with them an awareness of group identity already sharpened by cultural contact with other peoples," evidently seeing Irish interaction with the English as providing a sense of Irish selfhood.[19] Other scholars have disagreed with this supposition, pointing out that mid-nineteenth-century immigrants saw themselves as Corkonians, Galwegians, Dubliners, and so forth—the faction fights on American job sites serving as evidence.[20]

Discussions of public displays of Irishness have continued unabated since Handlin's work. Timothy Meagher looked at Irish Catholic immigrant groups coming together to raise a church building, for example, in *Inventing Irish America: Generation, Class, and Ethnic Identity in a New England City, 1880–1928* (1986). Stress on these public building projects has sometimes reduced evidence of ethnicity to a religious struggle between Catholicism and Protestantism, with these two strains of Christianity serving as separate categories of ethnicity, culture, and race. Meagher has contended that Irish and Catholic were inseparable.[21]

Carl Wittke was one of the first in the twentieth century to take issue with the Irish equals Catholic and Protestant equals Scotch equations; he was suspicious that such easy definitions gave "undue attention to ... one chapter, however important, in the story of the Irish in America."[22] He also found the categories of Irish (meaning Catholic), Scotch-Irish (meaning Protestant Irish), and Anglo-Saxon (meaning English) problematic; however, his introduction of the term "Celt" did not solve the problems of defining ethnicity or culture. His reliance on cultural markers to define Irishness, while interesting as a concept, did not, ultimately, explain the difference between stereotype and cultural inheritance. As Celt and/or Gael entered the discussion, scholars pointed out these terms presupposed a unified people where there was none. And, unfortunately, the new paradigm was simply Celt and/or Gael equals Irish Catholic.[23] Some studies have focused on the category *Celt* as it was used in the nineteenth century by Young Irelanders, for example; however, those studies have to acknowledge that, as used, it was euphemism for Irish Catholic.[24] Terms such as American Celts, American-born Irish, Celtic American, or native-stock Americans are created with a premise that implies that such categories are clear-cut.[25] The terms Celt/Celtic are thus fraught with as many difficulties as are surnames. While scholars might see Celtic as a group with a shared culture and/or ethnic characteristics living on the Atlantic seaboard of Europe, the term has been reworked and appropriated in recent years.[26] Ultimately, the term has come to mean "not English":

> Running through all these conceptions of Celticism, it is possible to see a continuous one-dimensional, oppositional definition, centred on the idea of being "not English"—a homogenizing outlook that has sought to shoehorn people and cultures into a common Celtic brotherhood defined by racial characteristics.[27]

There is no such thing as a "pure" race. In addition to Celtic and/or Gaelic, there was, as mentioned, Viking, Norman, English, Scottish, and other influence in Ireland, for example. Each group brought its own cultural markers into Irish society and culture—and the resulting mélange is *Irishness*.

The idea of the Irish being a people and a religion at the same time also draws heavily on the Jewish model again and completely ignores the reality that Christians are made, not born. People affiliate—or do not—with a sect of Christianity based on personal choice arrived at via familial, educational, political, and economic realities. The Reverend James MacSparran can serve as the example par excellence of the perils of such classification systems: Born in County Londonderry, where nearly half the population was Irish-speaking and Catholic, he was reared by his Presbyterian minister uncle; however, the family had Scottish Catholic roots. MacSparran became a Presbyterian minister, but later changed affiliation to the Church of Ireland and was ordained in England, and then served as a Congregational minister in Rhode Island for the duration of his career.[28] On the subject of religious affiliation's ties to ethnicity, Meagher has agreed with the observation that people change over time and we need to know more—about immigrants' class, status, education, profession, family, geographic location, and religion (including whether or not individuals were devout practitioners or merely on the rolls).[29] This book tries to do that.

Donald Akenson, *The Irish Diaspora: A Primer* (1996), agreed that equating Irish with Catholic and Gaelic is a problem. Akenson defined anyone born in Ireland as Irish, taking issue with the idea that emigrants had had no agency in their decisions to leave. He saw Kerby Miller's use of the word "exile" as erasing agency.[30] David Noel Doyle objected to this point as well.[31] Scholars have argued that before the famine, Irish emigrants went to Britain and America looking for higher wages and seeking greater social mobility and higher living standards.[32] In other words, the Irish were their own agents of change—making economic decisions for themselves and family members. Irish commercial networks have been trans-Atlantic for a very long time, and there was little victimization about it.[33] The southern counties of Ireland had a long-standing culture of seasonal migratory labor to the Newfoundland fisheries, for example. A number of firms stretched across the Atlantic, including that of Francis Anderson, who immigrated to Boston in the late 1790s and then to Belfast, Maine, around 1800. He came from County Down; his relationship to the Anderson, Child, and Child firm of Liverpool took him to New England. His mercantile business stretched from Belfast, Maine, to Wiscasset, Maine, where his brother John settled, and even to Boston, where Francis was a paid member of the Charitable Irish Society. A third Anderson brother settled in New Orleans. The Anderson brothers were Protestant.

Akenson has argued that "the bulk of the Irish ethnic group in the United States at present is, and probably always has been, Protestant."[34] Until 1980, the U.S. census determined nationality based on place of birth; therefore, the official U.S. stance was anyone born in Ireland was *Irish*. People are now given choice on the census forms. From 1998 until 2004, people living in Ireland would have agreed with the definition that those born in Ireland were Irish. As part of the Good Friday Accord peace agreement brokered in Northern Ireland, the Republic of Ireland revised Article 2 of its Constitution, using the following statement:

> It is the entitlement and birthright of every person born in the island of Ireland which includes its islands and seas, to be part of the Irish nation. That is also the entitlement of all persons otherwise qualified in accordance with law to be citizens of Ireland. Furthermore, the Irish nation cherishes its special affinity with people of Irish ancestry living abroad who share its cultural identity and heritage.[35]

The euphoria was short-lived, however. As a result of the then-powerful Celtic Tiger, Ireland found itself receiving immigrants, rather than watching "exiled" emigrants departing. Poles, Slovaks, Lithuanians, Nigerians, Thai, and a host of other nationalities entered the country in droves to live and work. Their children were and are being born in Ireland, which, until 2004, meant that those children were Irish citizens, even if their parents were not. Those new immigrants caused the people of Ireland to redefine their own definitions of self, and those discussions led to Ireland's very own nativist backlash and soul-searching. As of 2004, children born in Ireland to noncitizen parents are no longer considered native-born citizens.[36] If we cannot define Irishness by place of birth—which the 2004 amendment to the Irish constitution makes manifest—we must find another approach. Yet perhaps it is best to keep the discussion limited to the time frame under discussion. In the eighteenth and nineteenth centuries, ethnicity was still defined by place of birth and where people were most recently living. As Cian McMahon has pointed out, "differences among the white races were just as important as those separating whites from people of color" in the nineteenth century.[37]

Acculturation, too, has been used to calibrate Irishness for decades. In this mode of thought, the Irish ceased to be Irish if and when they became upwardly mobile. The rocky road to defining Irishness has been reduced to character traits: "[P]ride in an enviable past, unquenchable thirst for independence, great wit, relaxing charm, and a drive to accomplish that rests upon a firm belief in God and in the afterworld that is His."[38] President Kennedy's election, for some, seemed to culminate three centuries of Irish (meaning Catholic) people trying to "make it" in America—they had finally arrived; however, Protestant Irish already had laid claim to at least three U.S. presidents by the mid-nineteenth century—Andrew Jackson, James Knox Polk, and James Buchanan, for example.

The concept of diaspora has fueled a great deal of scholarly work. Lawrence J. McCaffrey's *The Irish Diaspora in America* (1976), for example, presented Irish immigrants as victims and refugees, "running ... from misery and death rather than rushing toward freedom and opportunity."[39] Timothy J. Meagher's definition of diaspora as a group of people who are outsiders in the receiving culture, still looking to home and the emigrant Irish worldwide, is succinct. The question is, though, were Irish immigrants really always "looking to home," or were they making a home for themselves and their children on this side of the Atlantic? Could they do both at the same time? Again, as a result of the diaspora concept, scholars have focused on how people are publicly Irish—in enclaves. This approach has traveled across the United States, and scholars have looked at most major urban areas—Boston, New York, Philadelphia, Chicago, San Francisco. It has also been applied to more localized areas, such as Butte, Montana, and Worchester, Massachusetts. Even though the place-names change, the spaces remain the same—public performance is the measuring stick. Catholic churches built, St. Patrick's Day parades or Orange Order parades marched in, or membership in the Masons demark Irishness—or

Scotch-Irishness. Scholars looking at Irish Protestants have had to contort the model as well. Ulster Protestants have been observed as public performers—generally depicted in Orange Order parades and/or Lodge membership. The implication is that their Protestantism is Scots, not Irish. (As the U.S. Catholic Church forbade its members to belong to a Masonic Lodge, on threat of excommunication, this avenue of community-building was denied to Catholic businessmen.) Knights of Columbus membership sometimes offered counterbalance. Do affiliations really create and/or support ethnicity or culture?

Current discussions still pull from biblical metaphors and the ideas surrounding God's chosen people. Exile, exodus, and diaspora remain loaded terms that mystify the experience of leaving Ireland, helping create a mythology of emigration/immigration.[40] In these scenarios the Irish Famine has become the central event. Early studies presented Irish Catholics as the hardest hit, and, therefore, the mid-nineteenth surge in Irish "fleeing" overseas was conceived as primarily a Catholic cataclysm. Recent scholarship, however, has shown that the Famine decade did not change religious affiliations in Ireland. What did happen, however, was those affiliations provided distinct lenses through which to view the Famine. While Catholics might have seen it as the grossest example of British misrule, Protestants could have seen it as a sign of divine providence. The Famine, too, has served as a measure of Irishness. The potato blight hit most of northern and western Europe—not just Ireland—nor was Ireland the only nation to be devastated by Famine. Ultimately, famines are caused by human responses to failures, such as British handling of the Famine. Scotland also suffered the potato blight and ensuing starvation; however, that event has not proven to be as much of a flash point as that which occurred in Ireland at the same time.[41] No such relief funds for Scotland received as much publicity. While many people learned about the Irish Famine, including the displaced Cherokee in Indian Territory, Oklahoma, and slaves in the United States, few reacted to Finland's famine (1856 and 1868), also laid at the feet of the British government through its military destruction of the area during the Crimean War.[42] Even groups in Belfast, Maine, hosted a number of events to raise funds for the Irish during the famine of the 1840s. No one raised funds in Belfast for the Finns.

Famine can be used as a tool for political gain or to subdue a people. Laissez-faire capitalism became a rationale for wiping out the poor or at best afforded an opportunity to do so.[43] While some among the English assumed that Irish poverty resulted from moral corruption, economic underdevelopment, and agrarian agitation, the truth of the matter (or one of the truths) is fewer than 10,000 families owned Ireland before the famine.[44] After the famine, half of Ireland was owned by a mere 1,000 of the largest proprietors.[45] Governments and their institutions have historically taken advantage of natural disasters to reshape society, driven by a search for profits.[46] In fact, while Britain's government kept detailed statistics on numbers of pigs and poultry eaten, it did not keep an accurate accounting of the number of people who died in the Irish Famine.[47] The Irish Famine was aimed not at a particular religion but at a particular class. All affiliated religionists—Anglicans, Presbyterians, and Catholics—subdivided holdings in the early decades of the nineteenth century, for example, when their sons married.[48] The three major denominations (Catholic, Anglican, and Presbyterian) had no distribution changes when comparing pre- to post-Famine Ireland.[49] All groups were hit equally hard—Protestant sects as well as Catholics—everyone faced starvation.

It was only in the second half of the nineteenth century that religious identities fused with political ideologies (nationalism versus unionism), deepening the chasm between Catholics and Protestants.[50] Famine refugee statistics support this, as 30 percent of the Irish dead in Toronto in 1847 were Protestants.[51] Before the Irish Famine, *The Republican Journal*, published weekly in Belfast, Maine, commented repeatedly on the evils of British governmental policy and its sneering dismissal of the laboring class. The newspaper also ran a great deal of coverage on issues affecting wage laborers. In that editor's eyes, then, class and status were the instigators of Ireland's destitution.

Despite what the U.S. census has offered as a definition, however, throughout much of U.S. history, Irish has been used to mean "Other." It has also been used as a pejorative.[52] Social status, economic class, non-English speaking, and/or Catholic religious affiliation have all played roles in the labeling process. If defining ethnicity and culture were only as simple as turning to the dictionary, life would be a lot less complex. Connotation can be more powerful than denotation because it is more emotional. Labels are powerful things. Those applying the labels also take unto themselves a lot of power. Perspective is part of the labeling process—whether one is an insider or an outsider determines the label. Belfast, Maine, provides an opportunity to look closely at insider (old-timer) and outsider (newcomer) interactions. Geography—as well as time in a community—must also play important parts in communal living. Many times recent arrivals find themselves at odds with those who have been a generation or two in a community, even if their ancestors came from the same country of origin. Many factors lead to insider status—length of time in a community, wealth, education, connections to the power structure, and so forth. The creation of insider (old-timer) and outsider (newcomer) communities and the ensuing competition between those two groups seems to be part of human nature. Folklorists have labeled this the "es-ex factor."[53]

Groups close ranks and use language, customs, manners, humor, and so forth to define themselves and to create identity. This is esoteric, which is one half of a dynamic system. Newcomers face a *culture of place* to which they must adapt, or at least acknowledge. If and when they become truly adept at reading the culture of place, they understand that they cannot assume insider status (exoteric). Ethnic identification and the creation of ethnic character descriptors mirror political struggles and social realities. Ethnic and cultural subgroups want to be liked by the insiders. In the eighteenth century, immigrants from Ulster wished to show their loyalty to the new political structure, perhaps because their hold on the new environment was tenuous. The cultural and ethnic markers reflected what society was looking for, because, ultimately, all culture is socially constructed.[54]

Sociological approaches have been applied since at least the 1970s. Ethnic persistence (acting the role of the "Other") in America was posited as an urban reality, tied to "the changing technology of industrial production and transportation."[55] Strong kinship and friendship networks were requisite if people were to survive the quickly evolving production landscape or so, scholars argued. Such studies also pointed out that group solidarity was tied to economic status, which also influenced even people's choices of mates. For example, most people in the late nineteenth century lived close to work so they could walk to and from as there was little in the way of public transport. Where people lived was determined by what they could afford. This meant that urban dwellers lived in neighborhoods with people from the same social class. This, in turn, influenced marriage-partner choices.[56] To be ethnic was to be the "Other." The practice of ethnicity required multigenerational families, shared social networks and institutions, and common occupations—and, of course, common class and status. As a result, the city was seen as the incubator of persistent ethnic behavior.

In his Herculean task of frequently updating the historiography of Irish studies, Kevin Kenny has weighed in, noting that scholars are divided over two approaches—transnational and/or cross-national. He has urged a merging of the two.[57] What all these studies have in common, besides their urban foci, is that many look at educated white-collar males or politically savvy labor leaders (and sometimes their related females) who made a big noise, politically speaking.[58] The Catholic Church in America and its leading clerics were also politically astute. These public performances of Irishness garnered—and still gather—public attention.

The actors in urban dramas were generally well aware of how to manipulate public perceptions and knew how to grab publicity. A number of these players, too, had the wherewithal to travel back and forth across the Atlantic—or at least their printed words could and did. (See, for example, Cian T. McMahon's "International Celebrities and Irish Identity in the United States and Beyond, 1840–1860," or "Ireland and the Birth of the Irish-American Press, 1842–61.") This trans-Atlantic Irish world meant that immigrants, in a number of cases, were still taking "the backward glance." Were they immigrants or merely ex-patriots? Or were they something else entirely—exiled public leaders trying to influence what went on politically in Ireland from afar? McMahon argued that the Young Irelanders, for example, were creating a kind of global nationalism.[59] Was that really the case, or were they merely climbing onto the world stage to bring public pressure to bear against a world power? How was this behavior any different than the ancient concept of hunger strike, using public humiliation of those in power to effect change at home? How did the perceptions of such people shade those tropes of Irish American studies as "exodus" and "exile"? What might it look like to be a political leader of Irish extraction in the United States, without the "backward glance"? Belfast offers several models of American politicians of Irish stock, who, while interested in issues "at home," were more interested in seeing where American power could take them.

A handful of studies have looked at Irish women's immigration, but, again, generally as "domestics" in middle class and wealthier homes in urban areas. Some of the first works to consider gender as part of the discussion were by Hasia R. Diner and Janet A. Nolan. Diner's *Erin's Daughters in America: Irish Immigrant Women in the Nineteenth Century* looked at the role of woman as culture bearer.[60] Diner focused on immigrant women's traditional domestic roles and how most parlayed those abilities into paid-for employment. While she presented Irish women as knowledgeable agents in their decisions to immigrate, she found them lacking in cooking skills, given the Irish peasant's reliance on potatoes and not much else. She based these conclusions on employers' anti-Irish diatribes and the lack of Irish cookbooks. In *Ourselves Alone: Women's Emigration from Ireland 1885–1920*, Janet A. Nolan, too, looked at the 700,000 young, single women who left Ireland during her study's time frame.[61] She looked at how Ireland's economics meant women suffered more—from loss of jobs, which meant greater economic dependency, and led to forced celibacy. As a result of lost economic power, girls became more highly educated than boys—*because* they had been preempted from the workforce. Education, however, stood them in good stead upon immigration. She asserted that Irish society was male-centric, noting that even radical campaigns, such as nationalism, discouraged women's active involvement. As a result, she hypothesized, women "liberated themselves from a society and an economy that had dispossessed them."[62] And there the discussion remained for more than a decade.

Any further discussion of gender was nearly ignored until the late 1990s and the early 2000s. More than thirty years after her groundbreaking research into the role of Irish women in culture creation and maintenance, Diner was taken to task because she had claimed that domestic service was liberating, focusing on women's roles in families, the labor force, and activism in American labor unions, social reform, and politics. Diner's early work did not have the vantage of close studies of previously taboo topics, such as nonmarital pregnancy and prostitution numbers and the severity of family dysfunction.[63] Janet Nolan returned to her discussion of Irish immigrant women's role in America's workforce in *Servants of the Poor: Teachers and Mobility in Ireland and Irish America* (2004). Irish women had to work—just as did men—after immigration. Nolan looked at how the feminization of teaching in America gave Irish women a chance at bettering their status, if not their class.[64] Her studies, however, are drawn from major urban areas, such as Boston, San Francisco, and Chicago.

While there have been a number of studies that have looked at rural experiments, such as Benedicta, Maine, or Graceville, Minnesota, these were rural "schemes" run by the Catholic Church in America in the nineteenth century. (See Edward T. McCarron, "A Brave New World: The Irish Agrarian Colony of Benedicta, Maine," in *They Change Their Sky: The Irish in Maine* (2004) and Bridget Connelly, *Forgetting Ireland: Uncovering a Family's Secret History* (2003).) The church sought to create rural enclaves of Irish Catholics, ensconced in rusticity, away from the evils of urban settings. The Irish miners of Butte, Montana, too, received their due, as have those of Pennsylvania. (See David M. Emmons, *The Butte Irish: Class and Ethnicity in an American Mining Town, 1875–1925* (1989) and Kevin Kenny, *Making Sense of the Molly Maguires* (1998) for examples.)

Throughout the 1990s, scholars opened up the discipline, trying to ascertain if deductions about Irish communities in the United States would be supported by evidence elsewhere in the worldwide diaspora of Irish immigrants. In *The Irish in New Communities: The Irish World Wide: History, Heritage, Identity* (1997), Patrick O'Sullivan called for an interdisciplinary approach to the field, urging the application of migration and feminist theories. He called upon academics to move outside their comfortable enclaves to look at immigration issues from other vantage points.[65] O'Sullivan argued that while ethnicity is a matter of personal choice, when language is lost, so, too, is much of ethnic identity.[66] This position does not allow for a discussion of cultural reconfigurations around language, such as Irish English. How does this influence or affect how the English-speaking Irish have been assessed? Irish English was noted, generally in comical/humorous contexts in publications throughout the eighteenth and nineteenth centuries, as a way of "Othering" the English-speaking Irish by other speakers of dialectical English.

By the 2000s, both Catholic and Protestant Irish immigrants were being looked at as Irish. Representatives from sociology, ethnic history, women's studies, and cultural geography joined the conversation. The themes of these past twenty years have ranged from looking at gender to trying to define Irish American identity. Meagher challenged his own earlier definitions in *Inventing Irish America: Generation, Class, and*

Ethnic Identity in a New England City, 1880–1928 (2001). This study of
the Irish in Worcester, Massachusetts, looked at ethnicity and assimilation. Meagher suggested that labor history might prove useful in discussing class shifts, from working to middle class. He urged an
interdisciplinary approach that might have more dexterity discussing
group boundaries, adaptability, and evolution. The problem, however, is
that Meagher continued to conflate ethnicity with culture, using the
terms "interchangeably." Assimilation, according to Meagher, ends any
idea of Irishness; he sought to answer what creates cultural persistence in
second- and third-generation Irish immigrants, trying to figure out
"when, how, and why ethnic groups or communities evolve over
time."[67] Many opted to see culture as part of a personal decision-making
process, a choice. Kerby Miller argued in his later works that ethnicity is
dependent on individual and collective identification, not necessarily
birthplace. Such personal choices are, of course, subjective and variable,
affected by "a multitude of shifting social, cultural, political, and psy-
chological circumstances."[68] Kevin Kenny, too, noted, for example, that
the Ulster Irish *chose* to be "not Irish" early in the nineteenth century in
the United States.[69] In Ireland, these people had identified as Irish because they were born and lived there. In other words, the Protestants of
Ulster chose to see themselves as Irish while in Ireland, as their "culture
and religion had diverged sharply from that of contemporary
Scotland."[70] Malcolm Campbell has argued that the "not Irish" label
was a result of anti-Irish immigration fervor, especially in America's
Northeast, where early Irish Protestant immigrants had settled.[71]

*Redefining Irishness in a Coastal Maine City, 1770–1870: Bridget's
Belfast* picks up the discussion of the "not Irish" decisions of New England
settlers at the pivot point from the eighteenth to nineteenth centuries. It
looks at private performances of Irishness, or as Kathleen Neils Conzen calls
it, "the process of adaptation as experienced by the individual immigrant."[72] How did Irish immigrants and their children navigate outside
America's largest cities? While the studies that have gone before have looked
at the headlines and speeches, this study proposes looking at the diaries,
weekly newspapers, and records from general stores, women-run boarding
houses, probate court, police court, local statistical records—including that
of the animal pound—to find out what life was like for Irish immigrants and
their children in rural America. This study also points out that rural did not
necessarily mean "out of the loop." Evidence clearly shows that rural Irish
could be just as politically savvy as their big city cousins—they just went
about their business a lot more quietly. The issues under discussion, too,
were different, with more of an American perspective. Life on the frontier
could be rewarding and less class rigid. Irish English is also evidence of a
cultural norm and should be analyzed as such.

Conzen, twenty-five years ago, called for such an approach, one that
gets away from analysis of a community and instead looks at individuals

and their children and their migratory lives, one that charts "the evolution of ethnic settlement systems through space, and ... explore[s] individual movement through and beyond them socially, culturally, psychologically as well as geographically."[73] *Redefining Irishness*, then, looks at how immigrant Irish and their children performed Irishness in a local, rural setting. What made their actions particularly Irish? How did stereotypes, perpetrated by the receiving culture, perceive Irish immigrants? How did the Irish react? How did such perceptions and reactions play out over a century? What truths were at the roots of those stereotypes? How did people enact cultural meanings daily through living—or performing—life? These daily encounters shaped people, through their reactions to "injustice, prejudice, and stereotyping."[74]

The micro-historical approach also affords the opportunity to trace migration routes once Irish immigrants alit. Did they stay in one place? How long? Did "the locals" stay in one place? Why or why not? How did the Irish differ from their "local" neighbors? Did they? Again, *Redefining Irishness*, given the small canvas, can point to larger trends—simply because the data are available in a way it would not be in a larger city. While Kerby Miller has looked at day-to-day Irishness (comparing similar folk traditions around wakes among Irish Catholics and Protestants, for example), *Redefining Irishness* attempts to access more fully the private performances of Irishness: Dialectical use of Irish English, defining what is meant by gift of gab, natural-born storytelling abilities, congeniality, and a drive to succeed (for a certain class). These private traits, while bordering on stereotype, are discussed in obituaries and some of the half dozen local written histories.

The original settlers of Belfast had fathers and grandfathers (mothers and grandmothers, too) who came from Ireland. Belfast's historians, however, worked assiduously to renounce anything and everything to do with Ireland or, worse, being Irish. The writers of the histories were not the originators of the city of Belfast, however. The history writers, members of a nascent professional class, came after the American Revolution, just before the War of 1812. These professional men claimed Scottish roots for the ancestors of Belfast's settlers. Some nineteenth-century descendants took that claim further, asserting they were the same as, if not better than, the Anglo-Saxons of England. Recent historical works have taken the nineteenth-century materials at their word; they concurred that Belfast was a creation of the Scotch-Irish (a term designating Ulster Protestant Irish not used widely until the mid-nineteenth century in America).

Belfast's early historians also remarked that many of those supposed Scotch ancestors had been 100 years in Ireland. What would being Scots look like after approximately five generations in Ireland? How long must people be in a culture before the "auld sod" is no longer the focus of culture? Would modern Americans, for example, accept the idea that people three, four, or five generations in the States are still foreigners? Would a fifth-generation Syrian-American be Syrian or American? Surely, such individuals are Americans with Syrian roots, which might mean that the cultural norms are primarily American (whatever that might mean); however, some family celebrations, names, and so on might still call forth or remember the Syrian roots.

A personal family example might help clarify the discussion. My husband, who considers himself a "child of Appalachia," was born in West Virginia but moved to Kentucky as a child. His father was from Alabama, having deep Southern roots, originally transplanted from Stewartstown, County Tyrone, Northern Ireland, several generations before; his mother was a seventh-generation West Virginian. While West Virginia's Unionist leanings led to its statehood in 1863, the term "Yankee" would never have been applied to my husband or his family. Yet, on his first trip to Ireland, Irish friends referred to him as a Yank. The Yankee designation, then, was applied by an outsider culture. Obviously, cultural insiders would understand cultural nuances and the political history—and would never use this designation for anyone from south of the Mason–Dixon Line. Old-timer and newcomer communities (or cultures), thus, may use different criteria to set up categories.

If culture is socially constructed, changing over time and place, perhaps the old-timer and newcomer labeling process is the place to start. The "Yankee" conundrum points out that there are always insider and outsider communities, and the process of labeling is always a matter of contention. In Belfast's microcosm, individuals stand out amid the receiving culture labels. *Redefining Irishness in a Coastal Maine City, 1770–1870: Bridget's Belfast* focuses on the extended family of newcomer Bridget Haugh McCabe, starting with the coverage in local papers of her gruesome death, and looks at her (and her family's) interactions with the old-timer culture of Belfast.

In the following eight chapters, I will look at the concept of Irishness from a number of vantage points. In "Chapter One: Irish in Public," I introduce readers to the individuals who made headlines in Belfast. I will use these individuals as baselines for how Irishness played in public. "Chapter Two: Irish Enterprise" focuses on how the professional class—Irish immigrants among them—rewrote Belfast's public and cultural history. In "Chapter Three: The Irish 'Other,'" I establish how the Irish—and Irishness—were perceived by old-timers in Belfast, Maine. Those perceptions changed over time, and participants operated out of their own worldviews. "Chapter Four: The Irish of Stereotype" traces the lack of evolution of Irish stereotypes over more than a century. Old-timers invariably perceived newcomers from Ireland the same way: It did not matter to them whether the newcomers were Protestant (Presbyterian) or Catholic. The stereotypes remained in place. I discuss how and why the "Othering" through stereotype changed tone in 1840s Belfast. "Chapter Five: Irish on the Move" discusses movement/migration as a fact of life in America. Because Belfast, Maine, provides a small canvas, I can trace generational shifts in and out of town. The fact that people moved frequently has to be considered when taking into account the culture of place. In "Chapter Six: Inventing Scotch-Irishness," I look at the foundation myths of the Scotch-Irish in America and the reasons for the creations of those myths. In "Chapter Seven: Bridging Social Boundaries," I look at several representative individuals and assess how cultures interact and inform one another—based on geography, rurality versus urbanity, generation, class, status, and gender, as well as time of arrival in a community. In "Chapter Eight: Making It Through the War," I look at Irish immigrants who went to war. When they did so, they marched off with their cohort—Belfastians with whom they had grown up, lived, and worked. Their decisions about that war, however, may have been influenced by the local economy of 1860.

The written materials of Belfast allow access to individuals' lives; however, those materials were produced by a literate elite. In this book, I attempt to look at the subtext and to "read between the lines" in order to glimpse into working-class Irish lives. I look closely at the interaction between old-timers and newcomers, and, with the aid of close textual readings, try to analyze how Irishness was performed in Belfast, Maine, from 1770 through 1870.

Notes

1 Peggy Levitt and Mary C. Waters, eds., *The Changing Face of Home: The Transnational Lives of the Second Generation* (New York: Russell Sage Foundation, 2002), 12.
2 Levitt and Waters, 18.
3 Levitt and Waters, 13.
4 Patrick Griffin, *The People with No Name: Ireland's Ulster Scots, America's Scots Irish, and the Creation of a British Atlantic World, 1689-1764* (Princeton: UP, 2001), 35.
5 George F. Willey, *Willey's Book of Nutfield: A History of That Part of New Hampshire Comprised Within the Limits of the Old Township of Londonderry from Its Settlement in 1719 to the Present Time* (Derry Depot, NH: George F. Willey, 1895), 145.
6 Sir Robert E. Matheson, *Special Report on Surnames in Ireland with Notes as to Numerical Strength, Derivation, Ethnology, and Distribution: Based on Information Extracted from the Indexes of the General Register Office* (Dublin: His Majesty's Stationery Office, 1909).
7 Matheson, 15.
8 Edward MacLysaght, *The Surnames of Ireland*, 3rd ed. (Dublin: The Irish Academic Press, 1978), x.
9 Matheson, *Special Report on Surnames in Ireland*, 25–30.
10 Matheson, 31.
11 Kerby Miller, "Ulster Presbyterians and the 'Two Traditions' in Ireland and America," in *Making the Irish American: History and Heritage of the Irish in the United States*, eds. J. J. Lee and Marion R. Casey (New York: New York University Press, 2006), 260.

12 Kevin Kenny, *Diaspora: A Very Short History* (Oxford: UP, 2013), 12. Kerby Miller, *Emigrants and Exiles: Ireland and the Irish Exodus to North America* (Oxford: University Press, 1985).

13 Wilkins Updike, *A History of the Episcopal Church in Narragansett, Rhode Island: Including a History of Other Episcopal Churches in the State* (Boston: Merrymount Press, 1907), Appendix A, page 45, note. See also *Lebor Gabála Érenn*, for a medieval example.

14 Brian Walker, "The Lost Tribes of Ireland: Diversity, Identity, and Loss among the Irish Diaspora," *Irish Studies Review* 15, no. 3 (2007): 267–82. https://www.tandfonline.com/loi/cisr20.

15 Kathleen Neils Conzen, "Thomas and Znaniecki and the Historiography of American Immigration," *Journal of American Ethnic History* 16, no. 1 (Fall 1996): 16–25, GALE.

16 Oscar Handlin, *Boston's Immigrants: A Study in Acculturation* (Cambridge: Harvard University Press, Belknap Press, 1959), 43.

17 Handlin, 64.

18 Handlin, 149.

19 Handlin, 151.

20 Noel Ignatiev, *How the Irish Became White* (New York: Routledge, 1995), 93.

21 Timothy J. Meagher, *From Paddy to Studs: Irish-American Communities in the Turn of the Century Era, 1880-1920* (Westport, CT: Greenwood Press, 1986), 13.

22 Carl Wittke, *The Irish in America* (Baton Rouge: Louisiana State University Press, 1956; New York: Russell and Russell, 1970), v.

23 Timothy J. Meagher, *Inventing Irish America: Generation, Class, and Ethnic Identity in a New England City, 1880-1928* (Notre Dame: University Press, 2001), 136.

24 Cian T. McMahon, *The Global Dimensions of Irish Identity: Race, Nation, and the Popular Press, 1840-1880* (Chapel Hill: University of North Carolina Press, 2015), 2.

25 Meagher, *From Paddy to Studs*, 2–13.

26 David C. Harvey et al. "Timing and Spacing Celtic Geographies," in *Celtic Geographies: Old Culture, New Times*, eds. David C. Harvey et al. (London: Routledge, 2002), 4.

27 Harvey et al., 6.

28 Kerby Miller, "Revd James MacSparran's America Dissected (1753): Eighteenth-Century Emigration and Constructions of 'Irishness'," *History Ireland* 11, no. 4 (Winter 2003): 17–22. JSTOR.

29 Timothy J. Meagher, "From the World to the Village and the Beginning to the End and After: Research Opportunities in Irish American History," *Journal of American Ethnic History* 28, no. 4 (Summer 2009): 118–35.

30 Donald Harman Akenson, *The Irish Diaspora: A Primer* (Belfast: Institute of Irish Studies, 1996).

31 David Noel Doyle, "Scots Irish or Scotch-Irish," in *Making the Irish American: History and Heritage of the Irish in the United States*, eds. J. J. Lee and Marion R. Casey (New York: New York University Press, 2006), chapters 3–5.

32 Roger Swift, "The Historiography of the Irish in Nineteenth-century Britain," in *The Irish in New Communities: The Irish World Wide: History, Heritage, Identity*, ed. Patrick O'Sullivan, vol. 2 (London: Leicester University Press, 1992), 54.

33 Maurice J. Bric, "Patterns of Irish Emigration to America, 1783-1800," *Eire/Ireland* 36, nos. 1–2 (Spring–Summer 2001): 10.

34 Donald Harman Akenson, "The Historiography of the Irish in the United States of America," in *The Irish in New Communities: Volume Two in the series The Irish World Wide: History, Heritage, Identity*, ed. Patrick O'Sullivan (London: Leicester University Press, 1922), 99.

35 Catherine Nash, *Of Irish Descent: Origin Stories, Genealogy, and the Politics of Belonging* (Syracuse: University Press, 2008), 26.

36 Nash, 28.

37 McMahon, *Global Dimensions*, 4.

38 Joseph P. O'Grady, *How the Irish Became Americans* (New York: Twayne Publishers, Inc., 1973), 158.

39 Lawrence J. McCaffrey, *The Irish Diaspora in America* (Bloomington: Indiana University Press, 1976), 7.

40 Patrick O'Sullivan, "Introduction," in *The Irish in New Communities, Volume 2 in the series, The Irish World Wide: History, Heritage, Identity*, ed. Patrick O'Sullivan (London: Leicester University Press, 1992), 9.

41 David P. Nally, *Human Encumbrances: Political Violence and the Great Irish Famine* (Notre Dame: University Press, 2011), 3.

42 Andrew G. Newby, "'Rather Peculiar Claims upon Our Sympathies': Britain and Famine in Finland, 1856-1868," in *Global Legacies of the Great Irish Famine: Transnational and Interdisciplinary Perspectives*, eds. Marguerite Corporaal et al. (New York: Peter Lang, 2014), 82.

43 Nally, *Human Encumbrances*, 8.

44 Nally, *Human Encumbrances*, 101. Miller, *Emigrants and Exiles*, 42.

45 Christine Kinealy, *The Great Irish Famine: Impact, Ideology and Rebellion: British History in Perspective Series*, ed. Jeremy Black (Houndmills, Basingstoke, Hampshire, England: Palgrave, 2002), 214.

46 Peter Slomanson, "Cataclysm as Catalyst for Language Shift," in *Global Legacies of the Great Irish Famine*, eds. Marguerite Corporaal et al. (New York: Peter Lang, 2014), 83.

47 Kinealy, *The Great Irish Famine*, 10.

48 Miller, *Emigrants and Exiles*, 54.

49 Paul S. Ell, Niall Cunningham, and Ian Gregory, "No Spatial Watershed: Religious Geographies of Ireland Pre- and Post-Famine," in *Global Legacies of the Great Irish Famine*, eds. Marguerite Corporaal et al. (New York: Peter Lang, 2014), 213.

50 Ell, Cunningham, and Gregory, "No Spatial Watershed," 223.

51 Mark McGowan, "Contemporary Links Between Canadian and Irish Famine Commemoration," in *Global Legacies of the Great Irish Famine*, eds. Marguerite Corporaal et al. (New York: Peter Lang, 2014), 282.

52 See Lewis P. Curtis Jr., *Apes and Angels: The Irishman in Victorian Culture* (Newton Abbot, Devon, England: David and Charles Ltd., 1971).

53 Roger Welsch, *Why I'm an Only Child and Other Slightly Naughty Plains Folktales* (Lincoln: University of Nebraska Press, 2016), 6. Welsch discusses this dynamism in modern terms, explaining why white people cannot use the "N-word," but Black Americans may. To translate this into the present discussion, I attended a party where a lot of people of Irish descent were telling one another the latest Paddy, Mick, and Bridget jokes they had heard. These were met with gales of laughter. An attendee with an English accent attempted to tell one as well—the room went deathly silent.

54 Discussion of ethnicity and culture being social constructs is not new. See, for example, William A. Yancey, Eugene P. Ericksen, and Richard N. Juliani,

"Emergent Ethnicity: A Review and Reformulation," *American Sociological Review* 41 (June 1976): 392; Mary C. Waters and Karl Eschbach, "Immigration and Ethnic and Racial Inequality in the United States," *Annual Review of Sociology* 21 (1995): 421; and Malcolm Campbell, *Ireland's New Worlds: Immigrants, Politics, and Society in the United States and Australia, 1815-1822* (Madison: University of Wisconsin Press, 2008), vii.

55 Yancey, Ericksen, and Juliani, "Emergent Ethnicity," 392.

56 Yancey, 396.

57 Kevin Kenny, "Diaspora and Comparison: The Global Irish as a Case Study," *The Journal of American History* 90, no. 1 (June 2003): 134–62. Downloaded from http://jah.oxfordjournals.org on February 4, 2016.

58 Ely M. Janis, "Petticoat Revolutionaries: Gender, Ethnic Nationalism, and the Irish Ladies' Land League in the United States," *Journal of American Ethnic History* 27, no. 2 (Winter 2008): 5–27.

59 McMahon, *Global Dimensions*, 3.

60 Hasia R. Diner, *Erin's Daughters in America: Irish Immigrant Women in the Nineteenth Century* (Baltimore: John's Hopkins University Press, 1983).

61 Janet A. Nolan, *Ourselves Alone: Women's Emigration from Ireland, 1885-1920* (Lexington: University of Kentucky Press, 1989).

62 Nolan, 95.

63 Deirdre Moloney, "Who's Irish? Ethnic Identity and Recent Trends in Irish American history," *Journal of American Ethnic History* 28, no. 4 (Summer 2009), 100.

64 Janet Nolan, *Servants of the Poor: Teachers and Mobility in Ireland and Irish America* (Notre Dame: University Press, 2004).

65 O'Sullivan, "Introduction," 1–2.

66 O'Sullivan, 12.

67 Timothy J. Meagher, *Inventing Irish America: Generation, Class, and Ethnic Identity in a New England City, 1880-1928* (Notre Dame: University Press, 2001), 7.

68 Miller, "'Two Traditions,'" 260.

69 Kevin Kenny, *The American Irish: A History* (New York: Pearson Education, Inc., 2000), 3.

70 Kenny, 14.

71 Malcolm Campbell, *Ireland's New Worlds: Immigrants, Politics, and Society in the United States and Australia, 1815-1922* (Madison: University of Wisconsin Press, 2008), 25.

72 Conzen, "Thomas and Znaniecki," GALE, page 2 of 7.

73 Conzen, "Thomas and Znaniecki," GALE, page 5 of 7.

74 Norman K. Denzin, *Performance Ethnography: Critical Pedagogy and the Politics of Culture* (Thousand Oaks, CA: Sage Publications, Inc., 2003), xi.

1 Irish in Public

The next murderous assault which we have to record was committed upon one Bridget McCabe, an Irish woman, who died from the effects of wounds given by persons unknown, during a disturbance at the house of her husband, Brian McCabe, on the 4th of January, 1861. A coroner's inquest failed to discover the guilty party.[1]

Four January 1861, Belfast, Maine. It was snowing—again. Bad weather arrived Christmas week and stayed: it snowed, rained, and sleeted on 20, 22, 24, 25, and 26 December. After a couple days' respite, the snow began again during the night of 30 December, dumping eighteen inches on the small city on the western shore of Penobscot Bay by noon the next day.[2]

The New Year's Eve storm was an omen. January 1861 proved to be miserable—Belfast got more than forty-four inches of snow before month's end—it snowed sixteen out of thirty-one days. The temperature dropped to nearly ten degrees below zero on the thirteenth. The average temperature was seven degrees colder than the previous year. It started snowing again around 3 p.m. on 4 January 1861.[3]

One person, however, was beyond caring.

Twenty-six-year-old Bridget Haugh McCabe took a couple of days to die during that first week in January in a dilapidated house down in Puddle Dock near harborside. No one intervened, even though people passing by heard "violent language" over the course of several days.[4] It was, after all, a house known to be home to a bunch of wild Irish; it was also a matter between husband and wife. The public consensus was that the screaming was the result of a drunken brawl. McCabe had been a Belfast resident for at least eight years—she married Brian McCabe in 1853. When she arrived is impossible to glean from public records, although her father, Thomas Haugh, is listed in the 1850 census.

Details of Bridget Haugh McCabe's death on 4 January 1861 emerged through two weekly newspapers, *The Republican Journal* and *The Progressive Age*. Miles Staples, coroner, gave at least two possible causes

DOI: 10.4324/9781003187660-1

of death—either Bridget's left arm had been submerged in scalding water, or she had suffered from "erysipelatous inflamation [*sic*]" caused by an injury to the arm.[5] At the time of death, gangrene had set in. Because no one had summoned a doctor, Staples declared, no one could say for certain what had happened—although he and the jurors had strong opinions about who was guilty:

> The jurors cannot conclude their verdict without, in the most unqualified terms condemning the studied and apparently concerted disposition on the part of the principle witnesses, including that of the father and husband.[6]
>
> Rum, beastly drunkenness, nightly rows, imprecations, outeries [cq] of murder, with the most abandoned brutality of conduct, witnessed and heard by good citizens, with from four to five misterious [*sic*] deaths of Irish persons, who were last seen in or about the premises of one individual and in two instances the wives of that individual; has justly caused this community to feel indignant and demand a full investigation by the jurors.[7]

Staples concluded that Bridget died when the inflammation reached her brain.[8]

This mention of "Irish persons" in the newspaper is one of the few public acknowledgments that there were Irish immigrants living in Belfast, Maine. Joseph Williamson, author of a two-volume history of Belfast, rarely discussed that community. He did, however, spend several pages explaining how the "Scotch-Irish" were mistaken for Irish, took time to talk about the patriotism of the non-Irish settlers who had emigrated from Ulster, and discussed the non-Irish settlement of Belfast in detail. While Williamson, an amateur historian, did not write about the Irish community, as judge of Belfast's police court in the 1850s he came into constant contact with members of that community who ran afoul of mainstream Belfast society.

In one instance Williamson overcame this limited viewpoint—he devoted several pages of his history to discuss William Brannagan, an immigrant from County Meath, who made enough money to pay for the construction of a Catholic church in Belfast, Saint Francis of Assisi.[9]

Brannagan arrived in Belfast in 1841 via mercantile channels, having first immigrated to Philadelphia, where he worked as a gardener. Within a few years of his arrival in Belfast, Brannagan was thoroughly integrated into its young men's groups, being one of the founding members of a temperance society.[10] He opened his own dry-goods and boot-and-shoe business in downtown Belfast.[11] After a few years, he sold out and became a salesman for others for the next thirty years. He never married, managed his money wisely, and remained firmly entrenched in Belfast's economic life.

Figure 1.1 Joseph Williamson Jr., amateur historian and lawyer. Courtesy of the Belfast Historical Society and Museum.

Bridget Haugh McCabe and William Brannigan may well have passed each other on Belfast's streets in the 1850s. And they were most certainly identified as Irish in their public gestures, behavior, and actions. Their stories, however, suggest that a spectrum of impressions and reactions, tinted by gender- and class-based understandings, combined to affect their public lives in this small community.

When Williamson included Bridget Haugh McCabe in his history, he did not present her as a woman, an individual, but as a victim of Irish violence. To be fair, no women, even those of higher social status, garnered a biography in Williamson's histories. He included Bridget's death story in a chronology of serious crimes committed in or brought to trial in Belfast. In Williamson's telling, McCabe was one of four women killed (or severely wounded) by men they knew.[12] Generally, women only earned mention in Williamson's necrology section.[13] And, as women were supposedly not involved in business, they were not deemed worthy of note. Williamson, however, seems to have intentionally overlooked the fact that a number of women he knew were involved in the business life of Belfast. After his wife died, for example, he boarded in the Field House, which was run by wives of elite Belfast males.

If not for Bridget's mysterious death, probably very few people in 1861 Belfast *would* have heard of Bridget Haugh McCabe. Irish immigrants made up less than 5 percent of Belfast's population. Bridget wasn't yet thirty, married to a man sixteen years her senior, and but was mother of three children, all under the age of six. She was also stepmother to Charles Spinks, fifteen years old, and William A. McCabe, ten, still at home, the sons of Brian McCabe's previous wife, Mrs. Margaret Spinks McCabe, a widow, who had married Brian McCabe in 1849.[14]

There are no death records for Margaret Spinks McCabe; yet just four years after *their* marriage, Brian McCabe married sixteen-year-old Bridget Haugh in 1853. As the coroner hinted, Brian McCabe was somehow implicated in Spinks' demise as well. Because Bridget was illiterate, the only written records of her existence have been left as a result of her interactions with the larger Belfast community. Her marriage to Brian McCabe is listed in city vital statistics. The U.S. census materials record her children's names and ages. Her death was noted in the city's vital statistics, as well as court records, and, of course, the two local weekly newspapers both ran articles on the event. She was not afforded the same deference other women in the community were given—even in death.

Figure 1.2 Surviving Puddle Dock house, still in use in the twentieth century. Courtesy of the Belfast Historical Society and Museum.

Bridget's death under mysterious circumstances on 4 January 1861 in the Puddle Dock area of Belfast, Maine, was the hot topic in town. Although her death garnered only about twenty column inches in the local newspapers, within that short space she was verbally stripped naked and her corpse displayed for the titillation of the paper's readers. What else remained to be said? The first written report of her death came a week after the fact, published in *The Progressive Age*:

> SUDDEN DEATH—SUSPICION OF FOUL PLAY—There was quite a sensation in this city on Saturday from the report of the sudden death of a woman named Bridget McCabe, wife of Bryan McCabe, which took place early in the morning of that day, and that she came to her death from blows inflicted by her husband or some other person.[15]

The story ran on page three—the one reserved for local stories—pages one and two being consumed by goings-on in Washington, D.C., and the unraveling political world in the weeks before Fort Sumter was fired upon by Confederate troops. *The Progressive Age* played up the sensational nature of her death. Half way through the first paragraph, the paper reported: "From the facts testified to, it seems that the body was found in bed in the morning entirely naked except a coverlit [*sic*] thrown over it." The paper went on to give a great deal of information garnered from the coroner's report, to whit:

> one of the arms from the shoulder to the wrist was much discolored as if from bruises; from the wrist, the flesh was entirely denuded of skin, the finger nails coming off with the skin and the flesh of the inside of the hand peeling off from the bones. Up and down the back the flesh was much discolored appearing as though mortification had taken place.[16]

The coroner, Miles Staples, noted that gangrene had commenced. Bridget, he determined, had died of infection of the brain. He also determined that she had been injured on Wednesday night, 2 January 1861, as a result of a drunken row.

The Republican Journal, the other Belfast weekly, quoted the coroner's report, including the accusation that Brian McCabe had had a nefarious hand in the deaths of his two wives.[17] It was thus only at the inquest into Bridget's death that the host community discussed in public documents the situation in Puddle Dock and speculated as to what had happened, not only this time, but in the recent past. It was at this juncture that the first Mrs. McCabe, Margaret Spinks, reentered the picture. Evidently, rumors had been afoot in Belfast that McCabe murdered his first wife. No such evidence exists—if it ever did. There is nothing in the *Vital Records* or the newspapers. There is no grave marker in any local cemeteries. Margaret Spinks McCabe simply disappeared, leaving behind four children and a widower. She left as quietly as she came into the public sphere.

Bridget's passing was not quiet. The public noticed that something untoward was afoot, yet, even though there had been screams over the course of several days before her death, no one in the host community intervened, no one checked to see the cause of the commotion, no one became involved. Closed doors evidently made the affair a private matter—something between husband and wife. But such was not always the case in Belfast.

Changing Mores

In 1829, a man named Hamilton was known as a wife beater, which raised hackles as well as eyebrows in Belfast, when "the shrieks of the poor woman gave notice ... that he was at his devils [*sic*] work."[18] A group of men grabbed Hamilton and roughly "rode" him around town on a rail seized from a nearby fence. They left the fence rail at his door with a sign attached: "Hamilton's horse is long and thin—When he beats his wife he'll ride him again."[19]

Why would community members involve themselves in domestic abuse in 1829 but not in 1861, a generation later? Brian McCabe apparently was in the same social class as Hamilton, so why was *he* spared a public drubbing? Had public sentiment really changed so much? Evidently, Margaret Spinks McCabe had not made a sound when she died, so her death went unnoticed publicly for ten years. The tone of the coroner's report, however, is one of moral outrage. Was Hamilton's wife seen as part of and accepted by the larger community? Was the "Irish" community considered off limits? In their lives and deaths, Margaret and Bridget, two immigrant women, were obviously outsiders, which made at least Bridget vulnerable to the public gaze.

In counterpoint to how press and community appear to have viewed Bridget, another comparison is pertinent. There was a sensational murder, a little more than a decade after Bridget's death in 1861 and just eighteen short miles away. Mrs. Almon (Emma) Gordon met a violent end at her husband's family farm in Thorndike, a small town further inland. Her husband and her seventeen-month-old baby had also been murdered and a six-year-old son hovered near death. Although Emma Gordon's death was highly sensationalized, the dead woman was treated in print far more circumspectly than was Bridget.

Buckets of blood and gore were paraded before readers, yet the body of Emma Gordon wasn't exposed to such naked interest as Bridget's had been. She died with her night clothes on:

Two stained and bloody sheets, shrouding with their ghastly folds, and indistinctly revealing the outlines of two human beings, lay upon the floor. Lifting these, through which the stains of blood and brains had spread, the blackened and bloody remains were discovered .... The wife, a woman young and small in person, but of beautiful form, lay upon her side, her long dark hair falling in curled masses upon the floor, saturated with her life blood .... Reverently, tenderly, the coverings were replaced....[20]

Why were the two murder victims treated so differently? Emma Gordon was allowed the dignity of being fully clothed in the newspaper pages, even if that clothing were made only of ash. Why was one reported to have been naked, while the other was described as having clothes "all cinders"?[21]

Both Bridget and Emma were mothers of small children. Both were in their twenties. Yet Bridget, the newcomer, was seen as beneath and besotted. Longevity in the area may have influenced the community response. The public presentation in the newspapers *allowed* the newcomer from Ireland to be stripped naked in reports of her supposed murder. Emma, on the other hand, had married into an established local family that owned a farm. In fact, there were Gordons in the voting rolls in 1800. The Gordons, unlike Bridget's family, had no interaction with the court system.

The impetus for the Gordon murders seemed to have been almost biblical in imagery—jealousy between brothers. The patriarch had decided to bequeath the family farm to the younger of his two sons. This was one of the many reasons presented to the reading public as to why the firstborn son stood accused of killing his brother, his brother's wife, Emma, and their infant, and of attempting to murder one of his nephews who slept in the same room as the married couple. Emma, as the wife of a landowner with a long-standing claim to roots in the community, wasn't gazed at in the same way as Bridget. In fact, the focus in the Gordon murder shifted to its biblical plot line—the father's favoritism toward the younger son led to a murderous hatred on the part of the elder. It was a morality tale. The Gordon murders, too, were the topic of conversation for weeks in the local newspapers.

Indeed, most of the information that came out at trial was about the alleged perpetrator and older brother, John T. Gordon, and the woman he had wooed. The object of his affection, Julia P. Edwards, reported, "I told him not to come again; he asked me to write to him; I said I should not; He said he was going away next day to Salem."[22] Julia had known John T. for a year. During that time she had received several unsigned letters that warned her against him. (The first letter informed her that John T. had broken into Harmon's store and stolen $28 worth of goods. The second letter warned her that John T. was spending late hours with another woman, who had a bastard child and that he was a mean drunk.)[23] John T. Gordon, for some reason, fixated on the idea that Emma Gordon, his sister-in-law, had written the letters, because a spiritual medium had told him so, according to the account given by Julia Edwards.

The fact that the men in Bridget Haugh McCabe's life were not given status and that she and her people were illiterate, Catholic, given to fisticuffs, and participants in an illegal liquor operation opened her life and death to public viewing in a most sordid way. Bridget did not meet nineteenth-century Protestant standards of public decorum for women. At one point, she *beat up* another woman. She was taken to court, found guilty, and fined—which was a very public procedure. Recent Irish immigrants found themselves in a culture that expected women to remain in the private sphere.[24] Women, especially white middle-class Protestant women, were to be pious, submissive, pure, and domestic.[25] Belfast, however, had numerous opportunities for women who did not fit neatly into such received wisdom. Women and girls, for example, could and did accompany their husbands and/or fathers on board those Yankee sailing ships that went around the world.[26]

Yet Irish immigrant William S. Brannagan apparently did meet nineteenth-century standards for public decorum. He never hid his Catholicism from people in Belfast.[27] He cooperated with Protestant businessmen and worked diligently to support the religious life of Catholics in Belfast, offering buildings he owned as locations for Sunday Mass. By his estimate, there were 150 Catholics in the city by the mid-1870s.[28] Through Brannagan's efforts, Saint Francis of Assisi Church was built in Belfast in the 1890s—he donated his money and land to the cause. As a reward for the donation, Brannagan arranged to live in the parsonage, a housekeeper provided. When he died in 1901, Brannagan was buried in Grove Cemetery, where, according to Williamson, "he lies, closely surrounded by the graves of his friends."[29] Those friends were Protestant.[30]

The Republican Journal reported in its obituary that Brannagan was

> an honest, upright man, of pleasant and friendly disposition, ... [who] had a host of friends, who honored him as a good citizen. In his friendships he knew no distinction of religion or politics, although he held decided views in both.[31]

We note that in a list of acceptable traits, religious persuasion was not part of Belfast's public measuring stick. Granted, Brannagan lived into the twentieth century, so the society Brannagan died in was quite different from the one he joined as a young man in the 1840s. Yet honesty and uprightness remained key in identifying good behavior. Being pleasant and friendly helped.

Williamson's second volume of *The History of Belfast* was completed by Alfred Johnson. In that volume, Brannagan merited a three-page biography, folded into the four pages devoted to the history of the Catholic community of Belfast. The writer, either Williamson or Johnson, gives a more detailed, personal description of the man:

> He is remembered by the present generation as a bright, active, dapper little figure, full of energy, though over eighty, always elaborately courteous, and habitually attired in a quaint black coat and a tall beaver hat: —by his inherent nature a true "gentleman of the old school." He had the quick wit and the sense of humor of his race, and was prepared to meet every comer with a ready answer. Always well supplied with the latest local news, he dearly loved a neighborly chat over a cheering "cup," and his none too frequent and ceremoniously short calls are still missed in more than one household of the older residents.[32]

Brannagan's biography thus exhibits a portrait of "Irishness": Ready with quick rejoinders, well informed on local gossip, chatty, and liking to share a drink. At the turn of the twentieth century, Brannagan's Irishness was considered quaint, lovely, and fun, if the obituary is taken at face value.

Ethnic Choices

Public Irishness has become, over the course of centuries, a desired ethnicity. That identity has been given positive cultural markers of late, such as "warmth, energy, humor, gregariousness, generosity, independence, tenacity."[33] In the twenty-first century, ethnic and cultural identity in America's mix of races, nationalities, ethnicities, and cultures means people pick their most attractive grandparents. People choose these identities for a number of reasons, not least of which is to maintain or enhance self-esteem. Because Americans do not have a "pure blood" or "pure culture" ideal that remains intact over generations, they have created a simple dichotomy: *Us* versus *them*.[34] These dichotomies frequently are a result of seeking to belong or to feel superior.[35] Perhaps people are merely seeking community in the anonymity of the city.[36]

Nothing, let alone something as convoluted as discussions of ethnicity and culture, is ever simple. The lives of Bridget Haugh McCabe and William S. Brannagan in Belfast, a town settled by those whose roots were in Ireland, allow us a glimpse into the vortex of conflicting categories at the core of ethnic and cultural studies. In the confines of its small town streets and squares, Belfast afforded newcomers and old-timers from Ireland ample opportunities to meet. In fact, just three blocks up a steep hill from the house where Bridget Haugh McCabe died near Puddle Dock ran High Street. From here, Belfast's "middling" classes could look out their windows down toward Penobscot Bay and upon the working-class Irish living and working at dockside. First-generation Irish Americans, newly arrived Irish-born people, Protestants, Catholics, rich, and poor met and interacted on High Street.

Class Standing

In a town the size of Belfast, the neighborhoods of the poor were not separated by long distances from the fiscally better off. Shortly after settlement, for example, Belfast's original eighteen families provided a population of 109 people. By 1790 that population had more than doubled, with less than half of the original settlers still in the area; in another ten years Belfast's population nearly tripled. By mid-nineteenth century, the town achieved equilibrium, numbering more than 5,000 people.[37] This modest population base meant that there was no comforting enclave that allowed old-world cultural ideas to remain unchallenged. Without such an enclave, immigrants had to look to the secondary labor market, in other words, the local economy—and businesses—for work, which meant it behooved immigrants to fit in with the locals rather than to remain aloof.[38]

The worlds of old-timers and newcomers in Belfast did not so much collide as interconnect. The large houses on High Street were the city's nucleus. The mercantile and professional classes lived there. The big houses pulled all economic classes together in a small space—Brian McCabe's first wife, the recently arrived and widowed Margaret Spinks, for example, did laundry for one of the women of High Street, a lawyer's wife.[39]

Bridget Haugh McCabe's stepmother (or perhaps her aunt) also worked for that woman: Abigail Davis Field, wife of the first lawyer who settled in Belfast after the Revolutionary War. Mrs. Field ran a boarding house out of her large home on High Street. Evidently being the wife of a lawyer did not mean Mrs. Field did not need to do her part for the economic well-being of her household. While the widowed immigrant from Ireland, Margaret Spinks, did laundry—the hardest, dirtiest, and lowest-status job a working woman could hold—not all recent immigrants were in such straits. William Brannagan started boarding in Abigail Davis Field's big house on High Street in 1842.[40]

Brannagan had an opportunity to meet the political and legal elite of Belfast as an equal, a role afforded to him as a resident of the Fields' boarding house. Maine's circuit judges and lawyers regularly took up residence there during court weeks. Politicians showed up every election year. Affluent summer boarders returned annually.

Others who lived at the Field House many a summer included Hugh Johnston Anderson and his extended family. Anderson served three one-year terms as governor of Maine from 1843 to 1845. His parents immigrated to Maine from Castlewellan, County Down, Ireland, in the late 1790s. He arrived in Belfast as a teen, assisting his uncle Francis in his mercantile business, which he took over when Francis died at age thirty-nine. Hugh ran the business for ten years, moving from the merchant class in Belfast into statewide Democratic politics, which carried him to the state governorship. He moved up in Democratic politics—to the nation's capital and later to San Francisco, where he was sent to clean up "defalcations and speculation with government funds" at the U.S. Mint there.[41]

At least for Brannagan and Anderson—one Catholic and the other Protestant, both considered Irish—class and status were earned through careers in mercantilism—in their ability to create wealth, which allowed them to move among power brokers. Their roles as male earners gave them entrée to American male society, one to which no female earners had access. It mattered, then, whether the Irish immigrant was serving the meal, washing the table linens, or eating the food at a table shared among Belfast's elites. Whether the immigrant was male or female also mattered.

Irishness

While the name of this small city on Penobscot Bay gives evidence of its origins in Ireland, there is little mention of the Irish in the half dozen nineteenth-century histories. Belfast, Maine, was settled in 1770 by men (and their families) from New Hampshire and Massachusetts, most coming from Derry, Londonderry, and Windham, New Hampshire. Those first settlers considered two names—Londonderry and Belfast—both names of cities in what today is called Northern Ireland. James Miller and John Mitchell settled the disagreement by a coin toss. Miller, the winner, came from Belfast, Ireland, via Londonderry, New Hampshire. He and Mitchell had been small children when they and their families left Ireland.

Belfast, Maine, was incorporated as a town in 1773 (disbanded during the Revolutionary War and reconvened in 1784) and as a city in 1853. The settlers of Belfast—and Londonderry, New Hampshire—obviously had warm feelings for their Irish birth homes. Even though the congenial controversy over the town's naming firmly transplanted thoughts of Ireland into American soil, these settlers' descendants were not so sanguine about being called *Irish*.

We might find that prejudice peculiar, as *Irishness* has become a privileged heritage in the United States in the early years of the twenty-first century. Data collected from the American Community Survey distributed by the U.S. census in 2008 show that more than 33 million Americans claim Irish ancestry, while another 2.5 million claim Scotch-

Irish ancestors. The numbers are astonishing—only those claiming German ancestry are higher.[42] Something has changed since the disdain toward the Irish in the eighteenth and the stereotypical "no-Irish-need-apply" advertisements of the nineteenth centuries.

Two "waves" of emigrants from Ireland, separated by some seventy years, faced the same local reactions, which gives an opportunity to discuss ethnicity, culture, class, and status in detail. The wonderful microcosm of Belfast, Maine, allows us to see how culture is defined, maintained, and/or recreated on the small scale. Belfast's size also allows us the luxury of looking at how communities are created, stereotypes and all—in this case, by individuals who traced their roots to the same homeland.

While there were no public parades celebrating Irishness and no Catholic church building until the end of the nineteenth century, Belfast was perhaps more accepting of the newly immigrated than many New England areas. For example, Grove Cemetery, which was laid out by a first-generation Irish American, has no separate Catholic section. Indeed, William Brannagan's grave, marked by a Celtic cross, celebrates his Irish roots—but does so next to the movers and shakers of his generation. Bridget's grave is not recorded.

Notes

1 Joseph Williamson, *The History of the City of Belfast,* Vol. 1 (Somersworth, New Hampshire: New England History Press in Collaboration with the Belfast Free Library, 1982), 380.
2 George Brackett, *The Republican Journal* 33, no. 2 (11 January 1861): 3, col. 1.
3 Brackett, 33, no. 6 (8 February 1861), 2, col. 7.
4 *The Progressive Age,* 7, no. 18 (10 January 1861), 3.
5 Dr. Thomas Maycock, M.D., Belfast Family Practice, personal note, n.d. In modern medical parlance, "an infection such as cellulitis; or the modern term, erysipelas, to describe a streptococcal or staph infection under the skin."
6 Brian McCabe was the husband; Thomas Haugh was Bridget's father.
7 Inquest on the Body of Bridgett [*sic*] McCabe 5 January 1861 [unpublished].
8 Inquest. The "one individual" was Brian McCabe. This is the only record of the "misterious [*sic*]" death of his first wife, Margaret Spinks.
9 Williamson, *The History of the City of Belfast,* Vol. 2, 58–61. Volume 2 of *The History of Belfast* was completed by Alfred Johnson upon Joseph Williamson's death.
10 William George Crosby, "Annals of Belfast for Half a Century," in *Early Histories of Belfast, Maine,* ed. Alan Taylor (Camden, Maine: Picton Press, 1989), 149. The group, Samaritan Tent, No. 17, Maine District, of the Independent Order of Rechabites, included *The Republican Journal* editors Benjamin Griffin and Cyrus Rowe.
11 Williamson, *The History of the City of Belfast,* Vol. 2, 59.
12 Williamson, Vol. 1, 375–80.
13 Williamson, Vol. 1, 525–82.

14 *Vital Records of Belfast, Maine, to 1892*, 405.
15 *The Progressive Age* 7, no. 18 (10 January 1861): 3.
16 *The Progressive Age.*
17 *The Republican Journal* (18 January 1861).
18 Crosby, "Annals of Belfast," 84. Crosby denigrates the man by not giving his first name, nor does he use an honorific such as Mister, which might mean that the man was in a social class lower than Crosby and his friends. In other Crosby stories, the man is shown as a not-very-bright "gofer."
19 Crosby. Crosby maintains it was the last time Hamilton beat his wife.
20 *The Republican Journal* (19 June 1873).
21 *The Republican Journal* (19 June 1873).
22 *The Republican Journal* (20 November 1873).
23 *The Republican Journal* (20 November 1873).
24 Barbara Welter, "Cult of True Womanhood," *American Quarterly* 18 (1966): 152.
25 Welter, 152.
26 Florence Ferguson Pendleton sailed to England on 5 July 1880, for her honeymoon voyage, with her new husband Captain James Nelson Pendleton of Searsport. Her first day in port, she had an English dentist pull an "ulcerated tooth" for five shillings ($1.25 American). PMM 39 Pendleton Collection, Penobscot Marine Museum, Searsport, Maine.
27 William Leo Lucey, S.J. *The Catholic Church in Maine* (Francestown, New Hampshire: Marshall Jones, 1957), 59.
28 Williamson, *The History of the City of Belfast*, Vol. 1, 316.
29 Williamson, Vol. 1, 61.
30 Belfast is unusual in that there is no separate Catholic cemetery. Brannagan's grave is marked with one of a handful of Celtic crosses to be found in Grove Cemetery.
31 William Brannagan obituary in *The Republican Journal* (24 January 1901), 1.
32 Williamson, *The History of the City of Belfast*, Vol. 2, 61.
33 Catherine Nash, *Of Irish Descent: Origin Stories, Genealogy, and the Politics of Belonging* (Syracuse, New York: New York University Press, 2008), 47.
34 James A. Morone, *Hellfire Nation: The Politics of Sin in American History* (New Haven: Princeton University Press, 2003), 12.
35 Patrick O'Sullivan, "Introduction," in *The Irish in New Communities: The Irish World Wide: History, Heritage, Identity*, ed. Patrick O'Sullivan (London: Leicester University Press, 1992), 10.
36 O'Sullivan.
37 Williamson, *The History of the City of Belfast*, Vol. 1, 843–7.
38 Mary C. Waters and Karl Eschbach. "Immigration and Ethnic and Racial Inequality in the United States," *Annual Review of Sociology* 21 (1995): 438.
39 Abigail Davis Field, Day Book, 19 September 1842: "Mrs. Spinks washed for me."
40 William S. Brannagan boarded at the Field House off and on for more than twenty years: 3 September, 28 November, and 4 December 1842, Abigail Davis Field Day Book. Brannagan returned to board in the Field House 25 February 1867 and "board[ed] from date" 10 March 1867, until Friday, 6 January 1868, when "Mr. Brannagan left us unceremoniously yesterday." Benjamin Franklin "Frank" Field Day Book.
41 Kenneth M. Stampp, *America in 1857: A Nation on the Brink* (Oxford: University Press, 1992), 29.

42 U.S. Census Bureau, American FactFinder, "Measuring America: People, Places and Our Economy," factfinder2.census.gov. As of 3 March 2014, the site shows people self-identifying as German ancestry number 33,666,142. Those who self-identify as Irish number 21,827,219. Those claiming Scotch-Irish ancestry number 2,543,749. See Michael P. Carroll, "How the Irish Became Protestant in America," *Religion and American Culture: A Journal of Interpretation* 16, no. 1 (Winter 2006): 25–54.

2 Irish Enterprise

There were no old men: new countries have no old men. We were all young men,--healthy, hearty, and in the full flow of joyous anticipation. There was nothing of that low, narrow, and contracted selfishness which disgraces the present generation. Highways, houses of public worship, academies, schools, and public institutions were the subjects of discussion to which every heart and hand were devoted. Our country and its prospects were everything: our trials, our perils and sacrifices, were nothing.[1]

After the Revolutionary War, professional men arrived in Belfast on Penobscot Bay. Dr. Herman Abbot was among them, settling just before the War of 1812. Abbot was the first to argue that Belfast was founded by Scots, eliding Irish/Irishness references. Another settler, William White, drew on Abbot's work and used secondary sources by Scottish writers, making sure the Scots origin story was firmly entrenched in Belfast's first public history. There was, however, another foundation myth afoot. This was based on class, status, education, and gender, according to the Belfast history by the elder Judge William Crosby. The world of Belfast was created anew by young men, at least as far as Crosby was concerned. It seemed that time began with the elder Judge Crosby and his contemporaries.

In his bold assertion that new countries have no old men, Crosby overlooked the preceding generation of elderly original settlers in the area with surnames like McKeen, Nesmith, Gordon, Stephenson, and McLaughlin.[2] In passing away, they passed out of Belfast's culture, at least as far as the newly arrived professional men were concerned. The culture of class and status rewrote Belfast's origins and aspirations.

In the invasion of the professional class, merchants looking for larger markets led the way, followed by lawyers and teachers. Frontier areas offered great rewards: "[It was] a commercial town, a place where merchants congregated to sell imported goods to the gathered loggers and farmers from the hinterland. This commerce inevitably produced

DOI: 10.4324/9781003187660-2

Figure 2.1 Judge William Crosby, Belfast's second lawyer, came from Billerica, Massachusetts. Courtesy of the Belfast Historical Society and Museum.

debts and disputes, from which a lawyer profited."[3] Where you have professional men, you also need schoolteachers to prepare the budding elite's sons for college and, ultimately, the professions.

Merchant Channels

Irish-born Francis Anderson, one of Belfast's earliest merchants, immigrated with his married brother John from Castlewellan, County Down, just before 1800. Francis, at least, may have spent some time in Boston, as he married a Boston woman.[4] His brother John and his wife Hannah settled in Pownalborough (modern Wiscasset), Maine. Francis represented the Liverpool firm Anderson, Child, and Child, which had both English and Irish partners.[5] The Andersons used an established network of Irish businessmen and merchants as they sought to make a place for themselves on the Massachusetts frontiers of the new republic. Both Francis and John were presented as potential members to the Boston-based Charitable Irish Society on 17 March 1802. The society, organized in Boston in 1737, provided aid to indigent or ill people from Ireland, or those of Irish extraction.[6] The society did not remark that those in need had to be of any particular religious affiliation. The society, supposedly composed of Protestants, also had Catholic members, such as

Matthew Cottrill and James Kavanagh, Irish Catholic merchants in Damarascotta, presented to the society on 17 March 1797.[7] The society held its annual gala on Saint Patrick's Day, which, evidently, was not viewed as an Irish Catholic-only holiday.[8] Francis's $5 dues payment was noted paid by the end of the year (17 December 1802).[9] Given their nominations as members, the Andersons apparently had some "Irish" feelings. If his paid membership in the Charitable Irish Society is any indication, Francis remained aware of the difficulties his fellow Irish immigrants and their children faced. In a more pragmatic sense, at least the society provided a good networking opportunity.

Sometime between 1802 and 1805, Francis Anderson moved to Belfast, where he participated in creating a competitive market town. He was a driving force on projects that, if they worked, promised a brighter future for Belfast. One of those projects was construction of a bridge over the Passagassawakeag River separating East Belfast from West Belfast. Anderson was elected clerk of the project. It was also an enterprise that involved risk. The toll bridge, 122 rods long, cost $18,000 in 1807, the monies for which were raised by nonresidents through sold shares.[10] Obviously Anderson, an immigrant less than ten years in the States, had enough wealth or, at least, access to those with wealth to sign on to a major construction project, one which promised to open new trade opportunities on both sides of the river then cutting Belfast in two.

Anderson's shop was a relatively new attraction in Belfast, as the village had not supported a merchant until the late 1790s; James Nesmith became the first trader in Belfast in 1799. Prior to the Revolution, settlers such as John Mitchell and William Patterson bought needed supplies in Stockton, Maine, ten miles farther east. But, by 1805, there were eight stores in Belfast, Francis Anderson's among them. By 1815, he was considered one of the principal traders among Belfast's sixteen merchants.[11]

The growth of the merchant class kept pace with the village population, which grew from eighteen families (comprising 109 people) in 1779 to 674 people by 1800. That number nearly doubled (to 1,274) by 1810. After Jefferson's Embargo and the War of 1812, population doubled again, to 2,839 by 1825. This growth was manifested in the number of buildings, which grew from forty-two, thirty of which were dwellings, in 1810 to 171 within a half mile of the lower bridge by 1825.[12] Maine became a state in 1820. Whether the result of the post-embargo economy or Maine's newfound statehood status, forty-two merchants were active in Belfast by 1827. Among them was Francis Anderson's nephew, Hugh Johnston Anderson, who was not just American-born but a Maine native.

Family ties may have drawn Hugh Johnston Anderson to Belfast around the War of 1812, when his father John Anderson died prematurely, leaving a widow and several children in Wiscasset. Fourteen-year-old Hugh went to work in the Belfast Anderson store. Hugh's widowed

Figure 2.2 Hugh Johnston Anderson, merchant, served three one-year terms as Maine governor. Courtesy of the Belfast Historical Society and Museum.

mother came with him to Belfast. Still in his teens just two years later when Francis died at age thirty-nine, Hugh took over the business. Francis's widow then married Abiel Wood of Wiscasset; so it appears the Anderson ties between the two towns remained strong. Hugh continued as a merchant in Belfast for the next ten years. He used his commercial position to segue into politics while still a very young man. He also used his Irish heritage to maneuver into obtaining the Democratic nomination for governor in 1843.

Lawyers and Money

The merchant class was not the only group expanding and putting down roots in Belfast. There was nary a lawyer east of Maine's Kennebec River until after the Revolution. As of 1797, there were only two in the entire Penobscot River valley.[13] The first lawyer in Belfast was Bohan Prentice Field, born in Northfield, Massachusetts, in 1774. Field graduated from Dartmouth in 1795. He read law and then set up practice in North Yarmouth, Maine. He and several other men seeking investment opportunities bought land in Belfast, and in 1801 Field moved his practice.[14]

Shortly thereafter, an enterprising young lawyer from Billerica, Massachusetts, after a dismal "prospecting" trip to Bangor for a potential location for a law practice, decided Belfast had more promise. William Crosby decided to set up in Belfast after consultation with

Bohan Field, who assured him there was enough work for two lawyers. Crosby moved permanently to Belfast in January 1802.[15]

Crosby's family had been in Massachusetts for several generations. Joseph Williamson's biography creates an image of an impoverished young man with grit. His father was a farmer, which might have been the son's livelihood except for a childhood accident. His right arm was crushed in a cider mill when he was seven, so Crosby would not have been able to do manual labor. His family decided he would need an education in order to make his way in the world. At age seventeen, he was poor and teaching school. Three years later he entered Harvard College, graduating in 1794. This was the family history—as presented in Belfast. The Crosby family, however, had deep pockets as well as roots—Simon Crosby Sr., the patrilineal American ancestor, was a slave-owning "wealthy landowner and influential Puritan both in England and Massachusetts."[16]

William Crosby was admitted to the bar in 1798 and opened an office in Billerica, where he practiced for three years.[17] Apparently, he thought he could do better—on the frontier. Within two years of setting up his practice in Belfast, Crosby felt comfortable enough to marry Sally Davis, from his hometown of Billerica; her sister Abigail married Bohan P. Field. Thus, it was that the first two lawyers in Belfast were related by marriage. Prior to Maine's statehood, Crosby had served as a Massachusetts state senator, representing the District of Maine. In Belfast, he served as county attorney until 1811; then he became chief justice of the Court of Common Pleas for the Third Eastern Circuit, a post he held until 1822. He was the first *educated* lawyer on the bench. Throughout the eighteenth century, judges on the bench had been "substantial persons," that is, prominent, well-to-do men with reputations for honesty.[18] After Maine achieved statehood in 1820, the judicial system underwent an overhaul. Crosby returned to his law practice, retired at age sixty, and lived another twenty-two years as a gentleman farmer. An avowed Federalist, Crosby did not enter Maine politics post statehood.

Belfast gained its third lawyer when Harvard-educated John Wilson arrived in 1803. Wilson's Irish-born father had emigrated as a child, living in Lexington, Massachusetts, and later Peterborough, New Hampshire.[19] Wilson's biography was written by the son of his "competitor" at law. William George Crosby, like his father William Crosby, read law and became a lawyer. He served as governor of Maine from 1853 to 1855.[20] Wilson, no doubt, loomed large in the Crosby household, if the stories are any evidence.

He liked friendly competition, and he considered the elder William Crosby a worthy adversary: "[Wilson] believed that honorable rivalry was the most effective stimulant to provoke the largest development of learning and talent."[21] The senior Crosby and Wilson competed for years, until Crosby became chief justice of the Circuit Court of Common Pleas, and Wilson was elected to the U.S. House of Representatives for two terms: 1813–1815 and 1817–1819.[22] He also served as captain in Belfast's cavalry militia, established in 1804. Prior to his service in the U.S. Congress, Wilson represented Belfast in the Massachusetts Legislature in 1806.[23] During the War of 1812, his house was confiscated by British army officers, who briefly took control of the town with 700 troops.[24] Wilson helped to separate Waldo County from Hancock County and suggested the name Waldo.[25] In working to create a new county, Wilson helped set up Belfast as the county seat. This would be the place where court convened, lawyers gathered, and business deals were recorded. One of the more mundane yet necessary tasks he worked on was a committee to establish a community graveyard.[26] He worked with Belfast's two other lawyers (Field and Crosby senior) to draft a measure urging repeal of the federal embargo. In the U.S. House of Representatives, he helped make sure a Collector of Customs position was housed in Belfast from 1818 onward. [27]

Wilson was active in Belfast's social life as well as in its governance. Dances, held in Huse's tavern or at Cunningham's hotel, drew thirty couples regularly. In 1808, twenty-five men of Wilson's acquaintance—including fellow lawyers Field and Crosby, and the leading merchants, such as Francis Anderson—planned a subscription series of four balls at Cunningham's hotel. The cost of the subscription covered one musician and food consisting of crackers, milk biscuits and buns, ham, cheese, brandy, wine, and so forth from 6 p.m. until midnight. Each subscribing male could bring one friend for whom he had to vouch. Every male had to dance in shoes and wear white gloves. Card playing was banished during the dance. The fact that it was forbidden in writing suggests that card playing (and betting) was a regular feature of entertainment, at least among Belfast's male community. Given that a shoe requirement was written down implies that shoes were not necessarily readily at hand and that a good many males may have been going around shoddily shod. Perhaps brogans (work shoes) were being singled out—men needed to have dance shoes, an unnecessary expense.

Any man living in Belfast regularly had to pay the subscription if he wanted to attend. The cost? A rather steep $1.25 per male subscriber per event.[28] Of the twenty-five men who worked on the committee to create the four-dance series, not one carried the surname of an original settler. The elite—those who could afford to spend $5 on a dance series plus dance shoes and gloves—were in a different social class than the hardy souls who had migrated from New Hampshire and Massachusetts nearly forty years earlier.[29]

Wilson was usually among the honored guests at any Belfast fetes. Fourth of July celebrations were generally prestigious affairs, involving an "excellent dinner" at one of the local establishments. The 1820 July

Fourth celebration was also an excuse to celebrate Maine's new separation from Massachusetts as a state in its own right. At Cunningham's hotel that year, Wilson was called on as master of ceremonies to offer a toast to commemorate the event: "'Maine an independent State. May her Legislators possess the patriotism of Fox and the intelligence of Pitt; her Judges, the science of Mansfield and decision of Holt; her Orators, the lightening [sic] of Cicero and the thunder of Demosthenes.'"[30] He was also called upon to serve on a planning committee to prepare a program to commemorate Thomas Jefferson and John Adams upon their deaths in 1826.[31] Wilson's first wife, Hannah Leach, was the daughter of bona fide Scottish immigrant and Belfast merchant Andrew Leach.[32] While we could argue that the couple shared an ethnic background, it is important to note that class also was involved—the daughter of a merchant married a lawyer. Members of the elite stayed within ranks.

In his biography of Wilson, William George Crosby used language common to all descriptions of those the community accepted. Wilson was "able," "ingenuous," and "an inflexibly, upright man."[33] Crosby made much of Wilson's honesty, courtesy, and popular manners, and named him "a universal favorite."[34] He took pains to limn in his

Figure 2.3 William George Crosby, lawyer and amateur historian, was born in Belfast. Courtesy of the Belfast Historical Society and Museum.

portrait a man of great physical abilities, calmness, and courage, traits we must assume were important to Crosby, if not to the community at large. In demonstration of Wilson's abilities, Crosby told the story—possibly apocryphal—of a witness who held a grudge against Wilson because of Wilson's treatment of him in the courtroom. The grudge-holding witness attacked Wilson in his offices when he found the lawyer alone: "It was but the work of a moment for Mr. W. to seize him by the collar and place him not very gently, in a horizontal position on the floor; he then very deliberately sat down on him." When a "brother lawyer" entered the office and cried out he feared the prostrate man was dead, Wilson deadpanned, according to his biographer, "Yes, I am aware of that, and I am the Coroner's Inquest sitting on the body!"[35] The droll sense of humor after violence is triumphantly overthrown is presented with a flourish by Crosby. We can safely assume that the "brother lawyer" was the elder William Crosby. This story was evidently well polished and told with relish. In a mere five sentences the younger Crosby gives a succinct tale of frontier justice and humor. We could also assume that the younger Crosby heard this tale many a time from his father and that it was most probably told for a laugh.

We learn more about the sense of place through the depiction of humor presented by the younger Crosby's written biography of Wilson. Wryly, Crosby recounts tale after tale showing Wilson winning whatever battle—*with just the right word*. According to Crosby, Wilson was a member of an early Belfast club—the Lazy Club. There were no written bylaws for this club, of course, but its members never ran when they could walk. Wilson ran downhill one day and was "reported to the Club."[36] He was tried by the club's members but argued in his defense that it was easier to run down a hill than to walk it. The ingenuous defense notwithstanding, Wilson's "pound of flesh" was extracted, which in deciphering Crosby's tales probably meant Wilson was responsible for buying multiple rounds of whatever club members were drinking. Again, the younger Crosby most likely learned these tales because they were part of his father's repertoire, tales told repeatedly to regale audiences of listeners. Crosby polished them for written delivery. He describes Wilson as having at least one stereotypical Irish trait: The gift of gab. While Wilson's father came from Ireland, John Wilson was born in New Hampshire. We do not know about his mother's ethnic roots. And, we must remember, these stories appear to have been told by Crosby senior, a man whose ancestors were several generations in Massachusetts. Are the traits the younger Crosby touts Irish, or are they American?

Education and Access

Among other Belfast elites who traced their roots to Ireland were Irish-born and Dublin College–trained schoolteacher William Lowney, who arrived in Belfast in 1804, shortly after the first lawyers.[37] His son, Nathaniel, born in Monmouth, Maine, in 1798, grew up in Belfast. Son Nathaniel also taught school for a few years and then read law in the Belfast office of Judge Alfred Johnson. Nathaniel was admitted to the bar in 1827. Judge Johnson, with whom he trained, was involved in Jacksonian Democratic Party politics. Lowney, his former law student, was, too.

The professional class prepared their sons for public lives, starting with their educations. Field and Crosby sons, as well as those of Hugh Anderson, attended Bowdoin College, the Congregationalist bastion in Brunswick, Maine. Other sons of the elite attended college in Waterville, the Baptist answer to Bowdoin. A handful went to Harvard. Education among Belfast's first generation of professional men had provided the tools that led to money and political power, which further enabled the members of that generation to pass on that kind of access to their children.

Belfastians were less apt to hark to Scotch-Irish predecessors in speeches or politics than New Hampshire professional men did in the mid- to late nineteenth century. Although *nineteenth-century* Belfast historian William White asserted that Belfast was settled by Scotch-Irish people, that was not an argument made in mid-century political struggles. Irish voters—especially in the Democratic Party—had clout. Local politicians worked hard to attract and keep Irish voters.

Hugh Johnston Anderson was not afraid to use his *Irish* ancestry in his rise from Belfast merchant to state and national political office holder. In fact, he and his supporters talked about his Irishness but did not mention his religious affiliation. Merchant Anderson, first-generation American, moved into the up-and-coming "middling" class even as a teenager. This class of people created a number of self-help groups, such as the Belfast Debating Society in 1825, of which he was a founding member.[38] By 1832, he had accrued enough wealth as a merchant to fuel his plan to become one of a handful of men behind the Waldo Bank, serving as a director. The bank, however, failed in the Panic of 1837.[39]

The two young men—Hugh Anderson and Nathaniel Lowney—participated in a number of joint ventures together. Perhaps we can infer that they understood one another, sharing a cultural and ethnic heritage. Both were members of a corporation formed to create a railroad between Belfast and Quebec in 1835. Transportation, they knew, was key to command growth in Maine. Yet the railroad project, too, withered in the economic collapse of 1837.[40] Opportunity may have appeared blighted, but both men rose rapidly to positions of real power in state politics, and,

Figure 2.4 The Anderson home on Primrose Hill in Belfast. Courtesy of the Belfast Historical Society and Museum.

at least, Anderson was able to translate that into a life-long career in federal service. Politics also provided "spoils" to victors: Jobs in various local and federal venues made these men wealthy.

Politics and Access

In the Irish Famine decade, Anderson made his first run for governor of Maine, then a position elected annually. He used his *Irishness* to his advantage to win the election. In that first campaign, Anderson competed against another first-generation American for the Democratic nomination—a man whose parents also came from Ireland. But, Edward Kavanagh of Newcastle, forty-four miles south of Belfast, was Catholic, educated at Catholic schools in Boston, Washington, D.C., Baltimore, and Montreal.[41]

Kavanagh, a lawyer, had been active in Maine politics for at least two decades. He wrote a petition to the Maine Constitutional Convention, urging that the state constitution do away with any disqualifications against Catholics, urging, "No religious test as qualification for public office [be] required; no ministerial tax in support of the clergy [be] allowed."[42] Kavanagh won a hotly contested U.S. congressional seat in 1830, the first Catholic from New England to serve in Congress.[43] He served as U.S. attaché to Lisbon from 1835 to 1841, and he was appointed one of four Maine commissioners on the Webster-Ashburton proposal for the northern boundary question. The latter appointment came back to haunt him in his run for the Democratic nomination for governor. The 1842 Webster-Ashburton Treaty settled the U.S.–Canadian boundary between Maine and New Brunswick, which had been a contentious issue for decades.

Kavanagh was elected to the state Legislature in 1842 and then chosen as president of the state Senate. His credentials, however, were no match for Anderson's political ties, nor were they able to overcome his affiliation with the Webster-Ashburton Treaty or his support of pro-slavery Southerner John C. Calhoun for U.S. president.

Kavanagh became the first Catholic governor in New England by happenstance. As president of the state Senate, he succeeded Governor John Fairfield when Fairfield resigned in 1843 upon his election to the U.S. Senate. Meanwhile, Belfast's Hugh Anderson was a friend and ardent supporter of Democratic former U.S. President Martin Van Buren, who had lost reelection in 1840 to Whig William Henry Harrison. Anderson had a deal with Fairfield—Fairfield would go to Washington to take the vacant Senate seat, and Anderson would get the Democratic nomination for governor. In a letter to Van Buren, Fairfield skewered Kavanagh's ability to outshine Anderson:

> Kavanagh, who is President of the Senate, will of course be acting Governor for the remainder of the year [21 days]. This may give him *some* advantage over Anderson, they being rival claimants for the next nomination, but I trust not much. Kavanagh's being a Catholic, having participated in the negotiations of the late treaty, and being in favor of [John C.] Calhoun, will, I think, more than counterbalance the advantage which he can derive from his position as Prest. [*sic*] of the Senate and acting Governor.[44]

When sitting Governor Kavanagh ran later that year for the Democratic nomination for a full one-year term, he lost to Anderson.

Rumors rumbled that Kavanagh had been denied the nomination because he was Irish Catholic. Yet *The Republican Journal* in Belfast argued in that election season that being Catholic was a nonissue. The newspaper asserted that Anderson's Irish credentials were bona fide—both his parents came from Ireland. The newspaper refused to equate *Irish* with *Catholic*, sidestepping any such discussion. The newspaper seemed to argue that reducing *Irishness* to Catholicism was not helpful. *Irishness* was more important a measure than being Catholic:

> The democratic party, which has ever been the firmest [of] champions of liberty of speech and of opinion would never proscribe a man for

his religious opinions. The Waldo Signal, which is a good authority upon no subject, gave currency to and probably invented, this falsehood some weeks since. The Bangor Democrat, in the course of an excellent reply to this slander, observes: .... The very men who are attempting to excite a prejudice against [Mr. Anderson] and a sympathy for Mr. Kavanagh, or rather to prevent Irishmen from voting the democratic ticket, would have appealed to another class of citizens to oppose Mr. Kavanagh if he had been nominated because he was an Irish Catholic.[45]

Anderson won the 1843 election—and two more (in 1844 and 1845).[46] He continued to pay homage to his Irish heritage, even after leaving elected office. He presided at a public meeting on 23 February 1847 to "co-operate in measures then in progress for the famishing poor in Ireland." The effort raised $193, which was "forwarded to the treasurer of the relief fund."[47] In subsequent years, Anderson went on to serve two terms in Congress, remaining a good friend of Martin Van Buren in the process and serving in the Franklin Pierce administration.[48]

In the Famine decade, Anderson was active in state "improvement" projects, helping to establish the state reform school, for example. By mid-century, the former governor was vice president of the Belfast Lyceum and frequently speaking at public events, such as the installation of a new minister at the First Congregational Society (Unitarian) and at Fourth of July celebrations.[49] He served on the Maine Board of Education and was involved in drafting a city charter for Belfast, which included a five-year audit of city expenditures, and presenting the proposed charter to the Legislature.[50] Soon after fellow New Englander Franklin Pierce became president in 1853, Anderson won appointment as U.S. customs commissioner in Washington, D.C. He later became commissioner of the San Francisco mint.[51] He retired to Portland, Maine. When he died in 1881, his body was returned to the place he considered his hometown—Belfast.

Nathaniel Lowney, his long-time partner in public projects, too, rose through the ranks, serving as register of probate from 1827 to 1837; clerk of the courts in 1838; chair of the Belfast Board of Selectmen for nine years; state representative in 1848; and collector of customs for the Belfast District, 1837–1841 and again in 1845.[52] Lowney was active in local committees, helping lay out Grove Cemetery.[53] He also served as treasurer of the Waldo County Bible Society.[54] Significantly, nowhere in Lowney's biography, nor anywhere in the *History of Belfast,* does Joseph Williamson Jr. describe Lowney's political battles. His political plum—Collector for the District of Belfast—was a federal appointment, made by the Democratic administration of President Martin Van Buren. Lowney served from 1838 through the first quarter of 1841—when William Henry Harrison's Whig administration took power in

Washington. In that first year, Lowney reported collecting $5,100.53 for the District of Belfast.[55] Among other matters, collectors oversaw a fund to "relieve ... sick and indigent seamen, from whose hard earned wages it had been accumulated."[56] When Democratic President James K. Polk reappointed Lowney in 1845, an unsigned remonstrance was sent to the U.S. Senate, accusing Lowney of "wrongful and extravagant expenditure of the Hospital money—either fraudulently or negligently."[57] The Senate voted to defeat Lowney's nomination in August 1846.[58] For five months and four days of work in 1845, Lowney earned $1052.66.[59] Government work could be lucrative.

Did lawyer Wilson, the merchants Anderson (Francis and Hugh), and teacher-then-lawyer Lowney move in well-connected circles because they were Protestant or because they were firmly entrenched in the middling classes? Was it possible that education, community, and political networks provided substantial rewards? Most likely, first-generation Irish Americans of the professional class moved easily into mainstream Belfast, becoming power brokers and molders of opinion. Catholic merchant William S. Brannagan—like his Protestant counterparts—did well, too. Perhaps the "frontier" aspect of Belfast helped all these men to "make it".[60] Education also played a supporting role in their class aspirations: These men could read and write, but there was more. Profits seemed to dictate acceptance of difference in nineteenth-century Belfast. Religious affiliation did not have the same onus—at least in public documentation—in Maine that it carried in other places. While Massachusetts nursed its anti-Catholicism for more than two centuries, Maine chose another route, with a few local exceptions.[61]

Notes

1 Joseph Williamson, "Autobiography of William Crosby [senior]," in *The History of the City of Belfast, Maine*, Vol. 1 (Somersworth, New Hampshire: New England History Press, 1982), 367–8.

2 Williamson, Vol. 1, 525–82. Williamson's "Necrology" section lists ages at death, drawn from data provided by Rev. Price, which he compared to town records.

3 Alan Taylor, "'Sprung up in a Day': Belfast, Maine Emerges as a Market Town," in *Early Histories of Belfast, Maine: Annals of Belfast for Half a Century by William George Crosby, Sketches of the Early History of Belfast by John Lymburner Locke, History of Belfast by Herman Abbot, a History of Belfast with Introductory Remarks on Acadia by William White* (Camden, Maine: Picton Press, 1989), v.

4 *Vital Records of Belfast, Maine to the Year 1892*, Vol. II, 12. Francis Anderson married Jane Dunlap of Boston. The bans were published on 14 July 1803.

5 Edward T. McCarron, "Facing the Atlantic: The Irish Merchant Community of Lincoln County, 1780–1820," in *They Change Their Sky: The Irish in Maine* (Orono: University of Maine Press, 2004), 73.

6 *Account Current with the Charitable Irish Society, Membership Account*

Book, 1837–1861, Vol. 12. Officers had to be "Natives of Ireland or any other part of the British Dominions of Irish Extraction, being Protestants, and, Inhabitants of Boston," unpublished. n.d., n.p.

7   *Constitution, By-laws and History of the Charitable Irish Society of Boston: Instituted 1737* (Boston: James F. Cotter & Co., n.d.), 105. The Society eliminated the Protestant-only requirement for officers around 1765; non-Protestant members had been accepted as early as 1740. Many thanks to Professor Emerita Catherine Shannon for sharing her (then) unpublished paper, "The Irish in New England," prepared for the Dublin Seminar for New England Folklife, 24 June 2012, now published as "With Good Will Doing Service: The Charitable Irish Society of Boston," *Historical Journal of Massachusetts* 43, no. 1 (Winter 2015), 12. See *Rules and Regulations of the Scots Charitable Society: Instituted at Boston a.d. 1684 and Reconstituted 1786*. The Scots Charitable Society was created in 1684; however, the immigrants from Ireland chose instead to create their own Protestant society, celebrating Irish identity. In fact, the Scots Charitable Society relaunched in 1786, because, "Many of the former members having removed during the late revolution, the remaining part applied to the Legislature for a charter." The charter was granted in 1786. We can speculate that those members of the Scots Charitable Society who "removed" remained Loyalists.

8   Shannon hypothesized that this was done in order to establish camaraderie: "After 1794 the annual meetings were always held on March 17th and from 1797 forward were always billed as a St. Patrick Day event which suggests additional progress in making the society more inclusive than in its beginnings."

9   *Account Current with the Charitable Irish Society, Membership Account Book, 1837–1861*, Vol. 12.

10   Crosby, 16. Jonathan Wilson, not to be confused with lawyer John Wilson, was the primary mover of the enterprise and the first toll collector on the bridge after its construction.

11   Williamson, Vol. 1, 694. Among Belfast's sixteen merchants in 1815 were John H. Conner, whose name sounds Irish, and Andrew Leach, who came from Scotland.

12   Williamson, Vol. 1, 843–7. Williamson's numbers conflict with those of William George Crosby, who says there were 1,259 people living in Belfast in 1810. Crosby, "Annals of Belfast," 2.

13   Williamson, Vol. 1, 384.

14   Williamson.

15   Taylor, "'Sprung up in a Day,'" v.

16   Christopher M. Spraker, "The Lost History of Slaves and Slave owners in Billerica," *Historical Journal of Massachusetts* 42, no. 1 (Winter 2014), 120.

17   Williamson, Vol. 1, 386.

18   Williamson, Vol. 1, 365.

19   Williamson, Vol. 1, 388.

20   Spraker, 128.

21   Williamson, Vol. 1, 388.

22   Williamson, Vol. 1, 389.

23   Crosby, 14.

24   Williamson, Vol. 1, 428.

25   Crosby, 162.

26   Williamson, Vol. 1, 696.

27   Williamson, Vol. 1, 698.

28 Williamson, Vol. 1, 763. The series, then, would have cost each subscriber $5, approximately $100 in 2018 dollars. Officialdatafoundation.org, downloaded 25 July 2019.

29 Williamson, Vol. 1, 763.

30 Williamson, Vol. 1, 777.

31 Williamson, Vol. 1, 786.

32 Williamson, Vol. 1, 535. Andrew Leach, born in 1753, came from Glencoe, Scotland.

33 Crosby, 162. William George Crosby, like his father, became a lawyer.

34 Williamson, Vol. 1, 162.

35 Williamson, Vol. 1, 162.

36 Williamson, Vol. 1, 162.

37 Williamson, Vol. 1, 399.

38 Williamson, Vol. 1, 321.

39 Williamson, Vol. 1, 702.

40 Williamson, Vol. 1, 668.

41 William Leo Lucey, S.J., *Edward Kavanagh: Catholic * Statesman * Diplomat from Maine, 1795–1844* (Francestown, New Hampshire: Marshall Jones, 1946), 70.

42 Lucey, 73–5.

43 Lucey, 96.

44 Lucey, 204-5.

45 Unsigned, "CATHOLICISM," *The Republican Journal* 15, no. 24 (11 July 1843): 2.

46 Williamson, Vol. 1, 880.

47 Williamson, Vol. 1, 737.

48 Joseph Williamson and Alfred Johnson, *The History of the City of Belfast, Maine*, Vol. 2 (Somersworth, New Hampshire: New England History Press and Belfast Free Library, 1983), 408.

49 Williamson, Vol. 1, 270, 325, 706, 777.

50 Williamson, Vol. 1, 149, 332–3.

51 "Death of Ex-Gov. Anderson," in *The Republican Journal* (2 June 1881): 2.

52 Williamson, Vol. 1: 399; U.S. Senate, 29 December 1845. *Journal of the Executive Proceedings of the Senate of the United States of America, from December 1, 1845 to August 14, 1848, Inclusive*, Vol. VII (Washington: GPO, 1887), 11.

53 Williamson, Vol. 1, 522.

54 Williamson, Vol. 1, 745.

55 *An Account of the Receipts and Expenditures of the United States for the Year 1839*. Prepared by the Register of the Treasury (Washington: Blair and Rives, 1840). This was a pittance on the national level but a sizable amount for Maine (0.01 percent of the Treasury balance of $36,891,196.94 for the year). Portland, with John Anderson (no relation to Hugh as far as I can tell) as collector, collected $126,742.04 in the same time frame—but that was clearly not the norm in Maine's smaller ports. Belfast was actually the third highest in Maine, following Portland and Bath ($14,210.72). The lowest amount collected was $26.03 (Wiscassat).

56 "The Case of Nathaniel M. Lowney, Collector of Belfast," unsigned pamphlet no. 1364 (Maine Historical Society, n.d.), 2.

57 "Case of Nathaniel M. Lowney," 1.

58 *Journal of the Executive Proceedings of the Senate of the United States of America from December 1, 1845, to August 14, 1848, inclusive*, Vol. VII. (Aug. 8, 1846), (Washington, D.C.: GPO, 1887): 153.

59 *Register of All Officers and Agents, Civil, Military, and Naval, in the Service of the United States on the Thirtieth September 1845 with the Names, Force, and Condition of All Ships and Vessels Belonging to the United States, and When and Where Built Together with the Names and Compensation of all Printers in Any Way Employed by Congress, or Any Department or Officer of the Government.* Prepared at the Department of State (Washington: J. & G.S. Gideon, 1845), 119.

60 Maine State Historical Society, Coll. 2791 Johnson Family of Belfast, Box 10 of 45, Folder 6 1804-1962. Acc. #2014.187. Alfred Johnson, and later his sons, served as Brannagan's estate lawyer. Brannagan's sister in Ireland, Mrs. Teresa Gunning, and his niece in Ireland, Miss Annie Cumiskey, inherited $27,495.34, nearly a million dollars in modern money. In addition to his Irish relatives, Brannagan bequeathed $5,000 to the Bishop of Portland to maintain Catholic services in Belfast; $1,000 to clear the cost of the parsonage in Belfast; $500 each to three Catholic priests in Maine–Rev. Fr. Patrick Gerrity of Winterport, Rev. Fr. M.C. O'Brien of Bangor, and Rev. Fr. J.E. Kealy of Belfast; $200 to the Society of Angel Guardian of Boston; $100 to James Haney, a long-time business associate in Belfast; $100 to Louise W. Johnson of Belfast, and Mrs. Caroline C. Willard of Cambridge, Mass., to be spent in his memory; $100 to the Belfast Humane Society; $500 to the Presentation Convent in Dublin; and $200 to Miss Margaret Havey of Belfast. His estate also had to pay $780.24 in inheritance tax (4 percent for anything more than $500. Lawyers' fees also took about $6,400.

61 During the Know-Nothing movement in the 1850s, the Reverend John Bapst, S.J., was tarred and feathered in Ellsworth, a result of anti-Catholic editorials in the local newspaper, involving Catholics' objections to using the Protestant Bible in public school education, the public conversion of two well-known local women to Catholicism also stoked anti-Catholic bias. Lucey, 130–2. Why was Maine's constitution more liberal, religiously speaking? It may have something to do with the participants in the final constitutional convention held in Portland on 11 October 1819. Of the 274 delegates, forty-five were involved in sea-related commercial enterprises; thirty-seven were lawyers; thirteen were doctors; seventeen civil servants; eight school teachers/principals; two editors; two surveyors; eight Baptist ministers; four Methodist ministers; only one Congregationalist minister; and eight farmers. One hundred delegates' vocations could not be ascertained by George Chamberlain, an Augusta school teacher, in 1890. See Chapter VIII in Ronald F. Banks, *Maine Becomes a State: The Movement to Separate Maine from Massachusetts, 1785–1820* (Somersworth: New Hampshire Publishing Company/Maine Historical Society, 1973), 150–83.

3 The Irish "Other"

THE FOURTH OF JULY IN CANADA. –The custom of firing cannons in honor of the 4th of July having extended beyond the 4th degree of north latitude, as far as Sherbrooke, Lower Canada, an effort was made on Tuesday last by a number of inhabitants of that town, armed with axe handles, to capture the offending cannon. This attempt was resisted by the other party, and a general melee ensued, in which clubs and axe handles were plied with no small damage of sundry heads and shins. –Two or three persons were hurt; one man had the bridge of his nose broken in, and another had a serious gash on the side of his head. The attacking party were beaten off, and the cannon kept by those who used it. Most of these engaged in firing and protecting the cannon, the Gazette says, were Irish.[1]

Unlike the professional men who ventured to Belfast between the Revolutionary War and the War of 1812, Irish immigrants of the mid- to late nineteenth century left no written histories of Belfast. In fact, most of the writing of the time was *about*—not *by*—the Irish immigrants of the nineteenth century. Their stories were told in public and some private documents—written by members of the receiving culture. They were the "Other" Irish.

In the 1850 U.S. census of Belfast, Maine, the first to note country of origin and the first to register Famine influx, 206 people listed Ireland as their land of birth.[2] The total population of Belfast at mid-century was 5,052. The immigrant Irish community was therefore a little over 4 percent—as far as census data can provide insight. People from Ireland (or their descendants) found their way to mid-coast Maine in a steady trickle from 1770 on, meaning that Belfast old-timers had roots in Ireland, even as newcomers arrived from the same island. Without something akin to the 1850 census data, however, it is difficult to as-certain if these individuals were Irish, of Irish extraction, or were American-born descendants several generations removed from Irish-born ancestors. Names sometimes give indications of ethnic origins, but those

DOI: 10.4324/9781003187660-3

labels are fraught. As there were few permanent church structures, let alone accompanying membership lists, there is little indication of immigrants' religious backgrounds.

The Irish immigrants of the nineteenth century, unlike the Ulster immigrants of the previous century, made no attempts to turn their backs on Irish roots—at least in the written evidence Belfast, Maine, provides. In addition, while Catholicism might have served as an Irish communal solidifier in large urban areas, it did not have the same power in the smaller, more rural economy. In fact, followers of Catholicism in Maine came from distinct ethnic groups speaking different languages: Passamaquoddy (Sipayik), Penobscot (Indian Island), Maliseet (Houlton), Mi'kmaq (Aroostook), Acadiens (Saint John River Valley), and Irish (even if English-speaking). Catholicism as a measurement of Irishness in rural Maine is, thus, not indicative of much.

Irish immigrants in Belfast formed no public associations—unless, perhaps, individuals joined a temperance group or an agricultural society. Freemasonry, often associated with the Scotch-Irish, was introduced to Belfast in 1817 but was put into abeyance after the "Morgan Murder" in 1826 when Masons were implicated. The Lodge was not reintroduced for twenty years.[3] Odd Fellows, Bible societies, Young Men's Christian Association, agricultural societies, and temperance societies formed throughout the nineteenth century. An Irish Catholic Knights of Columbus council wasn't created in Belfast until 1955: Belfast's group is named for immigrant William S. Brannagan.[4] Groups—including fire departments—were created by the "movers and shakers" in town—men of substance and the professions. While a Mechanics Association was established in 1841, with Benjamin Kelley as president and the editor of *The Republican Journal* as secretary, there is no evidence this attracted Irish immigrants as such. The Kelley family, for example, had been several generations in New England, so this was not necessarily an Irish organization.[5]

Irish Belfast

What is clear, however, is that, at least in the local weekly newspaper(s), Irish immigrants and their descendants continued to look back at the homeland—if the amount of coverage of things Irish can be used to ascertain a sense of Irishness. This did not mean, however, that Irish immigrants and/or descendants of earlier immigrants had any intention of returning "home" physically.

Through a close reading of *The Republican Journal* prior to 1845 and the beginning of the Famine exodus, popular ideas about (and perhaps from) the Irish in Belfast, Maine, are clear. For example, the debate over the Democratic gubernatorial nomination in 1842, between Irish Protestant Hugh Anderson and Irish Catholic Edward Kavanagh, created a new category of discussion that was not tied to Ulster Irish/ Protestant Irish versus Catholic Irish. *Irish* and *Irishness*, the editors argued, existed separately from and were more important than the category of *Catholic* or *Protestant* in making political choices. Democrats in Maine sought Irish votes—they did not care whether those votes were Protestant or Catholic. The implication then would be that *Irish voters* counted. In this, the local newspaper was perhaps more Irish than Catholic, in opposition to other "Irish-American" publications.[6]

What is in a Name?

While the majority of eighteenth-century immigrants from Ireland tended to be Presbyterians from Ulster, from the 1830s (pre-Famine) through 1920, 90 percent of immigrants from Ireland *were* Catholic.[7] It was only in Belfast's death records, with their paucity of data, that people from Ireland were identified: "1824 March 24: Daniel McCarvey, a native of Ireland, aged 21, while rolling a cask of water, fell between a vessel and the wharf, and was crushed to death."[8] McCarvey had the requisite "Mc" in front of his name denoting Irish. Not all those labeled "Irish," however, had such clear names: "1834 April 6: John Smith, an Irishman, was found dead from the effects of intemperance."[9] This cause of death might be a clue, but what of the following: "1860 March 12: Peter Welch, an Irishman, was drowned. His body was found seven weeks afterward"?[10] Was Bridget Fahy, age five, scalded to death on 15 February 1860, Irish? Or Cora A. Kelly, age four, burned to death on 11 December 1860, Irish?[11] How would we know that William White, Morris Harriss, Joseph Kerr, and James Convey were all natives of Ireland if the chronicler had not so noted?[12]

There are tantalizing hints of "Irishness" in the U.S. censuses taken in Belfast, beginning in 1800, based on surnames. A number of heads of households have Mc/Mac in front of their names—McFarland, McKeen, McLaughlin. These early settlers' *descendants* may have claimed Scotch-Irish heritage, so the theory that Mc designates Irish ethnicity is not a valid measure.[13] There were also men surnamed Ryan, Griffin, and O'Bryan in the 1810 and 1820 censuses.

Forty years after settlement, Connor, Bryan, and Burk [sic] were in the census rolls. The supposedly Irish name Burke comes from the Norman *de Burgo*. Does someone of Norman stock count as Irish? (If Ulster Protestants do not, why would descendants of Normans?) How many generations must a family live in an area before it is considered indigenous? The 1830 U.S. census provided more tantalizing names—Rourke, Tie (a misspelling for Tadhg, perhaps), McGroth, Boyles, Brown, Gammon, Kelly, Lowney.

Catholics in Maine

Even in the 1850 census, census takers did not always note the country of origin. For example, no census taker recorded that William S. Brannagan of Belfast was from Ireland, even though he came from Ashbourne, County Meath; he had the information carved into the Celtic cross erected to mark his grave in Grove Cemetery. The census did not record religious affiliation either, but Brannagan was proudly Catholic.

Statehood, and a new state constitution, changed possibilities for Catholics in Maine.

Maine was on the frontier rim with Boston at the hub. In 1820, as part of the Missouri Compromise, Maine became a state with its own constitution. That document guaranteed religious and political freedom to Catholics, doing away with Massachusetts' requirements that Congregational ministers be supported by taxation and that public officials take oaths, excluding Catholics from office.[14] Before statehood, when Massachusetts' law still required Congregational churches be established along coasts and waterways, Maine's residents in the hinterlands were left more to their own persuasions. Evangelical movements and denominations out of step with Boston's Puritan ethos, such as Baptists, had more traction inland.[15] While Catholic priests were banned

Figure 3.1 William S. Brannagan's grave monument at Grove Cemetery in Belfast is a Celtic cross. Photo by author.

Figure 3.2 William S. Brannagan was born in Ashbourne, County Meath, in 1811. He died in Belfast in 1901. The Knights of Columbus chapter in Belfast adopted Brannagan's name. There was no group in Belfast before 1955. Photo by author.

from Boston, on penalty of death, as late as the American Revolution, the handful of Jesuit missionaries on the Maine frontier serving Penobscot converts on Indian Island, or Passamaquoddy at Sipayik, or among the Maliseet or Mi'kmaq were mostly left alone.[16]

The total numbers of Catholics pre- and post-statehood changed dramatically, however. In the waning days of the eighteenth century and early decades of the nineteenth, Catholic numbers had risen slowly. As the century unfolded, however, more Catholics were to be found in Maine.[17] As a result, there were more Catholic schools in Maine.[18] Priests, however, were scarce.

The Catholic hierarchy feared the relative scarcity of practicing Catholics in Maine had a more prosaic cause than constitutions: Eighteenth-century unmarried Catholic male immigrants, for example, in Ballstown Plantation, located just south of what became Belfast, rarely saw a priest.[19] These fishermen who had come via Newfoundland or Boston married local Protestant women.[20] While priests and Jesuits included the Belfast Catholic community in their circuits, observant Catholics were lucky if they had access to the Sacraments every other month. Evidently, this lack of constant priestly leadership left people to their own devices, and the Catholic hierarchy feared it could lead to a loss of faith. The implication was that "loss of faith" meant marrying outside the religion.[21] Boston-based Bishop Jean-Louis Ann Madelain Lefebvre de Cheverus visited Irish Catholic communities, such as Damariscotta, Newcastle, and Whitefield, and found only *twelve* Catholic *families* with forty children in 1799. By 1820, there were *108* Catholic *families* in the same area.[22]

Statehood after 1820 led to rapid population growth overall. By the 1830s, Bangor, forty miles north of Belfast, for example, had become America's largest "lumber depot."[23] As the general population grew, so too did the number of Catholics in Bangor, from fewer than twenty in 1830 to about a thousand by 1836. This growth, however, took place in the decades *before* the Irish Famine. This would indicate that immigrants came for economic reasons, seeking employment. They were not necessarily fleeing from Ireland as much as coming to America.[24] Bishop Cheverus saw growth of only a little over 11 percent prior to 1820; after statehood, yet well before the Irish Famine, the influx of Irish Catholics to Bangor led to a rapid 20 percent rise in just six years.[25]

Catholics in Belfast

On a diocesan trip to Indian Island in 1827, twelve miles north of Bangor, Boston-based Bishop Benedict Joseph Fenwick, Cheverus' successor, traveled through Belfast. According to his journal, he sought Catholic Irish in the "low-rent" area nearest Belfast's docks, an area known as Puddle Dock—home of Bridget Haugh McCabe. Fenwick equated Irish with Catholic, as his diary made clear. So, by 1827, then, assumptions about religious affiliations of newcomers from Ireland had already changed: While in the third decade of the eighteenth century the stereotype equated Irish with Presbyterian, by the third decade of the nineteenth century the stereotype equated Irish with Catholic.

American-born Fenwick recorded the first mention of Catholics in Belfast in his diary in July 1827. The bishop asked his Belfast hotelier if there were any Catholics in the area and received a negative reply.[26] The bishop went in search, to no avail. After dinner, he made a second sortie, finding "a lady carrying a small child in her arms."[27] A later writer, recounting the incident, speculated that Catholics somehow "knew" each other simply by looking: "Something about her seemed to appeal to the Catholic shepherd in search of his wandering flock. That mutual recognition, that expressive bond of sympathy which not unfrequently [*sic*] leads us to half suspect the truth of our suspicions."[28] Another writer reported the same incident thus: "[Bishop Fenwick] approached a woman who appeared to be Irish but who identified herself to the stranger with great reluctance."[29]

Two twentieth-century Catholic writers, summarizing the bishop's diary, did a disservice. Fenwick was more specific in his account: "After dinner took another walk to the upper part of the town—had not proceeded far, when I met an Irish woman coming into town from the country with a child in her arms."[30] He had no doubts that the woman he was approaching was Irish. According to his diary, Fenwick asked the woman bluntly if she were Catholic. The woman in question "[surveyed him] cautiously with her eyes some moments" before answering in the affirmative.[31]

How did the bishop recognize the woman as Irish, and why did he suppose an Irish woman would be Catholic? In other words, what were his cues as to her nationality and religious persuasion? It appears that even the clergy drew on stereotype. The account in *Maine Catholic Historical Magazine* doesn't say what cues the bishop might have been reading but claimed "[t]hat most if not all of these Irish emigrants [sic] arriving in Belfast on this occasion mentioned by Mr. Williamson, were Catholics."[32]

In the years before the Irish Famine of the 1840s, Irish women wore a hooded cloak, generally colored blue, black, gray, or sometimes red.[33] Irish peasant women also traditionally wore red petticoats and/or red skirts with shawls around their shoulders.[34] Perhaps it was such attire that hinted at the origins of the woman walking in Belfast with her infant, and if that were the case, then the bishop could "read" such a public performance of culture rather easily. But, it would appear, the Irish woman couldn't read the bishop's attire nor even understand his dialect in his "performance" as Catholic cleric. When the bishop asked where she was going, she answered, "Mr. McGann's." When he asked her to let him accompany her, she pointedly responded, "'No,' for, what ha[s] **the like of [you]** [the emphasis is in the original] to do at Mr. McGann's?"[35]

She obviously saw the man before her as a threat. Fenwick wrote that he told her he wanted to meet all the Catholics in town. She sneered. (The bishop wrote she was "arch.") "'Surely,' she replied, 'you were not going to his house when I first saw you; why therefore do you wish to go to it now?'" When Fenwick explained he wanted to give "'[Mr. McGann] and the other Catholics a little good advice on the Sabbath day,'" the woman opined that perhaps he was a "Minister [sic]." Fenwick replied in the affirmative, whereupon the woman, wrote Fenwick, turned abruptly and said, "'neither [McGann], nor his family, want to see **the like of you** [emphasis is in the original].'"[36]

After more oral sparring, the woman pointed him to McGann's house, according to the two later writers. Once again, the bishop was much more forthcoming. When it started to rain, the bishop put up his umbrella over the woman and her child and walked with her.[37] She became exasperated and demanded to know what he was doing and why he was following her. When he told her it was his intent to accompany her to McGann's, she told him that was not where she was heading.[38] Fenwick wrote in his diary that he told the woman he would follow her until she told him where McGann lived.

In modern terms, this was stalking: A lone woman carrying a child could not get rid of unwanted male attention. He threatened her: He would not leave her alone until she told him where to find the Catholics in town. From his bishop's perspective, he was perfectly justified in his aggressive behavior. Given the bishop's reportage of her responses, readers have some clues as to what her views were regarding the incident.

Perhaps it was an act of desperation, trying to rid herself of this strange man, but she finally pointed out a house near the wharves. The bishop's hunch that the Irish Catholics would be near the water was borne out, and he adopted a self-congratulatory tone in his journal. No McGann appears in the census records; however, the bishop left a detailed record of what he found there:

> On entering a room of this house, I beheld on every side but objects of poverty and wretchedness, a sick woman groaning in a corner of the room, two other women with very poor clothes, seated on the floor, eight or ten children bunched around and only one man, and he also poorly clad. I soon learned from him that he and another had just arrived at Belfast with their families, that they had been able to get but little work since their arrival, that almost all of them had been, and some of them were, still sick, and that they were all perishing for the want of the necessaries of life. Seeing so much misery, I immediately informed him who I was, gave him money, and directed him to go without delay and purchase tea, sugar, bread, butter and milk, if he could find it at that hour of the day, and afterwards I should enable him to procure other provisions.[39]

The newly arrived Irish were living near the wharves, a marginal existence literally. The bishop had sought the Catholic Irish there in his first circuit through town; thus, it would appear that his definition of Irish included poor, newly arrived, and Catholic. Given the fact that the woman the bishop encountered was hesitant to define herself as Catholic or Irish, we can deduce that she may have felt that those two identifiers were dangerous labels in 1827 Belfast—even if Maine's new state constitution did not slight Catholics.

The Irish woman was suspicious of Fenwick. When she remarked that perhaps he was a minister, she was using pointed language. A minister is Protestant; therefore, from her Irish perspective, the bishop was not "performing" Catholicism—in other words, he wasn't Irish. (Although Jesuits use the term for their financial officers, this definition doesn't seem to be what the woman was saying.) Fenwick, who was born in Maryland in 1782, had an American accent.[40] If the Irish woman had encountered a priest in Maine before, the odds were that priest would have been Irish, for eleven of the fifteen clergy in Fenwick's diocese were Irish-born.[41] It would appear, too, that Fenwick did not notice the verbal clue when the woman referred to him as a minister.

Fenwick, like many an American, also used dialect differences to mark the woman's "Otherness" in his memoirs.[42] When the bishop and the woman met again, it was at McGann's. Fenwick teased her: "'There,' said I jokingly, 'is an Irish woman and a Catholic, who when asked by a stranger to show the way to a friend's house, refused to do it. She cannot be a true born Catholic.'" Fenwick gave her response as: "'And surely it was because I thought it was no good you were after.'"[43] The woman became flustered after being admonished by another woman who informed her that she was speaking to the bishop, and he reassured her that her behavior had been perfectly prudent, which implies that it was wise not to acknowledge one's Catholicism publicly. Once again, he showed her difference by presenting her dialect: "'No, no .... it is not for the likes of me to behave amiss to my own Clergy when I know them.'" [44]

Bishop Fenwick wrote he advised the Irish he met in Belfast that "sober and industrious" people would do well in the new land. Even if Fenwick were using sober to mean staid or businesslike, the implication is that the Irish would need to overcome some natural tendency. He then urged the new immigrants to go to Whitefield (ironically named for a Protestant evangelist of the mid-1700s), where there was a group of established Irish Catholic immigrants.[45] This might also indicate that Belfast was considered an entrance point to Maine, not a final destination—especially for Irish Catholics, at least by the Catholic Church hierarchy in the area. Given Bishop Fenwick's reportage, the stereotypes surrounding the Irish had remained intact: Poor, ill, and needing to be admonished to be sober and industrious.

While the Irish Catholics of Belfast, by Fenwick's estimate, consisted of few families in 1827, by 1832 he estimated there were 150 Catholics in Belfast.[46] Perhaps Fenwick overestimated this number in an attempt to get more support for Catholic clergy in Maine—or the group was quite transient. Not quite a decade later, in 1841, the Reverend Moyses Fortier of the Quebec diocese reported he heard confessions from a mere twenty-three adults and thirteen children—hardly the estimated 150 Catholics of 1832. Granted, perhaps Fortier heard confessions from the French-speaking contingent of Catholics in Belfast, which does not seem possible. If there were French speakers in 1840, every single one must have left before 1850.[47] In fact, those recorded as coming from the Canadian Maritimes had generally been born in Ireland.[48] Very few, if any, immigrants arrived in Belfast from Quebec. Saint Francis of Assisi, Belfast's Catholic church, claimed the Catholic population in Belfast reached 100 in 1895.[49]

Religious Stereotype

Not all nineteenth-century immigrants from Ireland were Catholic, however. When Francis Banan died in the Waldo County town of Knox in October 1843, his obituary gave the very familiar story of deprivation. The Banan family, arriving a quarter century before the flood of Famine refugees, was destitute when it landed in Belfast, Maine, in August 1819:

> He was poor having spent all his substance in his emigration.—He was in a strange country penniless and forsaken, and was necessitated to spend his first night in this country in the open air on one of the wharves in Belfast village, having been rejected by those who had good homes and all the conveniences of this life.[50]

Here was the stereotype of the newly arrived Irish immigrant, but this man was not Catholic—nor was he Presbyterian. He was a "native of Ireland," and yet he was known as a "systematic christian [sic], a member and Leader in the Methodist Episcopal Church."[51] The writer of the obituary mused:

> What must have been the feelings of that good man knowing himself so far away from his native country, poor, forsaken, and friendless, with no better comforts for a night's rest than a cold, damp wharf, for himself, wife, and three infant children?[52]

Just eight years later (1827), Bishop Fenwick encountered the poor Irish, who *were* Catholic, yet the bishop had assumed that all (or most) Irish immigrants were Catholic, which, as the Banans made evident, was not always the case.

Numbers in Ireland supported the stereotype. An 1834 Irish religious census claimed around 80 percent of the total Irish population in 1834 was Catholic: Church of Ireland membership was 852,000; Presbyterians numbered 642,000; and dissenter groups, such as Methodists and Quakers, were minuscule in comparison (only around 22,000).[53] It appears, then, that Catholics in Ireland outnumbered other religionists, but so they had in 1718. What had changed, evidently, was who was leaving. The 1834 statistics seemed to back the assertion that Irish equals Catholic; however, only 38 percent of those Irish Catholics went to Mass, and that varied by region.[54] Mass attendance was low throughout the west of Ireland, averaging 20–30 percent.[55] Only 20 percent in Connaught, for example, went regularly, while 72 percent in Wexford did.[56] In 1840, there was just one priest per 3,000 and one nun to every 6,500 parishioners.[57] In sixty years' time, the ratio improved: One priest per 900 parishioners and one nun to every 400.[58]

Statistics show, too, that across national boundaries Irish-born Catholics were, for the most part, non-practicing. In nineteenth-century Britain, for example, *nearly half* of Irish-born Catholics didn't meet their "minimal religious obligation, their Easter duties."[59] Catholicism, as demonstrated through practice, did no better in the United States, at least in the Sixth Ward of New York City, by the mid-nineteenth century. Half of the Irish population there did not attend Mass. Approximately one of ten Irish laborers went to Mass, and only half of Irish immigrants between the ages of twenty and twenty-five had made their First Communion or knew their catechism.[60] Chicago Irish were only nominally Catholic.[61]

There was also an anticlerical strain at work even within Catholic Ireland. For many years, only sons of the wealthy could train for seminary. Because of the Penal Laws, those who wished to train for the priesthood had to travel to the Continent for their studies. This meant that there was an economic divide between priests and their flocks. The first native seminary after a hiatus of many years, St. Patrick's, Maynooth, charged for everything. Poor parishioners saw this as gouging. In fact, secret societies perpetrated violence, punishing greedy priests, and in some cases parishioners were so upset that they affiliated with the Church of Ireland.[62] That anticlerical stance traveled to the United States. In Worcester, Massachusetts, a Catholic congregation rioted on Palm Sunday in 1847, dragging its "landlord" priest, Matthew Gibson, who was English-born, from the rectory, manhandling him along the way.[63] Violence against priests could, therefore, arise from a Catholic congregation, although Protestant-on-Catholic violence was much more prevalent.

Becoming American

The Know-Nothing Movement—anti-immigrant, anti-Irish, and anti-Catholic—incited violence against Catholic communities in Maine in the 1850s, even leading David W. Bacon, the Bishop of Portland, in 1855 to arrive at night dressed as a layman in order to avoid a riot. The Know Nothings arose in the aftermath of massive Irish immigration to the United States following the Famine. The Reverend John Bapst, S.J., was tarred and feathered in Ellsworth, not far from Belfast, in 1854. A mob burned Old South Meeting House in Bath in July 1854 when Catholics were using it for services, and a group burned a church in Lewiston the following year.[64] There was no such overt act of violence against Catholics in Belfast—at least none that was recorded. The fact, though, that the Irish woman could not "read" Bishop Fenwick's attire as Catholic might indicate that he was traveling as a "layman," just as Bishop Bacon did nearly thirty years later.

Many of those who arrived from Ireland either directly or via Canada in the mid-nineteenth century were illiterate, seeking work as laborers; thus, this group left few written records other than those created by the already established community—court records and deeds. Joseph Williamson Jr.'s two-volume history of Belfast is generally thorough but has few details of the city's largest immigrant population. Williamson, however, devoted several pages to a discussion of the character of the Scotch-Irish, their roles in settlement of the city, and their patriotism.[65] The re-categorization of immigrants from Ulster as something different, as Scotch-Irish, was complete—and successful—by the post–Civil War era.

Williamson was not ignorant of the fact that 4 percent of Belfast's population hailed from Ireland. He came into constant contact with the residents of Puddle Dock—the area where Bridget Haugh McCabe lived and died—in his role as Judge of the Police Court, beginning in 1853. He was appointed to the position by Governor William G. Crosby, also a Belfast native, his friend and neighbor.[66] Williamson was repeatedly reappointed until the position became subject to election. He was then elected to a four-year term in 1856.[67] Even as a student in Bangor, Williamson was well aware of the plight of those in Ireland during the Famine of the late 1840s and the early 1850s, for example. His brother William kept him apprised of events in Belfast, such as a fund-raiser for Irish famine relief at the Unitarian Church on 3 March 1847. William informed Joseph that the Thomaston Brass Band fell $11 short of meeting expenses, let alone raising funds for the Irish. William rather glibly summed up the event by saying, "I rather think that they won't come here again this winter."[68]

Crimes of the Irish considered by Judge Williamson ran the gamut from youthful mayhem, to drunkenness, to assault and battery. For example, eleven-year-old Henry Haugh, Bridget's young cousin, was incarcerated by Judge Williamson for throwing stones after the judge fined him $1 and costs, but Henry did not—or could not—pay.

The list of the Irish fined for drunkenness in the mid-1850s is extensive: Brian McCabe (Bridget Haugh McCabe's husband), James Murphy, John Doran, Antony Mally, Lewis Ryan, Michael Raridan (Reardon), Peter Welch (multiple times), Charles Haugh (Bridget's uncle), Daniel Sweeney, Daniel Clary, Eben Ryan, Daniel Sullivan, and Terry Owen were all found guilty of public drunkenness and fined, as was Ann Welch.[69]

A good number of arrests for drunk-and-disorderly conduct took place in 1853 around that quintessential American holiday—the Fourth of July—not Saint Patrick's Day on 17 March or Orange Day on 12 July. The immigrant Irish community in the mid-nineteenth century celebrated Independence Day with a great deal of hoopla. For example, the newly instituted Police Court of 1853 had a busy time of it around the Fourth of July that year: John Doran, Brian McCabe, Antony Mally, and Lewis L. Ryan were all accused of drunkenness, were found guilty, and had to pay fines and costs. These four constitute nearly half the cases for the day.[70] A very small minority of the local population (0.09 percent) was also arrested and fined for public drunkenness.

In Belfast, Maine, the newly arrived Irish did not bring into play sectarian and nationalistic sensibilities—they acted "American." In a way, they acted more American than the Americans. Those Irishmen charged with drunkenness on the Fourth were Irish Catholics. (McCabe was Catholic, and to the best of my knowledge so were the other three.) It would appear, then, this group of Irish immigrants *was* acting in a nationalistic and sectarian manner, but that nation and sect was at the very least—enthusiastic Americanism.[71]

As *The Republican Journal* reported, celebrating the Fourth of July had been taken over by the Irish in a loud and raucous fashion. As late as the 1840s, Sherbrooke, Quebec, was still a battleground between Irish supporters of American independence and the locals, who supported the British Crown, for example. Decades-long contention of the northern border, especially in Maine, could have helped fuel such exuberance. In fact, prior to the Webster–Ashburton Treaty, signed in 1842, Maine had nearly gone to war with Great Britain over lumbering rights in contested areas.[72] Edward Kavanagh's service on that unpopular treaty commission may have cost him the Democratic nomination for Maine governor.

The Republican Journal, supported financially by at least two first-generation Americans (Anderson and Lowney), weighed in on things Irish frequently, especially after Benjamin Griffin bought into the paper in 1841.[73] His brother George joined him as a partner briefly in 1843.[74] This period just before the Famine allows for a close look at how the Irish were viewed in Belfast—or viewed themselves—at least in this Democratic-leaning newspaper, before the influence of Famine refugees. As a point of comparison, the year 1843 serves as well as any—both Griffin brothers were involved in the paper, Maine Democrats were gathering power, and the rancor over the Aroostook War resolution with the Webster–Ashburton Treaty of 1842 still garnered many column inches in their four-page, six-column broadsheet. The so-called war was contention over the border between Maine and New Brunswick, and ensuing timber-cutting trespasses by loggers from both sides of the border. The issue became a point of controversy between Whigs and Democrats in Maine.[75]

A Backward Glance

Topics of American national import, while covered, did not receive the massive amount of coverage that some Irish issues did. Abolition of slavery, for example, was covered in only sixteen stories in 1843, while seventy-six news items that year were related to Ireland. Irish coverage in *The Republican Journal* ranged from criticism of the British government to discussions of Sir Robert Peel and the attempt to repeal Britain's Corn Laws. In some instances, coverage compared "bad" British expenditures made at Irish expense, as, for example, the following: "Parliament has contributed £50,000 for natural education in Ireland. This is £30,000 less than was lately appointed to enlarge Her Majesty's stables."[76] Members of the British government were often shown looking down on the United States and/or treating U.S. officials with disdain, as in the following:

> Lord Brougham, President Tyler and Repeal. –Lord Brougham made a furious onslaught upon President Tyler and his son in the House of Lords, a few evenings back, when the affairs of the sister country were being incidentally discussed. 'A *person* named Tyler, said to be a son of the President, has taken part in the Repeal agitation!' exclaimed the noble Lord, who proceeded to say that 'no one was answerable for his fooleries—the excessive fooleries of his family.' Lord Brougham while so excessively severe upon the son, styled the sire the 'accidental President of the United States;' but he could not believe unless he saw with his own eyes, that that functionary, had written the letter attributed to him in favor of repeal. [77]

In fact, this item followed immediately upon one noting that U.S. troops had been pulled from the Saint John Valley, the area in Maine under contention, recently secured by the unpopular (in *The Republican Journal*) Webster–Ashburton Treaty. Anti-British materials were often run in conjunction with sympathetic pieces about Ireland. The tone of a report on Peel's initial refusal to repeal the Corn Laws, for example, created the image of a hard-hearted British politician using policy to abdicate all responsibility for poverty: "Sir Robert Peel says it is impossible to legislate for distress—that no act of parliament can alleviate it—and so, I presume, the people and trade will be left to chance, and periodical revision."[78] At the same time, the newspaper printed sympathetic presentations of the destitution of Ireland, ascribed to Irish-born American Catholic Bishop John Hughes, who traveled to Ireland in 1843:

> Bishop Huges [*sic*] says he was glad to escape from the wretchedness and want and physical suffering which surrounded him everywhere in Ireland. He adds 'that it is not only the beggars who are poor and destitute; those who would fain gain something by work can hardly do so. Look at yon old woman sitting down in the market place of the town; she has come five miles on foot with her produce for sale; and what is it? Two eggs! On my credit, two eggs and nothing in the world beside; and for these perhaps, she will get two pennies (four cents) and wend her way five miles home to her hut, to wait till her single hen shall lay more.'[79]

The paper used considerable column inches to discuss Peel's reluctance to repeal the Corn Laws, landownership, poor wages, and Daniel O'Connell's call for a Repeal of the Act of Union with Britain. Even shipwrecks in Ireland garnered coverage. For example, hurricane destruction led to the loss of seventy fishing boats off Galway Bay; "seventy-three fisherman of Newcastle and Auralong have lost their lives, leaving destitute families."[80] Frequently, workers' pay would be compared to royal expenditures: "[T]here had been expended during the last eight years, in embellishing the royal palaces £458,000, and on the royal parks £344,000. This is pretty well for a country in which the lace workers are starving." The paper even reprinted an item from an English paper noting that Daniel O'Connell's son, using "an Irish method, truly, going so far abroad to carry a project at home," traveled to the United States for "[p]ecuniary, rather than patriotic motives."[81] The tone of disdain applied to O'Connell's son was applied by the English paper. Why did Belfast's paper keep that tone? Perhaps it did so to show the English as "snooty" and looking down on the Irish, the Irish in America, and, thus, Americans.

Setting a Tone

The Republican Journal coverage had a tone—the Irish were put upon and the British were caste-based, elitist, and disdainful of America and Americans. British royalty was costly; British governmental money was spent on fripperies. The British government and royal system was usually shown sneering at or looking down upon the working class, as well as American government and elected officials. This, the tone made clear, was insult upon injury. It used repeated juxtapositions of spending on fancy things by and for the royals with the appalling wages paid to piece workers (in the fabric and clothing industries), day laborers, mill workers, and so on, for examples.

Multiple articles talked about the poverty in Ireland, including the reportage of Bishop Hughes, who in 1843 was not yet under a cloud for his refusal to denounce American slavery. Ireland's troubles, at least as far as *The Republican Journal* made its case, were the result of British mistreatment and unequal distribution of land:

> IRELAND. –This Island [*sic*] is not quite as large as N.Y. State, and yet it contains 8,500,000 inhabitants. There are not over thirty thousand land owners in the whole Island. This fact tells the whole story of Ireland's oppression better than volumes.[82]

Daniel O'Connell's Repeal Movement was covered week after week. This coverage was straightforward and did not remark on O'Connell's long-standing call for an end to American slavery. The paper also ran an anecdote commending Ireland for not being part of the slave trade.[83]

In late autumn 1843, *The Republican Journal* ran an article that, in retrospect, proved to be an omen. New York state reported an outbreak of potato blight:

DEATH FROM DISEASED POTATOES. –The Utica (N.Y.) Gazette, notices the appearance in that neighborhood of a singular disease among the potatoes, which has already destroyed thousands of bushels. The disease first manifests itself by a black spot on the surface of the potatoe, [*sic*] which rapidly spreads till the whole root becomes rotten and worthless. Many farmers have lost their entire crops, the disease in many cases destroying the root while in the ground and large quantities have been also destroyed after having been dug or buried in heaps or stored in cellars. Potatoes affected with the disease are very poisonous, large numbers of hogs having died after eating them. Is not this subject worthy the attention of agriculturalists?[84]

Newspaper coverage of Irish subject matter conflated the ideas of democracy and republicanism with Repeal in Ireland. The paper would have spoken to those who were literate, but the majority of the 1850 Irish immigrants, the men working as day laborers, could not read or write. Illiteracy, however, "did not prohibit consumption of the printed word. Reading the newspaper was often a public event in the nineteenth century."[85]

So who were *The Republican Journal*'s readers in 1843? The subscription list is not available, but 1,150 people subscribed to it by 1837, more than triple its readership of 1829. Its mission statement, as it appeared on the front page of that first issue, was clear:

We propose to publish in Belfast a new paper of this name [*The Republican Journal*] to be devoted to Political, Local, Moral, Religious, Literary and Agricultural Information .... The political character of this paper shall be decidedly democratic, and we shall never hesitate to avail ourselves of every suitable opportunity to propagate republican sentiments.[86]

Newspaper material from the 1830s had not been so "Irish friendly." Something changed by the 1840s. The tone and content shifted once Benjamin Griffin acquired a share in the paper in January 1841.[87] His brother George joined him as co-owner in October 1843. The new dedication of the paper, from the brothers Griffin, was clear:

Democratic ... We shall endeavor to render the paper to all classes of readers, and to all occupations,—to the Farmer, the Mechanic, the Laborer, the Seaman, the Merchant, the Manufacturer,—and the ladies shall by no means be forgotten. We hope to make it a useful family paper....[88]

From the Griffin brothers' perspective, then, the working-class people of Belfast were the intended audience. Those people had an interest in

Ireland or so, the Griffin brothers assumed. Obviously, people would have had to be able to read in order to follow events in Ireland. Census takers, however, noted that the Irish immigrants of 1850 were illiterate.

Given that the paper's coverage in the 1840s was political, the language formal, and the topics ranged from education, to legislation, to verbatim transcripts from the House of Lords, and so on, the reading level would have had to have been at a higher than basic education level. The Irish immigrants of 1850 may not have been Griffin's target audience. His readers, however, must have had a long-standing interest in things Irish, as well as democratic and republican themes. Perhaps the paper was targeting Irish immigrants and their descendants who had been in the area for some time, who had become educated in their American sojourn.

Earning Acceptance

If Irish does not automatically equal Catholic, the discussion of what it means to be Irish is suddenly freed: "[Not using Catholicism as a cultural marker for Irishness] is a very interesting suggestion, for it opens the possibility that there is an Irish ethnic identity that is not tied to religion but is something different, deeper."[89] The nineteenth-century arrivals from Ireland, with Catholicism taken out of the equation, still faced the same stereotypes as had the Ulster immigrants of the previous century. Religious affiliation as part of the stereotype had shifted, but the remaining stereotypes remained intact.

In many respects, religion did not "ghettoize" recently arrived Irish in Belfast, while economic status and political activity allowed a degree of mobility. What is apparent when comparing the life stories of poor Irish Catholic immigrant William S. Brannagan (see Chapter One) with that of Francis Banan, the Irish Protestant who arrived penniless in 1819, is that they warranted special mention at their deaths because they had achieved success in Belfast, in America. Banan appeared worthy because his "true moral and intellectual worth" had become known in the community. His accumulations provided the evidence:

> He finally settled in this town [Knox, approximately twelve miles northwest of Belfast], and by his industry, prudence, and good economy, and the blessing of Providence, he accumulated a handsome property, which he left for the comfort of the afflicted family.[90]

William Brannagan's achievements, too, were measured in possessions: "[H]e has lived at his ease on an ample property acquired by industry and frugality."[91] His ability to give back to the community was also noted:

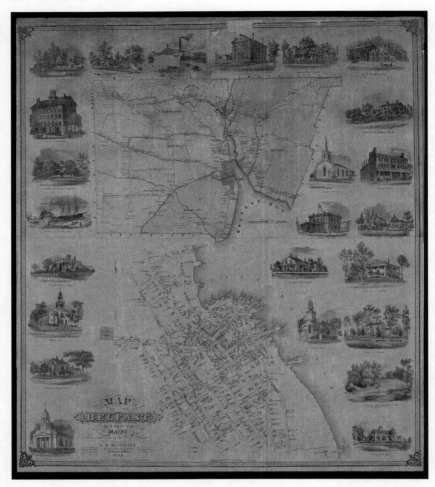

Figure 3.3 The 1855 map of Belfast provides an upper-class view of what mattered in Belfast before the Civil War. Courtesy of the Osher Map Library, University of Southern Maine. Map of the City of Belfast, Waldo Co. Maine from actual survey by D.S. Osborne. https:// oshermaps.org/map/46781.0001

Mr. Brannagan was a devout Catholic and took great interest in the local church. It was mainly through his efforts that the church was organized in this city, and the church edifice and parsonage were both gifts from him. He spent his money and time freely for the cause, and when old age came on made an arrangement by which he was to have a home in the parsonage.[92]

Their ability to accrue property perhaps gave them the ability to form friendships with people of status. Belfast judge, lawyer, and historian Joseph Williamson's younger brother, George, for example, was one of the pallbearers at Brannagan's funeral, as was Irish immigrant James Haney, who first appeared in the U.S. census in Belfast in 1870, where he was identified as a twenty-seven-year-old laborer born in Ireland.[93] Haney had been involved in Brannagan's business life for more than a dozen years, selling to and buying properties from Brannagan in 1889.[94]

Brannagan's funeral was a microcosm of Belfast's Irish heritage. The event brought together well-to-do, educated people from the elite with working-class Irish immigrants. Protestant and Catholic pallbearers participated in the public ritual surrounding his death. The Roman Catholic hierarchy of New England celebrated the funeral Mass and, no doubt, escorted the cortege to Grove Cemetery, where there was no separate Catholic burial space. First-generation American Nathaniel Lowney, whose father had been born in Ireland, helped layout and fence Grove Cemetery in the mid-1830s.[95]

Brannagan's and Banan's obituaries made use of a number of Irish stereotypes in describing their "heroic" rise to acceptance in Belfast and environs. Perhaps no greater compliment could be given to an Irish immigrant than the one given to Brannagan. When the census taker came to his rooming house in 1860, Brannagan was not designated as being from "Ireland." The land of origin was left blank—as it was for all Americans.

Perhaps we can define Irishness only by what people do that is considered uniquely Irish, which is not the circular definition it appears to be. Ethnicity and culture are also socially agreed upon constructs.[96] They are performed by people in reaction to unfolding events and changing times. They are not static creations.[97]

Being labeled "Irish" set people apart, designated them as "Other," as "lesser than." This denigration has been experienced by many colonized peoples, and the Irish were not alone in suffering such disparagement. As part of the process of creating the "Other," any difference was homed in on and used to create separateness, both at home in a colonized Ireland and in America, itself the result of colonizers who were also "Othered" in England. The irony has not lost its edge.

"Us versus them" uses a simple polarity: Me and not me. Because the Irish in England were forced to live in squalor amid social degradation, English discourse in Victorian Britain defined Irishness as demoralizing and degenerative, for example.[98] English capitalists and beneficiaries of the niceties of life created by new technologies did not, therefore, have to accept responsibility for the misuse of nature or workers. They could project their loathing of slums, tainted water, and stinking factories onto the laborers in their capitalist vineyards. If the English valued cleanliness, industry, temperance, deference to authority, and self-improvement, the

Irish were the antithesis of all things English. This made Irish workers well suited for the dirty job of keeping British capitalism running cleanly. In fact, at least one employer saw workers' Irishness as necessary for laboring in the factories of England, for "The English from the country parishes would not be suited to the work of the towns; the Irish adapt themselves more speedily to it, and are more importunate: they thrust themselves forward more."[99]

Categories such as race and ethnicity are social constructions.[100] What is of more importance is rank—old-timer versus newcomer. The urban immigrant enclave was an economic tool, one which provided immigrants with ready employment (even if not exactly lucrative remuneration).[101] Such employment did not require a great outlay on the part of the immigrant. Levels of education, region of residence, gender, marital characteristics, life span, and so on, all need to be part of the discussion across ethnic and racial groups.[102] It is self-evident that world economies put those with the least education and fewest skills at a disadvantage when seeking employment.[103]

In the United States, where "[e]thnic identity can be a means of locating oneself and one's family against the panorama of American history, against the backdrop of what it means to be an American," and where individuals are generally the products of intermingling of many nationalities, why do respondents to the U.S. census overwhelmingly opt to identify as "Irish"? "Irishness" is more than "a relatively comfortable version of whiteness."[104]

Grove Cemetery, like the city of Belfast, is home to people born in Ireland and some whose parents were. Protestants and Catholics are buried there—probably some agnostics and atheists, too. Besides Brannagan, Nathaniel Lowney and Hugh Johnston Anderson are buried in this city-center cemetery, as is James Haney.[105] These people all played their parts in creating Belfast. Their cultural and ethnic heritages helped form the character of the place.

Notes

1 *The Republican Journal*, 15, no. 27 (4 August 1843): 1, column 6.
2 That number includes children of immigrant couples born in the Maritimes.
3 Joseph Williamson, *The History of the City of Belfast, Maine*, Vol. 1 (Somersworth, New Hampshire: New England History Press, 1982), 743.
4 Knights of Columbus, William S. Brannagan Council, "Council History." Accessed 3 December 2020.
5 Kelley Family History, Belfast Free Library.
6 Cian McMahon, "Ireland and the Birth of the Irish-American Press, 1842-61," *American Periodicals*, 19, no. 1 SPECIAL ISSUE: Immigrant Periodicals (2009): 5.
7 Kevin Kenny, *Diaspora: A Very Short Introduction* (Oxford: University Press, 2013), 29.
8 Williamson, Vol. 1, 804.

9 Williamson, Vol. 1, 805.
10 Williamson, Vol. 1, 807.
11 Williamson, Vol. 1, 807.
12 The notices for these men ran in *The Republican Journal* in several issues in 1850–52. William White obituary ran on 26 April 1850, page 3. Morris Harriss obituary ran on 5 July 1850, page 3. Joseph Kerr obituary ran on 26 July 1850, page 3. James Convey obituary ran on 26 March 1852, page 3. This William White was born in Ireland and farmed in the Belfast area. He died of consumption, leaving an American-born wife and several children, all born in Maine. William White, author of *A History of Belfast with Introductory Remarks on Acadia*, was American born. Necrology information on Irish-born William White is found in the bound copy of the *1850 U.S. Census of Belfast*, 112.
13 Williamson, Vol. 1, 125.
14 William Leo Lucey, S.J., *The Catholic Church in Maine* (Francestown, New Hampshire:

Marshall Jones, 1957), 19. Lucey speculated that Maine's constitution creators were swayed by strong arguments from three wealthy Catholic citizens of Maine—James Kavanagh, Matthew Cottrill, and William Mooney—but he also pointed out that other dissident sects such as the Baptists would have insisted there be no public support of Congregational ministers. Edward Kavanagh wrote a petition, urging that there be no religious constraints in Maine.

15 Marie L. Sacks, "The Two Faces of Ballstown: Religion, Governance, and Cultural Values on the Maine Frontier 1760–1820," *Maine History* 43 (January 2007): 41.
16 Lucey, 51. French Jesuit Sebastien Rale was killed and scalped by Boston militiamen while living and working among Native converts at Norridgewock in 1724 during one of the frequent wars between England and France.
17 Lucey, 155.
18 Lucey, 118–35. Father Bapst, a Swiss Jesuit, had been in Maine 11 years when, in 1853, he began a series of lectures in Ellsworth on Catholicism. These lectures led to conversions. That, on top of a controversy surrounding Ellsworth's public schools requiring all students use the Protestant bible, led to altercations. The local editor led the opposition to Father Bapst, which culminated in his being dragged from his host's house, stripped and tarred and feathered the night of 14 October 1854. The manhandling of the priest was taken up by newspapers in Bangor and around Maine—in support of Bapst.
19 Ballstown Plantation is roughly modern Lincoln County, Maine.
20 Sacks, 51.
21 Lucey, 59.
22 Lucey, 33. Bishop Cheverus (1768–1836) was based in Boston. Benedict Fenwick became bishop of New England, also based in Boston, in 1825. The Portland diocese was not created until 1853 and served New Hampshire *and* Maine. New Hampshire became a separate diocese in 1884.
23 Lucey, 54.
24 James H. Mundy, *Hard Times, Hard Men* (Scarborough: Harp Publications, 1990), 31.
25 Mundy, 32.

26 The Catholic Church in Belfast, *The Maine Catholic Historical Magazine: Under the Auspices of the Rt. Rev. Bishop of Portland and the Maine Catholic Historical Society* 7, no. 3 (January 1917): 222-237.

27 *Maine Catholic Historical Magazine*, 225.

28 *Maine Catholic Historical Magazine*, 225.

29 Lucey, 58.

30 Benedict Fenwick, Second Bishop of Boston, *Memoirs to Serve for the Future: Ecclesiastical History of the Diocese of Boston* (Yonkers: U.S. Catholic Historical Society, 1978), 205.

31 Fenwick, 205.

32 *Maine Catholic Historical Magazine*, 223. The writer is referencing amateur historian Joseph Williamson's two-volume history of Belfast.

33 Margaret Lynch-Brennan, *The Irish Bridget: Irish Immigrant Women in Domestic Service in America, 1840–1930* (Syracuse: University Press, 2009), 13.

34 Lynch-Brennan, 14.

35 Fenwick, 205.

36 Fenwick, 205.

37 Fenwick, 205.

38 Fenwick, 205.

39 *Maine Catholic Historical Magazine*, 226.

40 Fenwick, vii.

41 Lucey, 86.

42 Fenwick, 205.

43 Fenwick, 206.

44 Fenwick, 206.

45 Fenwick, 206.

46 Lucey, 58.

47 Lucey, 59

48 U.S. census data.

49 St. Brendan the Navigator Parish: Roman Catholic Churches & Missions of Midcoast Maine, "St. Francis of Assisi Church's History." Accessed 3 December 2020.

50 *Republican Journal*, 15, no. 40 (3 November 1843).

51 *Republican Journal, 15, no. 40 (3 November 1843)*.

52 *Republican Journal, 15, no. 40 (3 November 1843)*.

53 Kerby A. Miller, *Emigrants and Exiles: Ireland and the Irish Exodus to North America* (Oxford: University Press, 1985), 41.

54 Miller, 73.

55 Timothy J. Meagher, *Inventing Irish America: Generation, Class, and Ethnic Identity in a New England City, 1880–1928* (Notre Dame: University Press, 2001), 28.

56 Miller, *Emigrants*, 73.

57 Meagher, *Inventing*, 28.

58 Meagher, Inventing, 29.

59 Donald Harman Akenson, *Diaspora: A Primer* (Belfast: Institute of Irish Studies, 1996), 214.

60 Miller, *Emigrants*, 327.

61 Ellen Skerrett, "The Development of Catholic Identity Among Irish Americans in Chicago, 1880 to 1920," *From Paddy to Studs: Irish-American Communities in the Turn of the Century Era, 1880 to 1920* (Westport, CT: Greenwood Press, 1986), 117.

62 Miller, *Emigrants*, 80–2.

63 Meagher, *Inventing*, 29.
64 https://portlanddiocese.org/diocese/history, "History: Diocese of Portland." Accessed 10 March 2021.
65 Williamson Vol. 1, 59–62 and 160.
66 Williamson Vol. 1, 400.
67 Williamson Vol. 1, 155.
68 *The Williamson Family Papers: Vol. 1: The College Years, 1844–1852* (Rockport, ME: Picton Press, 2003).
69 *Docket of the Police Court: City of Belfast. Commencing at the First Term of Said Court. March 1853. Criminal Docket ends. Aug. 1855 [cq]. Carried to Another Book.* (Courtesy of the Belfast Historical Society and Museum.)
70 Police Court Docket, cases #14, #15, #19, and #22.
71 Kenneth Moss, "St. Patrick's Day Celebration and the Formation of the Irish American Identity, 1845–1875," *Journal of Social History* 29, no. 9 (Fall 1995), 144.
72 Richard W. Judd, Edwin Churchill, and Joel Eastman, eds., *Maine: The Pine Tree State from Prehistory to the Present* (Orono: University of Maine Press, 1995), 347.
73 *The Republican Journal*, 28 January 1841, 2.
74 *The Republican Journal*, 13 October 1843, 2, column 1.
75 Judd, 347.
76 *The Republican Journal*, 15, no. 14 (5 May 1843), 3, column 2.
77 *The Republican Journal*, 15, no. 34 (22 September 1843), 3, column 1.
78 The Republican Journal, 15, no. 9 (31 March 1843), 2, column 6.
79 *The Republican Journal*, 15, no. 34 (22 September 1843), 3, column 2. For details on the Bishops trips to Ireland, see Ellen McKenna, "The Visits to Ireland of John Hughes, Archbishop of New York, from 1840 to 1862," *Clogher Record* 20, no. 1 (2009).
80 *The Republican Journal*, 15, no. 4 (24 February 1843), 3, column 3.
81 "VISIT OF O'CONNELL'S SON TO THE UNITED STATES," *The Republican Journal*, 15, no. 15 (12 May 1843), 3, column 1.
82 *The Republican Journal*, 15, no. 23 (7 July 1843), 3, column 3.
83 *The Republican Journal*, 15, no. 13 (28 April 1843), 1, column 5.
84 "DEATH FROM DISEASED POTATOES," *The Republican Journal*, 15, no. 45 (24 November 1843), 2, column 5.
85 Cian T. McMahon, *The Global Dimensions of Irish Identity: Race, Nation, and the Popular Press, 1840–1880* (Chapel Hill: University of North Carolina Press, 2015), 4.
86 "About the Republican Journal. (volume) (Belfast, Me.) 1829-Current," Library of Congress. https://chroniclingamerica.loc.gov/lccn/sn78000873/. Accessed 13 March 2021.
87 *The Republican Journal* (28 January 1841), 1.
88 "Democratic," *The Republican Journal*, 15, no. 37 (13 October 1843), 2, column 1.
89 Akenson, *Diaspora*, 214.
90 George Pratt, "Died," *The Republican Journal* 15, no. 40 (3 November 1843). Knox, of course, harkens to a Presbyterian past.
91 Obituary, "William S. Brannagan," *The Republican Journal* (24 January 1901), 1.
92 Obituary, "William S. Brannagan," *The Republican Journal* (24 January 1901), 1.
93 The older Williamson brother was acquainted with Brannagan. Joseph Williamson Jr., Judge of the Police Court, came into contact with him over a

stolen goods case. Rosalia Jane Norton had shoplifted from Brannagan's shop. *Docket of the Police Court: City of Belfast, Commencing at the First Term of Said Court.* March 1853. Case no. 112.

94 Deeds under William S. Brannagan (also found under William H. Branagan and William S. Branagan).

95 Williamson, Vol. 1, 522.

96 Noel Ignatiev, *How the Irish Became White* (New York: Routledge, 1995), 196, note 16.

97 William A. Yancey, Eugene P. Ericksen, and Richard N. Juliani, "Emergent Ethnicity: A Review and Reformulation," *American Sociological Review*, 41 (June 1976): 391.

98 Jim MacLaughlin, "'Pestilence on Their Backs, Famine in Their Stomachs': The Racial Construction of Irishness and the Irish in Victorian Britain" in *Ireland and Cultural Theory: The Mechanics of Authenticity*, Colin Graham and Richard Kirkland, eds. (London: Macmillan Press, 1999), 52.

99 MacLaughlin, 66.

100 Mary C. Waters and Karl Eschbach, "Immigration and Ethnic and Racial Inequality in the United States," *Annual Review of Sociology* 21 (1995): 421.

101 Waters and Eschbach, 438.

102 Waters and Eschbach, 424.

103 Waters and Eschbach, 425.

104 Stephanie Rains, "Irish Roots: Genealogy and the Performance of Irishness" in *The Irish in Us: Irishness, Performativity, and Popular Culture*, Diane Negra, ed. (Durham: Duke University Press, 2006), 130-160.

105 <cemetery.cityofbelfast.org> (accessed 6 March 2014).

4   The Irish of Stereotype

As the Jews had their Nazareth, the New-Englanders have their Ireland; but, as what is always due to too national a Spirit, they are as much despised in the other English Plantations, as any Teague is by them.[1]

America's cities always have been filled with foreigners. These outsiders have influenced and changed American habits.[2] This made old-timers (the receiving culture) nervous. Stereotypes became the weapon of choice in warding off, subduing the unknown newcomers. Stereotypes allowed old-timers to look down upon or to laugh at newcomers: Laughter can be used to defuse fear and/or to debase.[3]

The stereotypes applied to the Irish in what were the English colonies in America, and later the United States of America, remained amazingly stable from the early eighteenth to mid-nineteenth centuries. Interestingly, a good number of Irish-born immigrant old-timers applied the same stereotypes by which they had been "Othered" to newcomers from the same homeland—Ireland. This is especially relevant in any discussions of the three migrations of Irish into Belfast, Maine.

Caricature is a tool of stereotype.[4] Layers of tone are involved, ranging from satire to irony, sarcasm, parody, and burlesque. Ostensibly, this keeps the old-timers in control and the newcomers humbled, but humor can be used to seize the stereotype and, in its harshest use, become a weapon of revenge against the powerful (old-timers).[5] The use of humor in destabilizing stereotypes has long been an aspect of ethnic studies. Stereotypes, then, even given their negative power, can act as unifiers and, perhaps, even as aspects of culture creation. Stereotypes are "key sites to explore Irish identity in the popular media."[6]

As anti-Irish stereotypes were consistent over time throughout the American colonies, and later states, the question arises: Did this lead to any kind of unity among Irish immigrants? All Irish, not just Dubliners, or Kerrymen, faced equivalent stereotypes. Is there any evidence that the power of stereotypes was taken over, re-presented, re-appropriated, and re-distributed? What might that have looked like?

DOI: 10.4324/9781003187660-4

Irish Protestants

It would have been odd had Irish immigrants *not* made their way to Belfast, Maine, in the eighteenth and nineteenth centuries. In the Irish diaspora, between 1700 and 1820, a quarter to a half million emigrants from Ireland entered what is now the United States, 30 percent of all European immigrants during that period.[7] From 1776 to 1820 emigrants from Ireland provided 50 percent of all European arrivals.

By the mid-eighteenth century, Irish Protestants were firmly established in the colonies—some families having been in residence for nearly half a century. They had fled Ulster in droves at the beginning of the eighteenth century for economic, political, and religious reasons, the three terms being closely intertwined. Presbyterian minister James McGregor, who had "'no certain lodging in the parish [of Aghadowey],'" had written to Massachusetts Governor Samuel Shute seeking permission to immigrate; Cotton Mather supported his petition.

In 1718–1719, 2,600 Ulster Irish sailed to New England.[8] Still, even with permission, McGregor's group was not warmly received in Boston, so members of the expedition were shunted north to Casco Bay in Maine. Massachusetts authorities were not pleased when the newly arrived did not stay where told—Casco Bay in the District of Maine—and instead "squatted" at Nutfield, fifteen or so miles north of Haverhill, Massachusetts.[9] Those settlers from Ulster who had found the winter in Casco Bay too uncomfortable and returned to Boston were ordered out of town. A contingent of descendants from the group that squatted at Nutfield, New Hampshire, later re-christened Londonderry, ultimately bought what became Belfast, Maine.[10]

Many, but not all, of the Ulster immigrants of 1718 were Protestants practicing Presbyterianism. Their Protestantism, however, did not draw them closer to the already established American Protestant Christian community: Their Irishness, as well as their dissenter status, kept them separate and "Othered." Irish Catholic was further denigrated. When John Adams argued the defense of British troops who fired on a Boston crowd in the volatile "Boston Massacre" of 1770, he used a distinct term for Irish Catholic—"teague" (a misspelling of the Irish personal name *Tadhg*, replaced by Paddy in the nineteenth century). This term placed Irish Catholics, mulattoes, Blacks, and "jack tars" into a group defined by emotionality, illiteracy, and brutishness.[11] These stereotypes were added to the list: The Irish were seen as poor, diseased, violent, drunken, lazy, and deviant sexually.

Irish as synonymous with poverty began early, with this first large-scale immigration from Ulster in 1718. Those first America-bound Irish groups got the attention of British authorities in Boston. Thomas Lechmere, the British government's surveyor-general for customs in Boston, born in Worcestershire, England, arrived in Boston sometime after 1703. He married, his children were born, and he died in Boston. Lechmere saw shiploads of "Irish familys" from the north of Ireland in distinctive terms. In a letter, he cited rumors that if these families gave a favorable report back to kith and kin, "20 ministers with their congregations will come over in the Spring."[12] The word "minister" suggests he was referring to *Protestant* Irish families. Lechmere did not refer to these people as Scotch or as hyphenated Scotch-Irish. He complained that "these confounded Irish" in need of provisions, which were "most extravagantly dear, and scarce of all sorts," made life difficult for everyone—they were a strain on the colony.[13] These immigrants from Ireland were perceived as poor—and he did not concern himself with religious affiliation.

The facts show that the Ulster Presbyterians who landed in Boston and found themselves shifted north *were* poor. The newly arrived from Ireland *did* frequently ask for help. In fact, Casco Bay petitioners estimated that nearly 300 recent arrivals from Ireland had no provisions for the upcoming winter.[14]

The strain on the colonial government was severe enough that it had to be addressed, so when Governor Shute sought funds to alleviate suffering among the newly arrived colonists, he simply referred to them as "poor people from abroad, especially those that come from Ireland."[15] While Shute definitely saw these newly arrived people from Ireland as Irish, he wasn't alone in his definition of birth in Ireland equaling Irishness. This is sprinkled throughout the written materials of the era.

The Reverend James MacSparran, one-time Presbyterian minister and later Church of Ireland cleric, noted that newly arrived immigrants were often poor but that industry and hard work paid off:

> It is pretty true to observe of the Irish, in general, that those who come here with any Wealth are the worse for their Removal; though doubtless, the next Generation will not suffer so much as their Fathers; But those who, when they came had nothing to lose, have throve greatly by their Labour. He that lies on the Ground can fall no lower; and such are the fittest to encounter the Difficulties attending new Settlers.[16]

MacSparran was talking about Irish Protestants. He also identified the group that settled in Nutfield/Londonderry, New Hampshire, as Irish in his Irish emigrants' guidebook *America Dissected*: "In this Province [i.e., New Hampshire] lies that town called *London Derry*, all *Irish*, and famed for Industry and Riches."[17] The immigration generation suffered, unless they were already on the bottom, economically speaking, according to MacSparran.

In these early documents, there was a presumed connection between *Irish poor* and *disease-ridden* upon immigration. A ship from Ireland

arrived at Hull, Massachusetts, in 1718 with nearly 150 passengers reported to have smallpox. The colonial General Court sought to alleviate
the suffering, but it also wanted to make sure the disease did not come
ashore at Hull, the southernmost port on Massachusetts Bay. The
number of passengers down with the disease overwhelmed the Hull Pest-
house. Boston selectmen were ordered to find accommodations as soon
as possible and to provide fresh meat, greens, and firewood.[18]

Indeed, poverty pinched these immigrants. Those of later generations
who traced their origins to Ireland, understanding this, saw fit to take
care of fellow Irish-born or those of Irish extraction who suffered sick-
ness or shipwreck, establishing the Charitable Irish Society in 1737.[19]
The aim of the organization was to "administer that comfort and con-
solation, which is most suitable, for Irish Emigrants, or their descendants, in distress, in proportion to our social ability or individual
liberality."[20] While the bylaws stated that all group officers had to be
Protestants, Catholics were allowed to join.[21]

Benjamin Franklin Weighs In

In addition to *poor* and *diseased*, the propensity for *alcohol abuse* stereotype was already in place. Benjamin Franklin accused men of
Donegal, Pennsylvania, of having drunken habits in his "Narrative of the
Late Massacre," a diatribe against an armed mob that had murdered an
extended family of Conestoga in the mid-1760s.[22] In fact, Ulster
Presbyterian clergymen of the time raged against alcohol abuse among
their flocks, which may have helped fuel outside perceptions. Still,
Franklin was judicious in his use of the "Irish" label. While he launched
a written attack against the Paxton Boys, he never referred to them as
Irish, Scots-Irish, or Scotch-Irish.[23] He did, however, call the perpetrators the "white Savages of Peckstang and Donegall," and he did
comment on a physical characteristic with supposedly Irish connota-
tions: red hair.[24] Franklin said that the perpetrators of the massacre were
"Rum-debauched, Trader-corrupted Vagabonds and Thieves...."[25] Like
others of the eighteenth century, Franklin did not equate Irishness with
Catholicism; he saw Irish and Presbyterian as synonymous. He didn't
mind the Irish as much as he objected to Presbyterians, who were better
than the Germans, in his estimation, because the Germans spoke no
English.

His animosity was that of an insider—Franklin was a paying member of
the Presbyterian Meeting in Philadelphia, although not a regular at
Sunday services. As in many families, internecine strife can be scathing.
Franklin found the sermons delivered by Presbyterian minister Jedidiah
Andrews worse than tedious but admired those of his assistant Samuel
Hemphill.[26] When Andrews brought charges of heresy against his
younger—and more popular—assistant, Franklin became an active public

defender of the younger minister in writing. He used a syllogism to define the old-guard Presbyterian ministers as "Reverend Asses."[27] Franklin, like his contemporaries, did not refer to these Presbyterian ministers as Scots or Ulstermen; he called them "Irish." In a letter to his friend William Strahan, a Scottish printer and member of the British Parliament, Franklin was nearly giddy in recounting his written defense of Hemphill of thirty years before, bragging that his little piece had made him bitter enemies among the Irish Presbyterians.[28] (He did not tell Strahan that Hemphill had been found guilty of plagiarizing his sermons.)

A decade later, living in France, seeking political alliances during the Revolutionary War, Franklin wrote, "An Address to the good People of Ireland, on Behalf of America, October 4th, 1778." Although the publication was seized by the British before potential Irish readers saw it, Franklin spelled out parallels between American and Irish colonies: "We congratulate you however on the bright prospect which the western hemisphere has afforded to you, and the oppressed of every nation, and we trust that the liberation of your country has been effected in America."[29]

He was arguing that Irish—Protestant—colonists were part of the creative force in the American Revolution, that, indeed, the American Revolution was in effect the fruition of the Irish drive for independence from England. Franklin estimated that by 1776 nearly one-third of Pennsylvania colony's 350,000 inhabitants and their descendants were from Ulster.[30] He urged the Irish to remain peaceful at home and promised that America would develop stronger trade ties with Ireland "as far as her other engagements [would] permit."[31]

Still Franklin employed a number of Irish stereotypes in addition to *rum-debauched* and *violent*. He noted the Irish—and Scots—penchant for *witty repartee* and *humorous hyperbole*. Franklin poked fun at both Scots and Irish braggadocio (or hyperbole) in personal correspondence with his friend Strahan:

> Do you not remember the Story you told me of the Scotch Sergeant, who met with a Party of Forty American Soldiers, and tho' alone disarm'd them all and brought them in Prisoners; A Story almost as Improbable as that of the Irishman, who pretended to have alone taken and brought in Five of the Enemy, by *surrounding* them.[32]

Franklin's correspondence mirrors the idea that there was an ancient connection between Irish and Scots. He used a specialized vocabulary to explain the ethnic and cultural differences among Irish, Scot, and English. The English he saw as conquerors in Ireland who held their lands through confiscation. The land confiscated had been taken from "Caledonians" and "Britons," whom Franklin saw as "the original possessors in your island, or the native Irish."[33]

Franklin's letter suggests the Scots and Irish stereotypes were well established by the 1780s. In a later letter, Franklin described the Irish (and he was referring to Protestant Irish) as English speakers who quickly moved into positions of power in the new United States:

> It is a fact that the Irish Emigrants and their Children are now in Possession of the Government of Pensilvania, [*sic*] by their Majority in the Assembly, as well as of a great part of the Territory; and I remember well the first Ship that brought any of them over.[34]

Ulster Presbyterians

It would seem, then, that Franklin would neither define Irish as Catholic nor as speakers of Irish. Franklin's mentor, Irish-born James Logan, a Quaker and William Penn's provincial secretary, did use the term "Scotch-Irish" to refer to immigrants from the north of Ireland. He acknowledged that this was a local, Pennsylvanian term.[35] He also referred to them as "strangers."[36]

Even *Presbyterian* was not a term denoting unity. There were schisms and dissenting sects. Among Irish Presbyterians in the eighteenth century were followers of orthodoxy, liberal interpretation, evangelicalism, and prophetic traditions.[37] Many were unaffiliated with any congregation.[38] In fact, many so-called Irish Presbyterians were *not* practitioners in America.[39] That is not out of line with comparative studies of other Christian denominations in the American Revolutionary period: A mere 10 percent of white colonists formally participated in any recognized Christian church.[40]

If the accounts of the Irish in American colonial government documents are less than enthusiastic about the arrival of immigrants from Ireland on Massachusetts' shores, the bits that surface about how people were actually treated show true anathema on the part of the locals (or old-timers). A minister in Needham, Massachusetts, wrote in 1723–1724 that he "had had to plead with his people not to ill-treat the new settlers."[41]

This was not just a phenomenon in the New England colonies. The Reverend Charles Woodmason, an early eighteenth-century Anglican clergyman in Virginia, did not welcome Ulster Presbyterians, nor did he see their Presbyterianism as separate from their Irishness. Although Presbyterians shared the category of Protestant Christian with the Anglican, he labeled them differently. Woodmason pulled together the full list of undesirable Irish stereotypes when he described Ulster Presbyterians as "beggarly Irish Presbyterians....Ignorant, mean [and] worthless...the scum of the Earth and Refuse of Mankind."[42] Woodmason did not use Scots- or Scotch-Irish to describe the newly arrived group. The Anglican Church, with its ties to the English monarchy, at times has looked askance at all dissenters—Separatist, Puritan, or Presbyterian.[43]

As noted, the first generation of Ulster Irish to immigrate to the colonies in 1718 faced a great deal of animosity in Boston and environs. They had, however, ignored colonial authorities and effectively seized disputed territory in New Hampshire. Here some put down roots. Some fought in various colonial wars. Their children and grandchildren were born in New Hampshire. By the middle of the eighteenth century, these people were well entrenched in the colonies.

Work, or at least the promise of such, had brought the Irish to New England. Lumbering was the leading industry, especially in Maine and New Hampshire.[44] While some Irish workers may have "set out on foot or in coastwise vessels" for New England, after first immigrating to the Maritimes as Canada was often the first stop in migration, Belfast's founding investors were already in the colonies—and had been—for nearly fifty years.[45] The question then becomes, were the shareholders of Belfast, Maine, Ulster Irish or Americans of Irish extraction? What difference might that have made?

In the late 1700s, a foreign traveler to Belfast remarked that lumbering paid well enough that it made "these people careless of agriculture and husbandry."[46] This was the old stereotype in a new place: The locals who eschewed agriculture were lazy. While they may not have been doing "serious" farming, according to the visitor, they *were* working and making money in the lumber business. In 1805, cord-wood brought $2 a cord at the wharf in Belfast, whence it was shipped to Boston, where it could be sold for double that.[47]

The *poor, lazy,* and *scoff law* aspects of Irish stereotype, however, remained firmly entrenched—even in modern texts. The District of Maine, as it was designated, drew "desperate and impoverished yeoman farmers ... often bankrupt, [who] had not succeeded in the more populous regions of New England ... and therefore often represented the antisocial and maladjusted segments of society."[48] The border area also lent itself to smuggling—not an enterprise that left large volumes of paper evidence, nor did it earn migrants a great reputation.

Creating Scotch-Irishness

With the stability after the War of 1812 and Maine's statehood in 1820, Belfast's nascent male professional class began a new phase of settlement—one that was already retrospective. Herman Abbot, the first Belfast historian, writing around 1825, was one of the first to make a distinction among people *from* Ireland. While Abbot saw people from Ireland as Irish and people from Scotland as Scots, he took pains to establish that the "Scottish dialect was understood and spoken by several" of Belfast's early settlers who traced their roots to Ulster, Ireland.

Abbot saw Scottishness among Belfast's settlers prior to 1825 marked by an appreciation of Robert Burns' poems.[49] At least as early as 1825, then, such Irish Protestants were already considered something other than Irish by at least this particular local historian.

Still, the presentation of the Irish as *lazy* and *given to drink* continued unabated well into the nineteenth century. Local newspapers frequently ran items about the Irish, either in Ireland or as immigrants to American colonies. These early published pieces continued the litany of stereo-typical traits. In a letter ascribed in the pages of the *Hancock Gazette and Penobscot Patriot* to John Wesley, evidently written to a fellow preacher in Ireland, Wesley warned his co-religionist that "There is no country upon earth where [hard work is more a] necessity than in Ireland, as you are generally encompassed with those, who, with little encouragement [*sic*] would laugh or trifle from morning till night."[50] The writer of the letter also commented on perceived Irish vices, such as the use of snuff, a "silly, nasty, dirty custom," to which the Irish, like no others in Europe, were addicted. The final admonition, however, was reserved for alcohol:

> In Ireland above all countries in the world I would sacredly abstain from [a dram], because the evil is so general, and to this and snuff and smokey [*sic*] cabins, I impute the blindness which is so exceeding common throughout the nation.[51]

The stereotype of Irish immigrants being violent also remained stable from the eighteenth into the nineteenth centuries. A perceived propensity for violence served as fodder in Maine newspapers (popular culture publications) from the early nineteenth century through the post–Civil War period. As early as the 1820s, the *Hancock Gazette and Penobscot Patriot* presented stereotypes ranging from Irish-perpetrated violent crime to the Irish serving as the butts of jokes. Some stories reveled in gory reports from Ireland itself. Peasant revolts and atrocities perpe-trated against landlords were reprinted in Belfast's paper, providing a long list of negative adjectives, such as barbarous, savage, and brutal. Graphic descriptions of such "outrages" provided horrific scenes wherein law-abiding (and thus blameless) landlords were slain, such as the story about a Mr. Shea, a County Tipperary farmer, who

> had put out some under tenants, who held without lease, by civil bill of process, and had possessed himself of their lands. He was, in consequence, served with a notice that unless he restored the old occupants he should suffer for it. Shea then made preparations for defending his property and got two or three neighbours to assist him—All his precaution proved unavailing, for the next night his house was set on fire, in which there were sixteen persons, men, women and children.—He was the first to burst out on the assailants,

but was instantly shot, and thrown back into the flames, another who made a similar attempt, shared the same fate; and before the ruffians departed, every soul in the house was burnt to death.[52]

Interestingly, the editor of the *Hancock Gazette and Penobscot Patriot* admitted to having picked through Irish and English coverage of Irish "disturbances," which means he alone was responsible for choosing those presenting the most "savage brutality."[53] The editor used the *Dublin Morning Post* report that a Captain Waters from New Market had been assassinated and took time to describe in detail the fate of seventy-year-old war veteran Major Collis from Tralee Spa. The major had lost an arm in service. While he slept one night, a gang of "ruffians" broke into his home, cracked his skull with an iron bar, and shot him six times. The ruffians then ransacked and robbed his house.[54] Coverage of such "disturbances" continued. The Belfast, Maine, paper reported that a number of Irish locations—Kings, Kildare, Dublin, Tipperary, and Wicklow—were in states of emergency. The fact that one landowner had had "three dwelling-houses and thirteen office-houses" destroyed by fire was in no other way remarked on by the paper's editor other than to give the man's name and location. The *amount* of property *one* person owned was not questioned.

Other Irish landowners were more fortunate, merely having their houses plundered. Some were not so lucky. For example, in yet another description of a violent attack, the editor described how robbers had put an eighty-year-old woman on a straw-fueled fire to "make her confess where the money was concealed."[55]

News from the Boston papers, reprinted in Belfast, relished pointing out lawbreakers' Irish ties.

> Patrick Smith and Bridget, his wife, have been tried at Charleston for robbing the mail. The former was committed and the latter acquitted. Patrick Smith was convicted on two indictments for the same offence and sentenced to seven years imprisonment.[56]

A Massachusetts highwayman, "an Irishman, *Michael Martin* by name," was accused of robbing someone in New Hampshire as well.[57] Such Irish lawbreakers were merely one-step removed from scofflaws. In some instances the two were combined, such as in the following marriage announcement, presented in a whimsical manner:

> MARRIED, In St. John, N.B. 23d ult. Mr. Henry Hatton, to the amiable Miss Mary Campbell, lately from Ireland.—The ceremony was performed in jail, during the absence of the keeper; but the bride on his return was turned out of doors, leaving the loving couple the only consolation of taking a peep at each other through the gratings.[58]

Ideas about the Irish gift of gab and braggadocio that Franklin had remarked upon decades earlier survived intact in local newspapers. The editor of the *Hancock Gazette and Penobscot Patriot* in the 1820s used "filler" copy from English newspapers, which also seemed to have firmly entrenched notions of Irishness: "At a meeting of graziers in Norfolk, (Eng.) it was resolved to give a premium for the best *bull*. A cockney farmer, who was present, moved that no Irishman should be a competitor."[59]

At least one local newspaper editor's belief system saw people who claimed Ireland as the country of origin as violent by nature. During the summer of 1833, the Belfast editor reported an incident in Bangor Maine, forty miles north. Irishmen, he reported, flogged a sailor to death. He gave no reason for the violent act. The upshot, however, was a full-blown riot, wherein sailors from more than 100 vessels attacked Irish houses and beat the inhabitants:

> We understand farther that the Irish people were all driven from the town, but this we doubt. Bangor has become a young New York—they have their riots, and ever anon kill an Irishman or a sailor, with as little ceremony as real New Yorkers. Oh, the beauties of Bangor.[60]

In July 1833, there was indeed a series of riots in Bangor along the waterfront, led by rampaging sailors. The incendiary incident may have been the killing of John Harley, an Irishman, at a grog shop earlier that summer by a Maine local. It would appear a part-time employee at a Bangor grog shop, Moses Woodward, told Harley he could have all the wine he wanted for 25 cents. Harley drank three pints of port wine and died on site. The coroner ruled it an intentional death and Woodward was indicted for manslaughter. Evidently, Woodward forced the third pint down Harley's throat.[61] The case was under discussion from May into early summer.

On 6 July 1833, a group of Irish laborers in Bangor ganged up on a sailor and either beat or stomped him to death outside Joseph Carr's grog shop, an establishment frequented by both Irishmen and sailors. Whether Harley's death led to the sailor's death cannot be ascertained, but what happened next was an anti-Irish riot, led by sailors who were joined by local laborers. There were 125 vessels tied up at the wharves along the river. The beating to death of one of the sailors brought unity to the crews of the vessels. By the end of 7 July, rioting and well-armed sailors had burned Carr's grog shop and the tenement next door that housed Irish immigrants. Bangor's night watchmen were no match for "several hundred well-armed sailors."[62]

That was not the end of the violence. The next night, sailors rampaged through Bangor, pulling down Irish homes and beating Irish people, whereupon Irish families fled to the woods. The local government called in the local militia company, but it, too, was overwhelmed by sailors armed with clubs. By this second night of rioting, sailors were joined by native laborers. The riot spread out from the Irish section of the town into the streets of the well-to-do. A local lumber baron's mansion under construction was torched. Perhaps Irish laborers were considered a threat, but the Belfast editor did not speculate. The burning of a rich man's mansion grabbed Bangor leaders' attention, and through force of arms and loaded guns, they subdued the rioters on the third night. A number of sailors were arrested and charged with riot; they posted the very small sum required for bail and disappeared.[63]

The Republican Journal in Belfast expressed no sympathy for the Irish of Bangor. We might even conclude that the newspaper editor was sarcastic when he surmised that the violence did not actually drive the Irish away. The Irish and sailors, in the editor's definition, were of the same ilk: low class and violent. A death here and there was to be expected in such an environment, it would appear, if his "superior" tone is properly understood.

The pages of *The Republican Journal* continued the cultural stereotypes surrounding the Irish throughout the 1830s.[64] No mention was made of religious affiliation in the report of a fire at "the Babel," so named because it was the tallest structure in Belfast, but the newspaper editor's commentary was blunt:

> [The fire] proved to be in a room of the third story of the large wooden building on main street known as "the Babel," and occupied by an Irish family....We believe that there are few of our citizens who would regret the destruction of this Babel, if it could be done without loss of other property; it is a timely warning to level it with its foundation.—So mote it be, and all the people will say amen.[65]

That the editor of the paper in 1833 believed Irish and poor were synonymous is evident in the paper's pages. In a printed "spitting match" with another printer, he proposed that his adversary, whom he accused of publishing atheistic materials, should give the money to support two children of the late Captain Robert Emery: "Two of these children are supported by the bounty of a poor shoe-maker, an Irishman. They are related to this foreigner's wife. This generous man, labors hard, daily to procure bread for these poor helpless orphans."[66]

Access to Education

Irish poverty afflicted Irish learning, at least in early nineteenth-century newspaper "filler." The concept of a hedge school was not unknown to Belfast's residents of the 1820s, evidently, for the local editor made no attempt to explain such a thing to his readership. While the hedge schoolmaster was given his due as being a scholar of the classics, the fact that he dwelt in poverty was also limned clearly. As the story unfolded, readers learned the schoolmaster was paid only 5 shillings per quarter, teaching "in a miserable hovel by the road-side." Despite the desperate surroundings, the schoolmaster held his student to high standards, demanding a translation, "with true idiom" of Virgil's line, "*Obstupui, steteruntque comæ et vox faucibus hæsit.*" The Irish scholar, "Englished it thus, *obstupui*, I was bothered, *steteruntque comæ*, my hair stood up like the bristles of a fighting pig, *et vox faucibus hæsit*, and a devil of a word could I get out."[67] The Irish version of English drew the writer's ridicule, so even the translation from Latin, the mark of an educated person, was met with derision.

Such laughter at the expense of Irish education, given that Belfast's educational system for many years was not much above that of a hedge school, is significant. Locals raised money for erecting and running the first academy (around $3,500 plus an endowment), and in 1811 the Belfast Academy opened. Fees were to be "not more than $5 per term for each scholar," of whom there were to be no more than thirty-five.[68] A number of teachers spent a year or two teaching a session for local scholars from 1811 through 1852, but classes had to have met elsewhere after 1829, when the building was abandoned. In between times, the Academy was taken over and used as barracks by British troops in 1814. Occasionally, Unitarians met there, and in 1829, according to historian Joseph Williamson, a troupe of actors who thoroughly murdered Shakespeare came through. After that, the building was "left to take care of itself; its door open day and night, as an invitation to all tramps and night-walkers to enter and take possession; the haunt of the muses was no longer 'classic ground.'"[69] The teachers, who generally spent no longer than two years at the Academy, were all new college graduates—and all male. Nine Harvard graduates, seven Bowdoin College graduates, one Williams College graduate, and one Middlebury College graduate came through. Not a single one of these young men stayed in teaching or the area. About half entered the clergy, serving congregations from Bangor to New York state to Ohio—one died a missionary in Africa. The other half became lawyers—from Portland to Boston to New York City.

In comparison, by the middle of the nineteenth century nearly half the Irish population in Ireland was literate.[70] Universal education in Ireland, which was decidedly pro-British (and in English), meant that by 1790–1820, Ireland had a primarily English-speaking population.[71] Yet speaking English was not construed as enough of a similarity from Belfast's viewpoint, as the aforementioned hedge school item demonstrates. Local newspapers repeatedly demonstrated how Belfast editors viewed incoming Irish migrants—they spoke English, but with a decided flair and accent.[72]

Irish English

Irish use of English, however, remained the preeminent method of "Othering" the Irish. Phonetic spellings of Irish pronunciations were used as a form of pointed humor by native speakers of English regularly. Language deviance, like no other trait, separated the Irish from mainstream society. The phonetic spelling of Irish pronunciation was used to put down the newcomers: "males [meals]" of potatoes or bits of "carpits" [carpets] on "flures [floors]" drew literary smirks.[73] The odd pronunciations to native English speakers' ears were generally used in conjunction with a dig at the sagacity of the speakers:

> *An Original Anecdote.*
> An Irishman, one Pat McShane
> From Ireland came to State of Maine,
> An ostler; and was taken sick—
> Says landlord I will send, and quick
> A Doctor get—says, Paddy no
> Sir, if you *plaise* it shan't be so—
> To take my chance I had much rather,
> It was a Doctor kill'd my father.[74]

The pages of Belfast's weeklies, however, were not completely given over to such blatantly stereotypical stories. The editor of the *Hancock Gazette and Penobscot Patriot* also ran a story of several column inches regarding Irish patriot Robert Emmet's execution by the English and his purported last letter to the brother of the woman he loved. The tale of love lost because of a life cut short created a romantic portrait of Emmet. The article cited Washington Irving's *Sketches*, presenting lovelorn Irish pathos, yet also presented Emmet as a man of courage:

> [T]he firmness and regularity of the original hand-writing contain a striking and affecting proof of the little influences which the approaching event [his execution] exerted over his frame. The same enthusiasm which allured him to his destiny, enabled him to support its utmost rigor. He met his fate with unostentatious fortitude.[75]

As the nineteenth century progressed, and the Famine Irish arrived in large numbers in American eastern seaboard cities, nineteenth-century urban writers made—and published—class-based judgments against the Irish, whom they viewed as "lesser than." On the national scene, well-known editors in the Abolition movement, such as Lydia Maria Child, for example, made no apologies for their views on the Irish. Child, editor of *The National Anti-Slavery Standard*, while willing to speak highly of the Irish

in Ireland, especially Daniel O'Connell, who had publicly called for an end
to American slavery, had no such warm feelings toward the Irish immigrant, whom she viewed as base and ignorant.[76] She opposed reaching
out to the Irish community on the issue of abolition, especially as
American Catholic Bishop Hughes had come down on the side of anti-
abolition: "[T]heir moral and intellectual state is such, that they might
about as well attempt to call the *dogs* together for any purpose of reform."[77] Elizabeth Cady Stanton, leader of the women's movement initiated at Seneca Falls in 1848, was quick to second Child's fears about the
Irish and expressed her distaste at the thought of "Patrick and Sambo and
Hans and Yung Tung, who do not know the difference between a monarchy and a Republic, who never read the Declaration of Independence ...
making laws for Lydia Maria Child, Lucretia Mott, or Fanny Kemble."[78]
Stanton put the Irish on par with Black Americans, as well as German and
Chinese immigrants who spoke no or little English. Stanton, like John
Adams seventy-five years earlier, "Othered" anyone of the working or
laboring classes. Illiteracy, English fluency, and race also played their
parts. While Stanton argued that only those who had read the Declaration
of Independence were good enough to make laws for a Child, she evidently did not embrace Child's support of former male slaves being given
the right to vote before White middle-class American women.

Anti-Irish sentiments also were normative in the world of urban
published works, *especially* in those publications produced by the
Abolition movement. Child's anti-Irish immigrant stance was in direct
relation to her anti-slavery work, for example. Anyone who stood in
opposition earned her ire. She had harsh words for those Irish who rioted
after the Civil War draft was announced, turning their anger against
Black Americans in the city, burning an orphanage, and lynching Black
men. Yet she, like Stanton, "Othered" all immigrants. She described
immigrants in *her* city as former residents of European work-houses and
penitentiaries who led New York City to become "a sort of common
sewer for the filth of nations."[79] She used *ignorant* and *Irish* as syno-
nyms. She also harked back to the old standbys of lazy and drunken. The
Irish were, in her estimation, "idle, dissipated loafers."[80]

Her animosity may have arisen from fear. She would not have been
alone in those fears. The cities were, literally, filled with foreigners: By
1850, one in ten Americans was foreign born. Just a decade later, the
ratio was one in seven. Change worried people who had been here
longer; they worried about moral decline caused by newcomers.[81]

Child's animosity was stoked by the fact that these same "ignorant"
immigrants could vote long before American-born male former slaves or
White women. She was willing to hold off calling for White women's
suffrage, but she was outraged that immigrants would move ahead in
line of American-born former slaves who had been kept illiterate by
American law:

Thus thousands of foreigners, who cannot write their own names, or read their own votes, would be allowed to influence the elections of the country, while numerous native citizens, who are ignorant because our own laws have hitherto prevented them from obtaining the rudiments of learning, would be excluded from the polls.[82]

Child was not alone in her hostility. After the draft riots, many wealthy New Yorkers fired their Irish servants.[83]

Change of Tone

While national writers railed against the Irish in publications, however, the tone of reportage of things Irish in Belfast changed ever so subtly. *The Republican Journal*, published weekly, typically used "Pat and Mike" jokes as filler at the bottoms of columns, side by side with "silly female" and "darkie" jokes during the 1840s. Filler copy, then, highlighted the "Othered" of the 1840s—women, Black Americans, and the Irish. Women's call for citizenship rights, compounded by the same demands from Black Americans, threatened the status quo, as did "hordes" of Irish immigrants to large urban areas. Those fears may have spread even to rural areas; however, one reason for a subtle shift in tone in Belfast's weekly newspaper might have been because of who was paying the bills.

At least two financial backers of editor (and later owner) Benjamin Griffin's *The Republican Journal* were first-generation Americans: Hugh Johnston Anderson's parents came from Castlewellan, County Down. And, Nathaniel Lowney, born in Monmouth, Maine, was a former schoolteacher, who became a lawyer in Belfast. His father, also a schoolteacher, claimed to have been a student at Dublin College prior to immigration to Maine in the late 1790s.[84] So why did Griffin's paper run "Pat and Mike" jokes when two men with Irish heritage were helping underwrite it? Perhaps this co-opted the power behind the Irish stereotypes, subverting the power of such stories. Perhaps the proprietors saw their Protestantism as keeping them from identifying or being identified as Irish—yet at least Anderson used his "Irishness" to political advantage in his campaigns for governor of Maine, which he parlayed later into federal government positions.

The Republican Journal stories of the 1840s typically showed the Irish man or woman as "Other" through the use of dialect, a *patois* of Irish written in English or reflecting a literal rendition of Irish into English. These fillers from the 1840s used the standard stereotypes, frequently showing Irish, females as well as males, as violent. The scenes were typically courtrooms, depicting the Irish as having difficulties with established authority. They were flouters of the law and, although the characters used obsequious language with their supposed "betters," they went their own ways, even though the authority figure knew this to be childish and imprudent. The Irish were also shown as "thick." Close textual reading of a handful of such fillers helps explain why these features appeared in print.

In the 19 May 1843 issue of *The Republican Journal*, the polygamist Irishman called before the authorities gave his excuse for multiple marriages as, "'Why, plase your worship, I was trying to get a good one!'"[85] This shows the Irish polygamist in a proper subservient role to the judge, as one from below speaking to one above, yet the Irishman ups the ante. The judge is not "your honor" but "your worship," giving the judge God-like reverence, which *has been* used into modern times in the British Commonwealth for Lord Mayors. "Your worship" is an honorific, but does it "play" the same note for American readers? The speaker uses comparison shopping as his excuse, which is what makes the piece humorous. *The Republican Journal* editor was also trusting to context. His readers were also privy to a number of anti-female jokes or jibes; this "Irish" slight also plays as a battle in the war between the sexes jibe. For example, the paper ran the following, as an admonition to wives, just two months earlier:

> THE WIFE.—It is not unfrequent [*sic*] a wife mourns over the alienated affections of her husband, when she has made an effort herself to strengthen and increase his attachment. She thinks, because he once loved her, he ought always to love her, and she neglects those attentions which gained his heart. Many a wife is thus the cause of her own neglect and sorrow. The woman deserves not a husband's love who will not greet him with smiles when he returns from the labors of his day; who will not chain him to his home by the sweet enchantment of a cheerful heart. There is not one in a thousand so unfeeling as to withstand such an influence and break away from such a home.[86]

While modern readers may find the "husbandly" advice to women annoying, the same editor also discussed the plight of working women and sexual double standards frequently. So, again, even the seeming anti-female jokes may work as a kind of co-optation. For example, a page-one filler notes the following:

> When lovely woman stoops to folly, she is despised and the finger of scorn is pointed at her, –but man, who is the cause of all this, and much more, is merely called a wild youth, –and though he may have blighted the prospects, and sullied the fair fame of many a lovely female, –he still maintains his station in society, with a character unsullied by the breath of calumny, or reproach from the world.[87]

In the 3 March 1843 issue, Griffin also published a great deal of material on women's roles in other societies, a long piece on Sir Robert Peel's refusal to support repeal of the Corn Laws, as well as information about temperance societies. A Massachusetts temperance report proffered the following insights about poverty among immigrants, arguing it wasn't drink that reduced people to pauperism—it was economic realities:

> The largest number of these wretches have been reduced to poverty, not by liquor, but through the bad state of the times—the majority of them never having acquired any trade or profession, and depending merely upon the labor of their hands for daily sustenance.[88]

It is in context, then, that this particular editor's tonal shift becomes apparent; the jokes are less "laughing at" and more "laughing with." The tone is sympathetic.

Again, while the following might appear at first glance to trot out the stereotype that the Irish—male and female—were violent, the joke again creates a sense of camaraderie between male authority figures and the beleaguered—and scarred—Irishman. In the 11 August 1843 issue, Griffin ran a filler about an Irishman asked to prove he was married, whereupon the Irishman "bared his head and exhibited a huge scar, which looked as if it might have been made by a fire shovel.—The evidence was satisfactory."[89] Marriage and put-upon males losing the battle between the sexes seem to be the gist of this joke. If there is an anti-Irish slant, it is that the Irishman is a victim of the Irish woman.

The 18 August 1843 *Republican Journal* reported: "ACCIDENT.—An Irishman in Boston the other day, accidentally ran his head against a brick house, breaking through the bricks and doing other damage." The joke is that the Irishman's head can do a good deal of damage, as it is thicker than a brick; however, no other negative stereotype is affixed. There is no association with fisticuffs, liquor, poverty, disease, and so forth.

The Republican Journal continued to run considerable material concerning Ireland or those born in Ireland. In 1847, editor Griffin ran a short piece in which he (or some editor from whom he had pilfered the story) depicted the Irish-born as bloodthirsty and, in this particular case, as not playing fair or displaying un-American sensibilities:

> NAVAL.—Com. Conner has been removed from the command of the Gulf Squadron and Com. Perry placed in command.—Com. Conner is a native of Ireland, which together with his adopted country, he has disgraced, by hanging a marine, for comparatively no offence, and after he was recommended to mercy by the Court Martial.[90]

Yet, in addition to such a negative portrayal of the supposed Irish-born, Griffin reprinted a rather lengthy discussion of British parliamentary discussion of the Irish Famine, which he claimed to have gleaned from a number of European sources.[91] On the same page as that report, in which Lord Roebuck blamed Irish landlords and their extravagant life-styles for the troubles in Ireland, Griffin ran a short piece noting that the British government had promised to pick up the costs of transportation for any and all relief materials sent from the United States to Ireland.[92]

"Others," according to the old-timers, always had the same four fearsome traits: They drank too much; they were violent; they were poor; and they were sexually deviant. A begrudging respect for keen wit and a gift with words could be allowed, but only in so far as Irish English was not full of blarney. From 1718 through the Civil War, stereotypes against the Irish tended to remain the same. Urban writers, speaking to national readerships, were vociferous—and vicious—in their depiction of Irish immigrants. These national stereotypes were applied in Belfast, Maine; however, the tone of those applications—but not the stereotypes—changed over time. Part of the reason for that change was that the small city was founded by people with Irish roots; a number of its first professional men were first-generation Americans with one or both parents coming from Ireland (who helped bankroll the local newspaper); and by 1850 about 4 percent of the residents of Belfast were Irish born, albeit many were members of the working class.

Class and Status

Class and status took precedence over Irishness. For example, James D. Burn in "Three Years among the Working-Classes in the United States," published in 1865, remarked:

> It is worthy of note how the more prudent and industrious class of Irishmen succeed in the different walks of life, when they are favored with a fair field for the exercise of their genius and industry. In New York there is scarcely a situation of honor or distinction, from the chief magistrate down to the police, that is not filled by a descendant of some Irishman who lived in savage hatred of England beyond the pale![93]

The stereotype has been that newly arrived Irish lacked business experience, which meant they "lack[ed] ... the kind of individual ambition and entrepreneurial values that were vital to workers trying to move up in a capitalist industrial economy."[94] Yet, Irish entrepreneurs, with very little capital, managed to run a number of businesses in the service sector in Boston—groceries, butcher shops, fruit stands, saloons, restaurants, boarding houses, and hotels. A number of Irish peddlers roamed the streets. Their counterparts from another social class, those who *could* command capital, ran specialty shops for a different class of clientele; however, such people were still running businesses in the service sector. Working-class people were not in the market for fine cabinets, silver objects, musical instruments, and so on. That was hardly a sign of doom or failure. It was, however, a marker of an economic class divide.

Another reason there may have been less class-conscious "laughing at" newcomers from Ireland in Belfast was that wealth for all was slow to accumulate in the rural area. Was this caused by Ulster roots, or a result of Belfast being a small community at the hem of Boston's commercial frontier outskirts? In the early years of the *nineteenth* century, only one Belfast man owned a gold watch.[95] As late as 1850, only nineteen people paid taxes exceeding $100. Only after the American Civil War did Belfast's economy offer more individuals a chance at wealth. By 1874, 217 paid taxes of more than $100.[96] In addition, even though Belfast had been devastated by the "great fire of 1865," there were sixty-five more houses in 1870 than in 1860 and the number of polls, or the tax base, had increased by 126.[97] It would appear that not only Irish Famine immigrants faced a difficult economy for most of the nineteenth century but so did the locals.

In this look through Belfast's weekly newspapers, the stereotype of the drunken Irishman is missing. That is odd, given that Belfast's people were a heavy drinking group in the late eighteenth and early nineteenth centuries. As Belfast grew from village to town to city, cultural mores changed: Reports of inebriate workmen messing up road construction, or drunken truckmen losing their loads, led to a public call for temperance in Belfast, beginning with the Washington Movement in 1841. This, however, was taking coals to Newcastle. By 1842, there were six temperance societies in and around Belfast, including the following: The Belfast Society for Promoting Temperance (1828), County Temperance Society (1831), Belfast Temperance Society (1834), and Independent Temperance Society of Belfast (1841).

Even though the temperance movement began in Ireland, and people with Irish roots living in places such as Belfast were active temperance advocates, national temperance publications continued to tie Irishness to drink and garrulousness. An example is the one-volume *The Maine Law Museum; and Temperance Anecdotes*, by George W. Bungay. Published in Boston in 1852, the book says Ireland's Father Theobald Mathew started the temperance movement, but that didn't preclude the author from using the Irish as the butt of his jokes: For example, an English employer of an Irish worker tried to dissuade his employee from going to a local fair, using bribery because of the employee's previous encounters with demon rum there and having come home beaten bloody as a result. The Irishman, Darby, replied:

"I'm forever and all obliged to your honor, ... but does it stand to rason," added he, flourishing his shillelagh over his head, "does it stand to rason that I'd take five shilling for the great bating I'm to get to-day?"[98]

Darby had a great number of anti-Irish stereotypes attached to him in a short space—he was violent (carrying a shillelagh, a blackthorn cudgel), he was unreasonable (even while arguing that the "Boss" is unreasonable), and he was drink-driven. The stereotypes, evidently, were harder to lay to rest nationally than locally.

Notes

1 James MacSparran, "America Dissected, etc. in Sundry Letters from a Clergyman There: Letter 1: To the Hon. Col. Henry Cary, Esq.," in *A History of the Episcopal Church in Narragansett, Rhode Island: Including a History of Other Episcopal Churches in the State*, ed. Wilkins Updike (Boston: Merrymount Press, 1907), 43.

2 James Morone, *Hellfire Nation: The Politics of Sin in American History* (New Haven: Yale University Press, 2003), 2.

3 Jonathan O'Neill, "A Nod Is as Good as a Wink: Humor, Postcolonialism and the Case of Irish," *American Journal of Irish Studies* 13 (2016): 72.

4 Katie Barclay, "Stereotypes as Political Resistance: The Irish Police Court Columns, c. 1820–1845," *Social History* 42, no. 2 (2017): 258. http://dx.doi.org/10.1080/03071022.2017.1290343.

5 Joseph Boskin and Joseph Dorinson, "Ethnic Humor: Subversion and Survival," *American Quarterly* 37, no. 1 (1985): 81.

6 Barclay, 259.

7 David Noel Doyle, "Scots Irish or Scotch-Irish," in *Making the Irish American: History and Heritage of the Irish in the United States*, eds. J. J. Lee and Marion R. Casey (New York: New York University Press, 2006), 151.

8 Patrick Griffin, *The People with No Name: Ireland's Ulster Scots, America's Scots Irish, and the Creation of a British Atlantic World, 1689–1764* (Princeton: Princeton University Press, 2001), 26, 90.

9 *Massachusetts (Colony) General Court: Journals of the House of Representatives of Massachusetts 1718–1720*, Vol. 2 (Boston: Massachusetts Historical Society, 1921), 318. Accessed from Google eBooks 13 August 2013.
   The recommendation of the colonial General Court on 30 November 1720 was that the squatters be prosecuted if they did not move: "Whereas it appears to this House, that several Famielies [*sic*] lately arrived from Ireland, and others of this Province, have presumed to make a Setlement [*sic*] upon lands belonging to this province, lying westward of the town of *Haverhill*, which they call Nutfield, without any Grant or Leave obtained from this Court. *Resolved*, The the [*sic*] said People be warned to move off from said Lands, within the space of Seven Months, and if they fail so to do, that they be Prosecuted by the Attorny [*sic*] General, by Writs of Trespass and Ejectment." See R. Stuart Wallace, "The Scotch-Irish of Provincial Maine: Purpoodock, Merrymeeting Bay, and Georgia," in *They Change Their Sky: The Irish in Maine*, ed. Michael C. Connolly (Orono: UP, 2004), 43.

10 Charles Knowles Bolton, *Scotch Irish Pioneers in Ulster and America* (Boston: Bacon and Brown, 1910), 212–13. Among these were one single woman, one widowed woman, a couple with a small child, and a lame man.

11 "Adams' Argument for the Defense: 3–4 December 1770," *Founders Online*, National Archives, https://founders.archives.gov/documents/Adams/05-03-02-0001-0004-0016. [Original source: *The Adams Papers, Legal Papers of John Adams*, vol. 3, *Cases 63 and 64: The Boston Massacre Trials*, eds. L. Kinvin Wroth and Hiller B. Zobel (Cambridge, MA: Harvard University Press, 1965), 242–70.]

12 Thomas Lechmere to his brother-in-law John Winthrop, 4 August 1718. Collections of the Massachusetts Historical Society, 6th ser. V, Boston: Massachusetts Historical Society, 1892, 387 footnote. Accessed from Google eBooks, 13 August 2013.

13 Lechmere to his brother-in-law Winthrop, 387

14 R. Stuart Wallace, "The Scotch-Irish of Provincial Maine: Purpooduck, Merrymeeting Bay, and Georgia," in *They Change Their Sky: The Irish in Maine* (Orono: University of Maine Press, 2004), 44.

15 Samuel Shute, *Journal of the House of Representatives of Massachusetts 1718-1720*, vol. 2 (31 October 1718): 175.

16 MacSparran, 42

17 MacSparran, 41.

18 *Massachusetts (Colony) General Court: Journals of the House of Representatives of Massachusetts 1718–1720*, Vol. 2 (Boston: Massachusetts Historical Society, 1921), 172. Accessed from Google eBooks 13 August 2013.

19 Massachusetts Historical Society, Charitable Irish Society records 1737–2008.

20 Constitution of the Charitable Irish Society Adopted and Unanimously Accepted by the Society at a Full Meeting on Their Anniversary on 17 March 1804, Massachusetts Historical Society, Charitable Irish Society records 1737–2008. Article 11 of the constitution makes no distinction between Protestant or Catholic Irish. The only caveat is that the person applying for relief must be "of moral character and of Irish extraction."

21 Account Current with the Charitable Irish Society: Membership Account Book, Vol. 12, Massachusetts Historical Society. Maine settlers Matthew Cottrill and James Kavanagh, both Catholics, were invited to join the Society on 17 March 1797. While the calligraphy of the record clearly states that officers had to be "Natives of Ireland or Natives of any other part of the British Dominions of Irish Extraction, being Protestants, and Inhabitants of Boston," it appears that the word "Protestant" has been added by a different hand from the rest of the document and that it covers an erasure.

22 Benjamin Franklin, "A Narrative of the Late Massacres," in *The Heath Anthology of American Literature*, eds. Paul Lauter et al., Vol. 1 (New York: Houghton, Mifflin, 1998), 741.

23 Franklin, 741.

24 Franklin, 743.

25 Franklin, 741.

26 Kerry S. Walters, *Benjamin Franklin and His Gods* (Urbana and Chicago: University of Illinois Press, 1999), 136.

27 Walters, 138.

28 Benjamin Franklin, "From Benjamin Franklin to William Strahan, September 1, 1764," *Founders Online*, National Archives, https://founders.archives.gov/documents/Franklin/01-11-02-0092. Benjamin Franklin, "A Defense of Mr. Hemphill's Observations: Or, An Answer to the Vindication of the Reverend

Commission [30 October 1735]," *Founders Online*, National Archives, https://founders.archives.gov/documents/Franklin/01-02-02-0011.

29 Benjamin Franklin, "An Address to the Good People of Ireland, on Behalf of America, October 4th, 1778," in *Winnowings in American History: Revolutionary Broadsides, No. II*, ed. Paul Leicester Ford (Brooklyn, NY: Historical Printing Club, 1891), 21.

30 Public Record Office of Northern Ireland: Education Facsimiles 121-140: "18th Century Ulster Emigration to North America": No. 134.

31 Franklin, "An Address," 23.

32 Benjamin Franklin, "Letter to William Strahan, Passy, Augt 19th 1784," in *The Writings of Benjamin Franklin: Collected and Edited with a Life and Introduction*, ed. Albert Henry Smyth, Vol. IX (Norwood, MA: J. S. Cushing and Company, 1907), 261.

33 Franklin, "Letter to Baron Francis Maseres" (June 26, 1785), 349.

34 Franklin, IX, 264.

35 Kevin Kenny, *Peaceable Kingdom Lost: The Paxton Boys and the Destruction of William Penn's Holy Experiment* (Oxford: Oxford University Press, 2009), 32.

36 Griffin, *People with No Name*, 102.

37 Doyle, 151.

38 Kerby A. Miller, "Ulster Presbyterians and the 'Two Traditions' in Ireland and America," in *Making the Irish American: History and Heritage of the Irish in the United States*, eds. J. J. Lee and Marion R. Casey (New York: UP, 2006), 257.

39 Michael P. Carroll, "How the Irish Became Protestant in America," *Religion and American Culture: A Journal of Interpretation* 16, no. 1 (Winter 2006): 35.

40 Carroll, 37.

41 Bolton, 196.

42 Griffin, *No Name*, 163. Kerby Miller asserts that Ulster Presbyterians *in Ireland* increasingly formed alliances with Anglican unionists—it was the "most reliable protection against famine, eviction, or unemployment" for the poorer sort. Miller, "'Two Traditions' in Ireland and America," 267.

43 Martin E. Marty, *Pilgrims in Their Own Land: Five Hundred Years of Religion in America* (Boston: Little, Brown, 1984).

44 Stuart Bruchey, *Enterprise: The Dynamic Economy of a Free People* (Cambridge: Harvard University Press, 1990), 47.

45 Carl Wittke, *The Irish in America* (Baton Rouge: Louisiana State University, 1956, reprinted New York: Russell and Russell, 1970), 14.

46 Williamson, Vol. 1, 678.

47 Williamson, Vol. 1, 678.

48 Pauleena MacDougal, *The Penobscot Dance of Resistance: Tradition in the History of a People* (Durham, New Hampshire: University of New Hampshire Press, 2004), 110.

49 Herman Abbot, "Abbot's History of Belfast," in *Early Histories of Belfast, Maine* (Camden, ME: Picton Press, 1989), 233.

50 *Hancock Gazette and Penobscot Patriot*, October 19, 1820, I, no. 16.

51 *Hancock Gazette and Penobscot Patriot*, October 19, 1820, I, no. 16.

52 *Hancock Gazette and Penobscot Patriot*, February 6, 1822, II, no. 32.

53 *Hancock Gazette and Penobscot Patriot*, February 6, 1822, II, no. 32.

54 *Hancock Gazette and Penobscot Patriot*, February 6, 1822, II, no. 32.

55 *Hancock Gazette and Penobscot Patriot*, 18 July 1821, II, no 3.

56 *Hancock Gazette and Penobscot Patriot*, 11 July 1821, II, no. 2.

57 *Hancock Gazette and Penobscot Patriot*, 29 August 1821.

58 *Hancock Gazette and Penobscot Patriot*, September 5, 1821, II, no. 10.
59 *Hancock Gazette and Penobscot Patriot*, 15 March 1821, I, no. 37, 4.
60 *The Republican Journal*, 18 July 1833, 5, no. 24, 3.
61 James Mundy, *Hard Times, Hard Men* (Scarborough, Maine: Harp Publications, 1990), 34.
62 Mundy, 35. The sailors, according to Mundy, were armed with belaying pins.
63 Mundy, 36.
64 *The Republican Journal* commenced publication in 1829 and continues to publish. It was shut down by authorities briefly during the Civil War.
65 *The Republican Journal*, 18 April 1833.
66 *The Republican Journal*, 2 May 1833.
67 *Hancock Gazette and Penobscot Patriot*, August 1, 1821, II, no. 5.
68 Williamson, Vol. 1, 330–1.
69 Williamson, Vol. 1, 332.
70 Louis M. Cullen, *The Emergence of Modern Ireland: 1600-1900* (New York: Homes and Meier Publishers, 1981), 238.
71 Timothy W. Guinnane, *The Vanishing Irish: Households, Migration, and the Rural Economy in Ireland, 1850-1914* (Princeton: Princeton University Press, 1997), 106.
72 "Died," *The Republican Journal* 15, no. 40 (3 November 1843), 3, column 5.
73 Jon Gjerde, ed., *Major Problems in American Immigration and Ethnic History* (New York: Houghton Mifflin, 1998), 105.
74 *Hancock Gazette and Penobscot Patriot*, January 30, 1822, Vol. II, No. 30.
75 *Hancock Gazette and Penobscot Patriot*, December 14, 1820, Vol. 1, No. 24, page 1.
76 Lydia Maria Child, *Selected Letters, 1817–1880* (Amherst: University of Massachusetts Press, 1982), 167–8.
77 Child, 169. See also Joseph E. Capizzi, "For What Shall We Repent? Reflections on the American Bishops, Their Teaching, and Slavery in the United States, 1838-1861," *Theological Studies* 65, no. 4 (December 2004). Gale Academic OneFile, downloaded 15 June 2020.
78 Daniel Okrent, *Last Call: The Rise and Fall of Prohibition* (New York: Scribner, 2010), 48.
79 Child, 435.
80 Child, 440.
81 Morone, 3.
82 Child, 468–69.
83 Child, editor's note, 434.
84 Williamson, Vol. 1, 399. For information on Hugh Johnston Anderson's parents, see Edward T. McCarron, "Facing the Atlantic: The Irish Merchant Community of Lincoln county, 1780–1820," in *They Change Their Sky: The Irish in Maine*, ed. Michael C. Connolly (Orono: University of Maine Press, 2004), 73. William George Crosby asserts that William Lowney was a graduate of Dublin College. See his "Annals of Belfast for a Half Century," in *Early Histories of Belfast, Maine* (Camden, ME: Picton Press, 1989), 133. I found no trace of William Lowney (nor any variant spelling) in *Alumni Dublinenses: A Register of the Students, Graduates, Professors, and Provosts of Trinity College, in the University of Dublin 1593-1860*, eds. George Dames Burtchaell and Thomas Ulick Sadlier (London: Williams and Norgate, 1924); second edition (Dublin: Alex Thom and Co., Ltd., 1933).
85 *The Republican Journal*, 19 May 1843, 3, col. 2.

86 *The Republican Journal*, 31 March 1843, 1, col. 6
87 *The Republican Journal*, 3 March 1843, 1, col. 3.
88 *The Republican Journal*, 3 March 1843, 3, col. 3.
89 *The Republican Journal*, 11 August 1843, 1, col. 4.
90 *The Republican Journal*, 5 March 1847, 3. Editor Benjamin Griffin's source, however, was in error. Commodore David Conner, 1792–1856, commander of the Home Squadron in the Gulf of Mexico during the Mexican-American War, was born in Harrisburg, Pennsylvania. He was viewed as a war hero for landing more than 8,500 men at the city of Vera Cruz, assisting General Winfield Scott's invasion of central Mexico. He ended his career as commander of the Philadelphia Naval Yard. http://hdl.loc.gov/loc.mss/eadmss.ms016014. He was actually the son of an Irish-born immigrant, and the reason given in his papers at the New York Public Library for handing over the squadron to his second in command was that he was seriously ill. https://www.nypl.org/sites/default/files/archivalcollections/pdf/connerd.pdf.
91 *The Republican Journal* March 5, 1847, p. 2, col. 4.
92 *The Republican Journal*, March 5, 1847, p. 2, col. 6.
93 James Burn, "James Burn Describes Irish and German Immigrants in New York City, 1850," in *Major Problems in American Immigration and Ethnic History*, ed. Jon Gjerde (New York: Houghton Mifflin, 1998), 105.
94 Timothy J. Meagher, *Inventing Irish America: Generation, Class, and Ethnic Identity in a New England City, 1880-1928* (Notre Dame: Notre Dame University Press, 2001), 48.
95 Williamson, Vol. 1, 846.
96 Williamson, Vol. 1, 847.
97 Williamson, Vol. 1, 845.
98 George Washington Bungay, *The Maine Law Museum; and Temperance Anecdotes: Original and Selected* (Boston: Stacey and Richardson, 1852), 61.

5 Irish on the Move

[After the American Revolution] there had been a large influx of population and of the right class; men who did not come to spy out the leanness of the land nor squeeze out its fatness, but to lay the foundation of homes for a lifetime.[1]

"Settlers" are inherently transient, and that volatility leads to creativity. "To settle" can have an air of defeatism about it, implying that people have given up looking for anything better. After the settlement phase, what comes next? The cultural phase? How is culture created in such a place? People came to Belfast, participated, and went somewhere else. Did the steady flux create its own kind of migratory community that was somehow cohesive in a transitional way? Ultimately, the question is, how was community defined?

Steady in-migration of Irish people or people of Irish extraction to Belfast lasted for a century. Not everyone stayed. Economics drove people. When people settled in rural areas—or in cities—they were responding to "the specific economic context they encountered."[2] Immigrants were not ignorant of fiscal realities in the places to which they traveled. Their "decisions [were] based upon hopes for greater material prosperity or desires for superior political and religious liberties, [and] were considered, calculated, and deliberate."[3] Immigrants settled where land and/or work were available. *When* a group arrived in the U.S. affected its experience.

While East Coast port cities were growing quickly from 1743 to just before the American Revolution—New York 72 percent, Charleston 66 percent, Philadelphia nearly 60 percent, and Newport 44 percent—Boston lost population. The speculation as to why is multifaceted, having to do with economic fallout from the Anglo-French wars (Massachusetts was heavily invested); depreciation of paper currency; "bad" paper from Rhode Island's land banks; and "the limited capacity of its hinterland."[4] It also had less capital.[5] And, ultimately, Boston was reliant on the shipping trade, which the embargo of the early nineteenth century nearly destroyed.

DOI: 10.4324/9781003187660-5

Still, early critical studies of the Irish in America reported on Eastern seaboard communities, and Boston, a port city, received a great deal of attention.[6] People have moved in and out of the geographically constricted city regularly: "By 1850, only half the descendants of the Bostonians of 1820 still lived there."[7]

What led to such massive movement? There are several possibilities, not least of which is that New England was poorest of all American colonial regions.[8] Wealth was unequally distributed, as it was everywhere in the colonies. In New England, however, fewer hands held more wealth. The richest 10 percent of householders controlled 56.8 percent of the total wealth of New England.[9] The rise of the merchant and professional class led to further imbalance. Belfast was tethered to Boston until Maine statehood in 1820.

Settlement

What becomes readily apparent in the microcosm of Belfast is that movement was the only constant. In 1773, Belfast had just fifty inhabitants of all ages and of both sexes.[10] In the early days after the American Revolution, Belfast reconfigured and recreated itself. There were only fourteen families in place in 1784, when eight families from New Hampshire joined them.[11]

When the Revolutionary War descended on Belfast, the village had consisted of 109 people, mostly women and young children, with only eighteen heads of families (men) tallied.[12] After the war not all of the original male settlers came back to the area. John Mitchell never returned, for example, which was ironic as he had been the driving force behind creating the corporation that purchased the area from the Waldo heirs. John Mitchell's family was devastated by the war. Three of his sons—George, Samuel, and Joshua—died in military service. Robert, who was taken prisoner of war to Europe, returned briefly after the war and then moved to New Orleans, where he died. The eldest, John (junior), a ship's master, whose home port was Boston, died in 1782 of smallpox in Martinique. John (junior) had married John Cochran's daughter in Belfast. While three of the elder Mitchell's five daughters married and continued to reside in Belfast, the remaining two married and moved out of the area, one to Connecticut, the other to Chester, New Hampshire. Thus, only three of John Mitchell's ten children remained in the area. Two other original settlers—John Davidson (junior) and Matthew Chambers—did not return after the war either.[13]

The group that joined the settlement in 1784 was no more settled than the original inhabitants. John Robinson, "a native of Ireland," was never associated with the "Scots colony" in Ireland by Belfast's local historians.[14] He came to the colonies as part of Wolfe's army during the French war.[15] He settled in Londonderry, New Hampshire, and fought in the American Revolution. He was paid "£105 in depreciated Massachusetts securities," which he used to buy his Belfast land (Lot #47) from Massachusetts land-speculator "Lord" Timothy Dexter, arriving in Belfast in 1784.[16] He was a practical weaver, raising his own flax, which his wife spun into thread and he wove into linen; however, he moved to nearby Greene Plantation and lived there until his death in about 1808.[17]

The Belfast of 1800 was vastly different from that of 1770. Within those thirty years, Belfast had become a small mercantile hub. When merchants moved into the area—including Ulster immigrant Francis Anderson—a blatantly striated society ensued. A subscription dance series put together by Belfast's leading male citizens, including Anderson, highlighted the chasm in class and gender difference.

While William Crosby, (senior), the second lawyer in town, saw his generation of professional men as "of the best kind," creating the community from whole cloth, the reality was quite different. In the retrospectives created by his son, William George Crosby, and by Joseph Williamson, both lawyers and amateur historians, the hardships faced by their class—the professional class—took precedence. Williamson's account cast a romantic glow over the original settlers' lives: "All the early inhabitants of Belfast were in comfortable pecuniary circumstances. Their lands were paid for, and they were therefore exempt from the demands of mortgages or adverse claimants."[18] Perhaps he should have said, people of a certain social class had no mortgages or legal battles to win. Williamson described self-sufficient yet genteel people doing without "a single carpet, mirror, clock, book, picture, or article of ornament or luxury."

The city that Crosby and Williamson described, however, was created by the professional class, which began arriving in the late 1790s. Belfast's original settlers, descendants of immigrants from Ulster, had been squeezed out of city limits by the professional class, which led to class skirmishes. The hinterlands of Belfast had led to squatters on land owned by absentee landlords (harking back to the eighteenth-century settlement of Londonderry, New Hampshire, and its environs). A goodly number of the little more than two dozen who had ventured to Belfast in 1770 had moved out of the city proper by 1800—west to Greene Plantation (today's Belmont, Searsmont, and Morrill), Knox, or Montville; south to Northport; east to Searsport; north to Brooks, Swanville, or Prospect, just outside Belfast's jurisdiction, starting over in peripheral areas outside Belfast.[19] Theirs was anything but a world of gentility:

> The records of the Hancock [Belfast's county before Waldo was created] and Lincoln County Courts of Common Pleas reveal that during the ten years 1796-1805 residents of coastal, commercial Belfast and the inhabitants of backcountry towns confronted each

other in 134 debt cases. In nine out of ten cases (119 of 134) the Belfast resident was the plaintiff and the backcountry inhabitant the defendant.[20]

The trade embargo of 1807 and the ensuing War of 1812 were partly responsible for New England's economic instability, which affected the merchant and professional classes particularly, including Yankee ship captains in Belfast. Sea trade nearly went extinct. Backcountry residents became ever more vulnerable to debt and ejectment as those who owned the "debts" demanded payment. Backcountry citizens retaliated against merchants and professional men who demanded debt payments. Some of these residents disguised themselves as "Indians" and were dubbed Greene Indians (or White Indians of Greene Plantation). They confronted deputies who ventured into the marginalized areas and destroyed the paperwork of eviction and legal claims. Sometimes, a Belfast posse would swoop in to arrest a White Indian of Greene Plantation, but that led to armed confrontations.[21]

This class animosity was captured by local poet Joseph Dolliff, himself a resident of Belmont, which bordered Belfast. Belfast residents fell victim to rumor one evening in 1807, hearing that the Greene Indians were planning a retaliatory raid on Belfast for an arrest in Greene Plantation earlier in the day. (It later turned out that a number of local youths had fueled the rumor and had fired off guns in the woods to give it credence.)[22] In "The Greene Indian War," Dolliff satirized the new merchant class of Belfast in the person of James Nesmith, Esquire, the first trader in Belfast, who arrived in 1799.[23] Fearing the onslaught of Greene Indians, the Nesmith of the poem commands, "his 'boy' to rise;/ He says, 'Be sure my trunk secure,/There all my treasure lies.'/'James, take this trunk, and skip and jump,/And to McFarland's run.'" Captain Ephraim McFarland ran the coaster to and from Boston. Evidently travel on the boat was not for the delicate, but the good captain supplied everyone an "eye-opener" on board before breakfast every morning.[24] Nesmith, in addition to having a treasure chest, also had access to rum and brandy with which to entice Belfast's fighting men to arms in the middle of the night. Dolliff went through rollcall, which contained a number of the original settlers' names, but it also listed the new lawyers in town: Bohan P. Field and William Crosby. Crosby didn't fight, according to the poem, because his "limbs were bad." (William Crosby had had an arm crushed in a cider press when he was a child.) The Browns, Pattersons, Whites, Durhams, and Millers were listed as representative surnames of the original settlers, but newcomers' first and surnames were given: "To risk their lives, protect their wives,/they all marched off to war." The Reverend Alfred Johnson, Belfast's first full-time minister, took a drubbing, too. Leading the troops to meet the Greene Indians, Johnson heard a noise, looked behind him, and found his army had fled.

As the poem reached its climax, the good reverend dropped to all fours and crawled to Whittier's Tavern, where he happened to run into Judge Read. By morning's light, those at Whittier's were "warm as wool" and all the citizens of Belfast claimed victory.[25]

Satire is an old tool used to put authority figures in their place and had a long history in Ireland. It continued as a tool of the dispossessed in Maine. Dolliff's poem was purported to have been composed orally and handed down generation to generation in the same manner—even though the poet requested that "Good people, all, both great and small,/Give ear to what I *write*" (emphasis added).[26] Williamson provided two descriptions of the poet from two individuals who claimed to have known him. (Williamson's first volume of Belfast's history was published in 1875.) In the first, Dolliff was presented as a "harmless, inoffensive man" who occasionally sold a few shingles in Belfast. In this iteration he was presented as poor. A second description claimed he

> was a man of quick wit, rich humor, and wonderful facility in stringing together verses in which there was apt to be more reason than rhyme, and but little to spare of either; and that he usually found in this locality [i.e., Belfast] ampler field for the development of muse and muscle than he did at home [i.e., Greene Plantation].[27]

In other words, Dolliff composed a lot of poems at the expense of Belfast's elite male class. There is no record if Joseph was kin to two former Belfastians who removed to Greene Plantation: Brothers Daniel Dolliff (who left Belfast before 1800) and John Dolliff (who left after 1810).

Political Landscapes

Belfast's lawyers, however, were more concerned in this era with national events and how those events had devastated the local economy. In an attempt to loosen the near death grip around New England traders' necks, first-generation American lawyer John Wilson worked with Belfast's two other lawyers—Field and Crosby—to rescind the trade embargo at the federal level. In an ironic twist, Wilson had his home seized and used by British officers during the brief British incursion into Belfast during the War of 1812.

After the war ended in December 1814, the economy started to recover as well, as evidenced by resumed lumbering in the area. On one particularly memorable day, 21 February 1815, between 300 and 400 sleighs and ox teams loaded with lumber, hay, and provisions arrived at the Belfast wharves.[28] Belfastians, however, barely had time to resume lumbering and ship-building before the "year eighteen hundred and starved-to-death" struck. Weather caused massive upheaval in Belfast, as well as the rest of New England. Maine had snow every month of 1816, including a sleet storm in July. Crops froze in the fields in August.[29] The bizarre weather pattern, which resulted from a volcanic eruption in Southeast Asia spewing ash into the atmosphere, affected climate worldwide.[30] From a New England perspective, points west looked more inviting. When Kentucky and Ohio lands promising a more moderate climate opened for settlement, between 10,000 and 15,000 Mainers migrated.[31] Stories of fertile lands and moderate climate after 1816 continued to draw thousands of Mainers westward.[32] Only one of the original Belfast settlers who had been squeezed out into the wilds of Knox moved as far as Ohio. After all, the original group of settlers was aging.

Migratory Medical Men

Even a cursory look at migration patterns of Belfast, Maine, shows that people traveled into and out of the small coastal city regularly. Just a quick glance at one professional class—medical doctors—from 1800 through the War of 1812 years demonstrates the transitory nature of this society. Before 1800, Belfast had one physician, who arrived in 1792. Dr. John Scollay Osborn, from Epsom, New Hampshire, lived in Belfast until his death in 1831. From 1800 to 1815, ten doctors arrived in Belfast, with three remaining in Belfast their entire careers: Dr. Herman Abbot, one of Belfast's amateur historians, stayed from 1810 until his death in 1825 at age forty-two; Dr. Charles Hall arrived in 1807 and died in 1819. Dr. William Poor arrived in 1815 and practiced in Belfast until his death in 1829, age fifty-three.

Those doctors who moved out of the area did so for a variety of reasons. Two served as military physicians during the War of 1812—Dr. Thaddeus Hubbard and Dr. Caleb Boutelle. Hubbard returned after his military service, but set up a practice in Searsport, five miles farther east, and then moved to Norridgewock, Maine, where he spent the rest of his career. Boutelle was taken prisoner of war, held in Gibraltar, and died in 1819. Of the remaining five doctors: Dr. Joseph Underwood came and went, not acquiring "much of a reputation." A Dr. Webster put in a brief appearance in 1803. Dr. William Crooks deserted his wife and had been removed from his position as surgeon's mate in a regimental unit in 1793. A Dr. McMillan moved from Belfast to Knox, Maine, and thence to Ohio.[33] Dr. Edward Cremer came to Belfast in 1808 but died in Jamaica in 1810. Dr. Eben Poor moved from medicine into politics and back again. He arrived in 1814 from Andover, Massachusetts, via Andover, Maine. He lived in Belfast eight years, then moved to Castine (also spending time in Penobscot), Maine, to become Clerk of the Courts, which office he held seven years. Then he returned to Andover, Maine, and resumed his medical practice. He served as a state senator in 1822, just two years after

Maine became a state. Professional men were, clearly, migratory. We could find similar patterns in subsequent years, at least among Belfast's doctors. What also becomes clear is that professional men had short life spans. Achieving the age of fifty was a milestone for most.

Professional careers in the nineteenth century required people to travel. Many men, as they took positions with companies or in politics, moved to places like Boston, New York, or Washington, D.C. Jobs could (and did) take people to California, the Caribbean, Minnesota, and many points in between. Hugh Johnston Anderson, first-generation American, lived and worked in Washington, D.C., for a decade, moving from the governorship of Maine into federal positions in Democratic administrations. His federal career sent him to San Francisco for a few years.

Economics and Migration

Migrations do not occur at the national or even state level.[34] Local family economies and cultural-economic regions drive migration. In other words, individuals migrate based on individual choices made within economic, historical, religious, political, familial, and other circles. In Belfast's microcosm, we can see how economic upheaval affected migration within the United States. Many of Belfast's early merchants themselves moved on to Boston. The 1840s, especially, were a volatile decade for people who had been in Belfast since the 1820s: Samuel Moulton arrived in 1822 and set up a tin plate and sheet iron-working business with a partner. That business was dissolved by 1824, and the partner moved to Portland, but Moulton stayed on in Belfast until 1844, at which point he moved to Boston.[35] He returned to Belfast in 1853 and stayed there the remainder of his life. He was one of the few to return. Watchmaker Freeman C. Raymond lived and worked in Belfast from the mid-1820s until 1840, when he moved to Boston permanently.[36] Henry Colburn, born and raised in Belfast, worked as a clerk, then became a merchant, and later ran a tavern, but moved to Boston in 1849. He lived there the remainder of his life, but upon his death in 1874 his body was shipped back to Belfast for interment.[37] Mayo Hazeltine was a long-time merchant in Belfast, beginning in 1827. He, too, moved to Boston, where he died in 1843.[38]

As Belfastians headed to Boston in the 1840s, many Bostonians were moving out of the city's orbit. At the same time, Irish immigrants were arriving in great numbers.[39] Belfast ships plied the waters to Boston regularly. Lumber continued to drive the Belfast economy throughout the 1840s, providing employment for a host of coasting schooners, fifty of which sailed from Belfast to Boston or Salem, Massachusetts, making at least ten trips a season. Boston, then, was a central hub, which meant Irish immigrants *could* find work there, albeit of the unskilled variety, which may explain why a good many stayed within city limits. Canada, before the 1840s, provided a cheaper entrance to the United States via Halifax, Nova Scotia, but commerce in Halifax, or Saint John, New Brunswick, was at the mercy of the Saint Lawrence River to the north, which freezes in winter.[40] Harbors in Belfast and Portland do not. During the 1840s, Irish immigrants could travel directly from Liverpool to Portland, Maine.[41] On the other hand, the Cunard Line steamship, partly owned by the British government, had a terminus at Boston, which is one reason Irish immigrants continued to arrive in Boston.[42]

The work Irish immigrants found in Boston generally did not require massive amounts of training (which required money), nor did they have to make large cash investments. The Irish were ubiquitous among the Boston servant class: Waiting tables and working as blacksmiths. Most hostlers and stablers were Irish. Many more Irish laborers worked in the building trades. The Irish found little in upscale retail, wholesale, cabinet making, maritime, silversmith, musical instrument manufacture, and so on, which was part of their skill set.[43] The Irish, however, were grocers, butchers, fruiters, peddlers, saloonkeepers, restaurateurs, and boarding house or hotel keepers.[44] In other words, the Irish excelled at providing the necessities of life.

The decade of the 1840s in Boston and Belfast, thus, was marked by a great deal of migration. The impetus for movement spiked in 1849, when California's gold fields beckoned many who were attracted to glittering streets of promised gold—on the prairies, in the northern woods, or California.[45] The marker of "making it" was increasingly fame and fortune (and no longer having to work hard). The obituaries of Irish Catholic William Brannagan and Irish Methodist Francis Banon seemingly support that definition. As discussed previously, these two Irishmen were accepted and noted in Belfast because of the wealth they amassed in their lifetimes.

Gold Fever

In 1849, Asa Faunce and his partners built the *Suliote* in Belfast, proposing to sail to San Francisco, if forty people subscribed for the voyage. That number was quickly reached. They filled the ship with as much merchandise from local stores as they could hope to sell, and off they went. Among those who left were *The Republican Journal* owners for most of the 1840s, Benjamin Griffin and Cyrus Rowe (who bought out George Griffin).

Griffin's coverage of Irish topics in the paper had brought a new tone into the discussion of things Irish in Belfast, and with a substantial subscription list of well over a thousand people, his approach evidently was appreciated by his readership. Under Griffin's editorship, *The Republican Journal* presented Sir Robert Peel's unwillingness to repeal the Corn Laws as callous. His choice of articles on Daniel O'Connell's call for a Repeal of the Union with Great Britain was always supportive. He ran many articles that used a caustic tone when speaking of the British government, and he consistently showed members of the House of Lords as "snooty." This was a marked change from the coverage of the 1830s—and previous editors. Two of his financial backers were first-generation Americans whose parents had been born in Ireland—Hugh Johnston Anderson and Nathaniel Lowney.

Griffin remained in Belfast for not quite one decade, but during that time he became an integral member of the community, part of an inner circle of "movers and shakers." Arriving from Boston in 1841, he ingratiated himself in Belfast happenings by 1844. When the town purchased a new fire engine, he was among sixty young male volunteers of the new fire company, serving as secretary.[46] He also served as secretary for the Mechanics Association, which was reorganized in 1840. It met in the Masonic Hall in the building known as Old Babel (this was the tallest building in Belfast, but one which also housed immigrant Irish families). Benjamin Kelley served as president.[47] Griffin joined one of the many temperance societies flourishing in Belfast—the Independent Temperance Society of Belfast.[48] He was also a sought-after speaker, such as being "keynote" for Samaritan Tent No. 17 Independent Order of Rechabites, a total abstinence temperance organization.[49] By the late 1840s, he was elected to the Board of Education.[50] In one of his final Belfast appearances, Griffin spoke at the major event of 1849—preparing for the launch of the *Suliote* for California. He planned to leave Belfast and sail to California with thirty-nine other passengers. Former Governor Anderson presided at the gala festivities.[51]

The five men from Belfast who boarded the *Suliote* for California via Cape Horn were a disparate group. Griffin, identified as a printer and editor, was joined by a carpenter, a boat-builder, an artist, and a sailmaker. According to his obituary, Griffin headed to California with a nest egg of $10,000. That figure is startling—and more than a little suspect. The story Griffin spun about his days in California is equally questionable. Supposedly, he bought a printing office and established a newspaper in San Francisco, wherein he doubled his investment in short order. The office was worth $25,000. He didn't have insurance. A fire bankrupted him in one night:

> Thus stripped of all earthly possessions, and it being in the heighth [*sic*] of the gold excitement in the mountains, he, with a party of his former employees in his office, started for the gold diggings. But misfortune did not come singly. The exposures and hardships of such a life threw him into a fever, recovering from which left him the legacy of a life-long attack of inflammatory rheumatism.[52]

Griffin returned to the East Coast and resumed journalism for the rest of his career, editing the *Providence [Rhode Island] Daily Post* and later the *Syracuse [NY] Democrat*. He died at age fifty-three in 1874 while working for *The Weekly Recorder,* published in Fayetteville, New York.[53] Despite the lack of extant correspondence, someone who had known him in Belfast wrote an appreciative obituary, albeit unsigned:

> He was much esteemed for his many excellent characteristics. Of brilliant talents, extensive information, a rare conversationalist, and a gifted and ready writer,—these qualities, added to a personal fascination that won the hearts of all acquaintances, made him in his day the most popular gentleman of this vicinity.[54]

He was also praised for his writing: "His editorials in the 'Journal' were distinguished by vigor of thought and simplicity of style."[55]

Just a few months after Griffin left Belfast in 1849, Cyrus Rowe, his former partner at *The Republican Journal,* traveled overland with six men from Belfast for California. Upon arrival in Sacramento, he claimed to have met sixty-one "Belfast" men in California—more than 2 percent of the total male population of Belfast, Maine.[56] Rowe never returned to Belfast, remaining a short time in California and then moving to Nevada, where he died. Indeed, Belfast travelers sought out other Belfast

Figure 5.1: By the 1870s, Belfast's harbor and the Puddle Dock area were crowded with trains, as well as ships. Courtesy of the Belfast Historical Society and Museum.

travelers. Even local historians Williamson and Crosby kept track of who went where—but only of those men from their social class (men of note).

The *Suliote* was not the only Belfast speculation during the California Gold Rush Year of 1849. Three other Belfast-built vessels sailed for San Francisco that year—the schooner *Mary Read*; the brig *San Jacinto*; and the bark *William O. Alden*. Nineteen of the thirty-eight adventurers who sailed to San Francisco in the bark *William O. Alden,* named for the captain, were from Belfast.[57] Nearly thirty years later, only four had returned to Belfast; three were still living in California; and six had died. The fates of the other six are unknown.

Belfast's young men on the make weren't the only ones drawn westward. Belfast's Collector of Customs in 1849, a federally appointed position, was from the town of Camden, a few miles south of Belfast on Penobscot Bay. When his tenure was up, he, too, headed for San Francisco. He remained there, "occupying a judical [*sic*] station."[58] Even a professional man could be migratory, always looking for something else.

Irish immigrants, therefore, who traveled westward in the United States did so with the rest of Americans. Nearly half of the San Francisco Irish, for example, had lived in the Eastern United States before migrating.[59] Some Irish Catholic immigrants—and migrants Catholic or Protestant from the East Coast of the United States—to San Francisco did well, holding high-status occupations—lawyers, doctors, and merchants.[60] This, however, was not just a phenomenon on the West Coast of the United States. Professional men did well financially on the frontier.

The Vast Frontier

In Crosby's assessment of Belfast migrations, published as a series of sketches in *The Republican Journal* in the mid-1870s, no second generation of many a family seemed to stay in the area. Some moved a few miles out of town, but out of city limits. Of the eight leading traders in 1805–1806, for example, only three left progeny who remained in the area upon Crosby's writing his *Annals*. One man of the eight had sold his business to his brother and then decamped to Boston. Another, Irish immigrant Francis Anderson, died, leaving his teenage nephew in charge of the family business, but, as discussed earlier, even nephew Hugh Johnston Anderson made his home elsewhere after living more than twenty years in Belfast.

Crosby was intrigued with this onward migration of the younger generations. He pointed out that of the thirty-six men he considered the backbone of the community in Belfast's early years—professional men, such as lawyers and doctors; skilled tradesmen, such as blacksmiths, house wrights, shoemakers, masons, tanners, hatters, tailors, painters and inn holders—only thirteen had descendants still in Belfast. Crosby did point out, dryly, that one, Abel Baker, a tailor, had left the area, running off with a married woman after having committed tax fraud. Evidently, Baker had an excuse for leaving, in Crosby's estimation.[61] Crosby's observations about Belfast's transient population hold true on the larger scale. In many cases, the idea of a better life entailed accruing wealth or moving beyond a subsistence economy. U.S. history is filled with people going to places where the latest "mother lode" could suckle many a newborn enterprise.[62] Immigrants from Ireland were part of a centuries-long exodus and trek ever westward. They, like the rest of European America, continued their westward migrations as the American continent was seized from local peoples. Settlements, by nature "unsettled" places, meant society was unsettled, too. This state of being unsettled allowed social fluidity. Social strata were not solidified—the edges were permeable. Some men born in Ireland who served as Belfast, Maine, lawyers, school teachers, politicians, and merchants, whether Catholic and Protestant, did quite well financially. A number of those men rose to the rank of professional through education. Belfast's frontier status fifty years before the supposedly astonishing class and status leveling out west shows that the *frontier*, north or west, offered class mobility, if not riches.

Class and Status

Some working-class Irish immigrants to Belfast stayed. Some just moved nearby. Bridget Haugh McCabe's extended family provides a case in point. Her father's brother, Charles Haugh, may have immigrated to Belfast as a result of the Irish Famine. He was the first in the family to arrive in Belfast. His first appearance in public records is the 1850 U.S. census. He was forty-five and a laborer; his eighteen-year-old son John, supposedly, had been born in Maine. That would mean our assumption that Haugh arrived post-Famine would be wrong; however, census takers made mistakes frequently.

Wife Margrett [*sic*] was thirty-nine in the 1850 census. There was a ten-year age gap between the eldest son John (age 18) and Henry (age 8). The other two children listed in the 1850 census are Hannah/Johanna (age 3), and Charley (9 months). By the 1860 census, Margaret was listed as forty-five. Was she really thirty-nine in 1850? She had three more boys: Franklin eight (born circa 1852), Thomas (perhaps named for his father's brother, born circa 1854) six, and William (born circa 1857) three. What happened to these Belfast-born children? Did they stay in Belfast? Did they migrate elsewhere?

Eldest son John married twice: Nancy Burke in 1852 and Mary A. McLaud [MacLeod] in 1876. He married both women in Belfast. Second son Henry served as a private in Company D, 20th Infantry, in the Civil

War. He transferred to the Navy, dying at age twenty-two onboard the *Mendota* near Fortress Monroe in 1864. That same year, daughter Johanna, seventeen, married local Belfast sailor Charles T. Tewkesbury, age twenty-two, whose father was a tin "pedlar [*sic*]" from New Hampshire and whose mother had been born in Palmyra, Maine. Johanna divorced Tewkesbury and by 1868 was remarried to John H. Brown, also a seaman. There is no record of William past the 1860 census. Franklin (Frank) married Mary E. Jamie in 1874. Thomas married Miss Frank S. Walker in 1879. Both young men married in Belfast.[63]

It appears, then, that the Haugh family stayed in the area for nearly thirty years, but none of the children, even though they married "at home," lived in Belfast as of 1860, at least in so far as the census was concerned. By 1870, even Charles' (senior) household was not listed in the U.S. census, but by 1880, Charles senior was dead and Margaret lived alone back in Belfast. Perhaps the family had moved into a neighboring jurisdiction, but none of the first American generation remained in Belfast.

Men were not the only ones who searched for better opportunities. Belfast was home, at least for a few years, to Eliza Spinks. Hers, we remember, was not the happiest of childhoods. Part of the extended family of the allegedly murdered Bridget Haugh McCabe, Eliza was the dead woman's stepdaughter. Eliza's mother, Margaret Spinks, born in Ireland, was a widow immigrant with three children. She married Bryant [*sic*] McCabe in 1849—the same year the *Suliote* sailed for San Francisco. Eliza's mother disappeared from public records, but her stepfather remarried—sixteen-year-old Bridget Haugh. The new wife was only two years older than Eliza. There were accusations Eliza's mother, too, had been murdered by McCabe, but those weren't made public (in printed records) for nearly a decade.[64] After her mother's death, Eliza was given a court-appointed guardian 7 April 1852, lawyer Nathaniel Lowney, himself a first-generation Irish American.[65] By 1860, however, Eliza was working as a laundress in the Physicians Hospital in San Francisco. There was at least one other familiar Belfast name in the San Francisco hospital's census materials: Jane Carr, born in Ireland, one-time resident of Belfast, worked as a cook there.

Eliza's elder brother John Spinks left no public records after 1850, and that was just a census listing. Her younger brother Charles Spinks mustered into Company I, 26th Infantry, in 1862, served his time, and re-enlisted in 1863. He died of fever at Barrancas, Florida, in 1865.[66] His entire estate went to his half-brother William A. McCabe, who still lived in Belfast and who remained there the rest of his life.[67] Perhaps Eliza was dead by 1865, or she could have married, been estranged from Charles, or Charles and William had no idea where she was. To all intents and purposes, she ceased to exist. In other words, of Margaret Spinks McCabe's four children, only one remained in Belfast—her son with Brian McCabe, the son born in Belfast.

Family Networks

Irish immigrants to Belfast in 1850, for the most part, traveled in family groups. This fact may have made the group as a whole more settled. The influx to Belfast of new settlers from Ireland in the years immediately following the Famine did not conform to the notion that most Irish-born emigrants left Ireland single in that decade.[68] Belfast's immigrant travel patterns do, however, reflect an earlier reality. Nationally, from 1831 to 1841, 60 percent of Irish immigrants traveled in family groups, and they continued to do so throughout the Irish Famine years.[69] People who traveled to Belfast were no different. According to the 1850 Belfast census data, forty families and under two dozen single people made up Belfast's Irish immigrant community. Of those, twenty-three families (or at least their remnants) remained in Belfast ten years later, and at least two of the men listed as single in 1850 had married (or perhaps had been married prior to immigration and then sent for wife and children) and remained in town.[70] It is not possible to trace Irish immigrant women who might have married, given that they changed surnames. Fourteen families of those counted by the 1850 census enumerators were headed by individuals forty or older; twenty families were headed by people in their early to mid-thirties; and six young families, parents in their twenties, were also part of the mix. Obviously, most of those who came to Belfast were older, more established family units. Of these 1850 households, nine were composed of married couples with no children—the childless couples were nearly evenly split across the age groups. Larger family sizes included blended and extended families. Only twenty-three Irish-born individuals were single in the 1860 census. Some childless older couples could well have been traveling with married children and their families, but the census records make it impossible to track, especially if the older couple were the parents of the woman.

Belfast census data do not support the assertion that a great many Irish-born settlers arrived in Maine via Canada, but, of course, the census enumerators did not necessarily get all the information or get it correctly. For example, William S. Brannagan is not listed in the 1850 census, even though he was resident in the community starting in the early 1840s, given records from Abigail Davis Field's Day Books.[71] Still, Brannagan often traveled on business. He may have been "on the road" when the census taker arrived at the Field House. In the 1860 census, he was erroneously listed as American born.[72]

Of the forty Irish immigrant families in Belfast in 1850, only two came through Canada, at least in so far as the census data can tell us. All six of the Donnelly children of Irish-born William and Eliza were born in Nova Scotia. Irish-born David Mitchell evidently married Sarah in Nova Scotia, and two of their three children were born there. The youngest, age one, was born in Maine.

Maintaining intact family circles was a factor in migration. For example, Irish-born Fred A. McDowell, a man noted as being a physician in the 1850 census, evidently settled in Vermont upon arrival from Ireland. He remained there long enough to marry and have three children in Montpelier before traveling to Belfast. McDowell remained in Belfast only long enough to be recorded in the 1850 census, and there is no evidence that he practiced medicine in Belfast. According to public records, he (and his family) went to Lowell, Massachusetts, where he died in 1853.[73] His widow remained in Lowell through the 1860 census, housing the extended family from Vermont, including her father, Nathaniel Packard, age eighty-eight, and her sister/widowed sister-in-law, Seraph Packard, age fifty-five, and Ellen Packard, age twenty, who was attending school.

McDowell's eldest daughter worked as a milliner. She married, whereupon the young couple moved to Newark, New Jersey, thus beginning a chain migration.[74] By the 1870 census, McDowell's widow was living in Jersey City with her two adult sons. The sons remained in the area the remainder of their lives, albeit moving frequently in and around northern New Jersey and into New York City.[75]

Assessing the evidence of blended families is also tricky; the seven-member Banon family of 1850 serves as example. Besides the parents, James, age forty, and Catherine, age fifty, there were five younger Banons, also Irish-born. This family was not related to the Francis Banon family of 1819, as far as I have been able to establish. The eldest daughter, according to the census taker was twenty-eight; the remaining four offspring were eighteen, seventeen, fourteen, and twelve. If we can assume any validity in these ages, we have an interesting family grouping. These immigrants were no longer in Belfast at the 1860 U.S. census, so we cannot double-check ages. The wife is listed as ten years older than the husband, and there is a ten-year gap between daughters Ellen and Mary. What might this tell us? Perhaps Catherine, the woman of the house, was widowed and Ellen was a child from a previous marriage, as forty-year-old James Banon would have been too young to have had a twenty-eight-year-old daughter; however, if the eighteen-year-old daughter was indeed his, then James would have been twenty-two when he married Catherine, who would have been in her early thirties. The remaining children were quite close in age. Perhaps the twenty-eight-year-old Ellen was James' younger sister. The census taker did not note whether these were sons and daughters, only that they lived in the same household. Age gaps between children could also be explained by deaths. Census data will not let us speculate any further.

In addition to the possibility of blended families, there is also the fact that many households included members of the extended family. For example, Irish immigrants Patrick and Mary Carey, both twenty-six, arrived with two teenagers with the same surname. Edmund and Susan were seventeen and fifteen, respectively. These two children could not, obviously, have been the young couple's children. There was, however, also a Mary senior, age fifty, whose surname is also listed as Carey. We can speculate then that Mary senior was Patrick's mother; the census taker recorded Patrick and Mary junior as marriage partners. Edmund and Susan must therefore have been Patrick's younger siblings. Patrick, who was older than twenty-one, was listed as head of house, even though his mother was living.

While we might expect such extended family arrangements among Irish immigrants, we should note that such an arrangement was not abnormal in the receiving community either. For example, even the very wealthy James W. Webster, originally from New Hampshire, his wife, and two unmarried young adults, ages twenty-one and twenty, plus an eleven-year-old, occupied the household where Irish-born and single Bridget Brien served as a domestic. Again, there is nearly a decade between Webster's older children and the eleven-year-old. Is this a second wife for Webster? In addition to the husband, wife, two unmarried adult children, and a pre-teen, Webster's seventy-eight-year-old widowed mother-in-law also lived in the house.

The 1850 census has a few oddities, showing the difficulties of relying entirely on the census takers' acumen. In a couple of instances, some Irish-born laborers were listed twice, or at least appeared to be. For example, John Bogan was listed as a hostler. He was listed at different addresses and given different ages. A few possibilities present themselves: (1) there were two John Bogans; (2) there was one John Bogan, and his employer listed him as being part of the employer's household, while his landlord/lady did the same; (3) there was one John Bogan, and the census taker(s) did not record his age correctly. John Bogan, age *thirty-five*, was hostler, for a public house. John Bogan, age *twenty-eight*, hostler, shared a room with Thomas Bogan, twenty, a tailor. Both Bogans were living in the household of Irish-born couple Henry and Sarah Gowan, who had two Maine-born children under the age of two. Henry was a blacksmith. Given that both *John* Bogans were hostlers, I would argue that the age is simply listed incorrectly by his employer. It would appear, too, that John and Thomas were related, perhaps brothers. It also seems reasonable that the Gowans might have been supplementing a blacksmith's wages by boarding the Bogans. The census, however, did not list such a business relationship. If, in fact, the Bogans were boarders, that would mean that Sarah had her own home-based business, which would not have been an unusual occupation even for old-timer resident females in Belfast, including women of higher social status.

Migration Patterns

The Irish of Belfast were always on the move. Settlers from Londonderry, New Hampshire, and its environs moved to Belfast and then fled to various refuges during the Revolution. Some returned to Belfast after the war and, when confronted by debt and the newly established class system enforced by the newly established legal system, removed themselves to the area surrounding Belfast. Others headed west. Migration evidently could be perpetual for some. It is this aspect of Irish immigration, or indeed any influx of people "from away," that is intriguing. How long do people need to be bound to a community in order to influence its development? How is culture affected, given human movement into and out of communities? What motivates some people to stay and others to go? Do economic necessities alone determine the answers? Do some people need to be near family, the basic circle of dependency?

Belfast's microcosm provides some answers. Williamson and Crosby imply in their written works that all those professional men (including tradesmen) who were active in the village as it evolved into a town, and, later, a city, made their marks on the community. Many of such migrants to Belfast spent the greater parts of decades, if not longer, in the community. Their energy helped create Belfast's culture. Belfastians who settled in family groupings tended to be more centered in Belfast—even if the young people moved outside city limits—especially if they were members of the working and/or laboring class.

Belfast's population migration westward recommenced around 1860, as northern New England (Vermont, New Hampshire, and Maine) did not grow much in population. Most rural areas in those three states actually lost population.[76] People, asking how they might get ahead, evidently decided that farming in New England was not the answer.

Many people who moved away, evidently, still considered Belfast home, as a number of them had their bodies returned for burial in the family plots laid out in Grove Cemetery. Hugh Johnston Anderson and Henry Colburn were not alone in this. Daniel Lane, born in Buxton, moved to Belfast from Portland, Maine. He came to Belfast to be the Collector of Customs. After leaving Belfast, he moved to Boston and later died in Newtonville, Massachusetts. His body, however, was sent north for burial in Grove Cemetery. These men who had moved away for the greater portions of their careers returned in death. For some reason they still considered Belfast home—perhaps it was where their parents, children, or extended families were buried.

Notes

1 William George Crosby, "Annals of Belfast for Half a Century," in *Early Histories of Belfast, Maine*, ed. Alan Taylor (Camden, Maine: Picton Press, 1989), 23.
2 Crosby, xi.
3 Crosby, 3.

4 Stuart Bruchey, *Enterprise: The Dynamic Economy of a Free People* (Cambridge: Harvard University Press, 1990), 92-95.

5 Bruchey, 98.

6 See Oscar Handlin, *Boston's Immigrants: A Study in Acculturation* (Cambridge: Belknap Press of Harvard University Press, 1959).

7 Handlin, 12.

8 Bruchey, 97.

9 Bruchey, 102.

10 Joseph Williamson, *The History of the City of Belfast, Maine*, Vol. 1 (Somersworth, New Hampshire: New England History Press, 1982), 117.

11 Williamson, Vol. 1, 191.

12 Williamson, Vol. 1, 188.

13 Williamson, Vol. 1, 191.

14 Williamson, Vol. 1, 195.

15 The Treaty of Paris ended the Seven Years' War in 1763. General James Wolfe led the victorious British troops in taking Quebec in 1759 but lost his life in the battle.

16 Williamson, Vol. 1, 195.

17 Williamson, Vol. 1, 195.

18 Williamson, Vol. 1, 118.

19 Williamson, Vol. 1, 119.

20 Alan Taylor, "'Sprung up in a Day': Belfast, Maine, Emerges as a Market Town," in *Early Histories of Belfast Maine: Annals of Belfast for Half a Century by William George Crosby, Sketches of the Early History of Belfast by John Lymburner Locke, History of Belfast by Herman Abbot, A History of Belfast with Introductory Remarks on Acadia by William White* (Camden, Maine: Picton Press, 1989), x.

21 Taylor, xi.

22 Williamson, Vol. 1, 428.

23 Crosby, 2.

24 Crosby, 8.

25 Williamson, Vol. 1, 430-433.

26 Williamson, Vol. 1, 430.

27 Williamson, Vol. 1, 429.

28 Williamson, Vol. 1, 678.

29 Crosby, 35.

30 Anthony Reid, "Lessons of Tambora Ignored, 200 Years on," https://www.eastasiaforum.org/2015/04/25/lessons-of-tambora-ignored-200-years-on/ accessed 16 March 2020. Scientists estimate that 160 cubic kilometers of pyroclastic material was spewed into the atmosphere, lowering global temperatures a degree, which caused worldwide climate change. The explosion "[triggered] the westward migration of New England farmers rendered desperate by the failure of their 1816 crops."

31 Crosby, 35.

32 Crosby, 35.

33 Williamson, 412. Perhaps Dr. Crooks was the man who attacked John Wilson, Esq. in his offices and got thumped for his troubles.

34 Dirk Hoerder, "Recent Methodological and Conceptual Approaches to Migration: Comparing the Globe or the North Atlantic World?" *Journal of American Ethnic History*, 29, no. 2 (Winter 2010), 83.

35 Crosby, 54.

36 Crosby, 59.

37 Crosby, 71.

38 Crosby, 72.

39 Handlin, 12 and 25.

40 John F. Bauman, *Gateway to Vacationland: The Making of Portland, Maine* (Amherst: University of Massachusetts Press, 2012), 21. Bauman notes that by 1880, 57 percent of Portland's population was first and/or second-generation Irish, 85.

41 Bauman, 21.

42 Handlin, 49.

43 Handlin, 64.

44 Handlin, 63-65.

45 Williamson, Vol. 1, 678.

46 Williamson, Vol. 1, 718.

47 Williamson, Vol. 1, 746.

48 Williamson, Vol. 1, 756.

49 Williamson, Vol. 1, 758.

50 Williamson, Vol. 1, 333.

51 Williamson, Vol. 1, 706.

52 Williamson, Vol. 1, 706.

53 "An Old Journalist Gone," *The Weekly Recorder*, VIII, no. 38 (19 March 1874), 3.

54 Williamson, Vol. 1, 353. U.S. Seventh Census, Table II, "Population by Subdivisions of Counties," Waldo County, Belfast, 6. The total number of males in Belfast, including free "colored," was 2,538 in 1850.

55 Williamson, Vol. 1, 353.

56 Williamson, Vol. 1, 708.

57 Crosby, 168.

58 Crosby, 167.

59 Malcolm Campbell, *Ireland's New Worlds: Immigrants, Politics, and Society in the United States and Australia, 1815-1822* (Madison: University of Wisconsin Press, 2008), 95.

60 Timothy Sarbaugh, "Exiles of Confidence: The Irish-American Community of San Francisco, 1880-1920," *From Paddy to Studs: Irish-American Communities in the Turn of the Century Era, 1880 to 1920* (Westport, Connecticut: Greenwood Press, 1986), 161.

61 Crosby, 13-14 and 18.

62 Autobiographies give insight into this behavior. See Benjamin Franklin, *Autobiography and Other Writings*, ed. Russel B. Nye (Boston: Houghton Mifflin, 1958); Anne Ellis, *The Life of an Ordinary Woman* (Lincoln: University of Nebraska Press, 1980); Elinore Pruitt Stewart, *Letters from a Woman Homesteader* (Lincoln: University of Nebraska Press, 1961); Mark Twain, *Roughing It* (New York: Book of the Month Club, 1992).

63 Belfast, Maine, *Vital Records to the Year 1892*, Vol. II, 198.

64 Myles Staples, Coroner, "Inquest on the Body of Bridgett [*sic*] McCabe Jan. 5 1861," photocopy of the handwritten report.

65 Probate Case #1673.

66 Williamson, Vol. 1, 514.

67 The probate records give the grand sum of $158.32. Probate Case #2834.

68 Timothy W. Guinnane, *The Vanishing Irish: Households, Migration, and the Rural Economy in Ireland, 1850-1914* (Princeton: Princeton University Press, 1997), 104.

69 Guinnane, 104.

70 Michael Casey, single in 1850, by 1860 was married to Mary and had six children, ages thirteen, eight, seven, five, two, and one; James Gillam, single

in 1850, by 1860 was married to Bridgett [*sic*] and had four children, ages seventeen, fifteen, eight, and six. Gillam was supposedly thirty-four in 1860 (possibly thirty-eight, given his age was listed as twenty-eight in the 1850 census). The name is spelled Gilum in the 1860 census.

71 Abigail Davis Field, Day Book, "3 September 1842 Mr. Brannagan here.... 28 November Mr. Brannagan left here for Boston...4 December Back from Boston..." She was also purchasing materials at his store that fall. "3 November [1842] to 30 yrds sheeting at Mr. Brannigan's [*sic*] at 1 shilling per yrd 3:84, shoes from Brannigan's 1:38, to muff-from Brannigan 2:25."

72 William Brannagan was born in Ashbourne, Co. Meath. The Celtic cross erected to mark his grave in Grove Cemetery says so. In 1860, Brannagan was a resident of the American House, which was filled with Irish immigrant employees: Patrick Conner, waiter; Bridgett [*sic*] Conner domestic, Catherine Crowell, domestic, Jane Floon, domestic, widower Charles Kimball, hosteler, and his two sons, Frank and Edgar, Arnold Moody, age twelve [no adults with this surname] and John Bullard. There is no indication that the last two named individuals worked at the American House. The census enumerator listed Brannagan as a clerk, age forty-five and Maine-born. By December 1866, Brannagan was again resident in the Field House. (Benjamin Franklin Field, Day Book, 9 December [1866] "Mr. Brannigan came...6 March [1868] Mr. Brannigan left us unceremoniously yesterday.")

73 Probate records, Middlesex County, Massachusetts, 20 September 1853. (Ancestry Library-downloaded 27 July 2017.)

74 New Jersey Episcopal Diocese of Newark, New Jersey, Sunday, 27 March 1892, cert. #1096. (Ancestry Library-downloaded 27 July 2017.)

75 Berkley B. McDowell was living in Charlestown, Massachusetts in 1866, according to a city directory, working as a clerk. Just four years later, he was in Jersey City, New Jersey, according to the 1870 census. In 1883, he married in New Jersey. Two children were born there, but by 1895 he was in the shoe trade and living in Brooklyn, New York. (Ancestry Library-downloaded 27 July 2017.)

76 Guinnane, 4.

6 Inventing Scotch-Irishness

The closest the Scotch-Irish would come to a 'plantation' in Maine came shortly before the American War for Independence, when several residents of Londonderry, New Hampshire, became proprietors and early settlers of Belfast.[1]

Throughout eighteenth-century writings, most people in America's receiving communities labeled immigrants from Ireland *Irish*. They also applied stereotypes to their definitions of what it meant to be Irish or to display Irishness: poor, ill, abusers of alcohol, violent, and so forth. Many of those immigrants who originated in Ulster also referred to themselves as Irish; however, stereotypes which attached to Irish and Irishness in the American colonies caused other immigrants to chafe at the label.

Belfast, Maine, traces its roots to people from Ulster who immigrated in 1718. Arriving in Boston, they were shifted by Massachusetts' authorities to Casco Bay in Maine, then part of Massachusetts. Some of the group later squatted at Nutfield, renamed Londonderry, New Hampshire. It is imperative, then, to trace the development of this predecessor community in New Hampshire and to analyze attempts by some of its members to redefine Irish and Irishness.

Among those from Ulster who immigrated in 1718, the Reverend James McGregor was one of the first who tried to rework the labeling process. He sought to create a label that gave the Ulster immigrants equality with local English settlers, implying unity under the concept of Britishness. His attempt, however, did not gather strength (or followers) until the nineteenth century. So it took a century—after the immigrant generation had died out—before any idea of a hyphenated identity was introduced in New Hampshire and/or Massachusetts. The hyphenated Scotch-Irish identity, however, was used early in Pennsylvania, which caused Presbyterian minister John Elder to bristle, as he heard the term as an "ill natured title."[2]

DOI: 10.4324/9781003187660-6

Origin Myths

Stories have power. They are used to create history.[3] Myths are simply stories about origins, explaining who we are and how we got here. Immigrants from Ireland, through dispersal from the homeland (diaspora) and having to deal with domination (colonization), were subject to relocation, dislocation, and re-situation, which *could* have led to renewal.[4] Collective memory is created through such origin stories. Stories from Londonderry, New Hampshire, written nearly 200 years after settlement, disagreed on whether there were unified ethnic or cultural norms among the early colonists. Settlers were, according to the storytellers, "divided in both civil and religious allegiance."[5] The purpose of the stories of the nineteenth century was to create a collective memory. We can see the process in practice in the published materials of nineteenth-century ministers, academics, politicians, and public speakers, who had evidently overcome any distaste for the Scotch-Irish label. Descendants of the Ulster Presbyterians who settled Londonderry, New Hampshire, for example, used their pulpits, speech stumps, lectures, and oratory to help create the Scotch-Irish identity in New England, if not in America as a whole. The question is, why?

Those who arrived from Ulster in 1718 found there was a long list of stereotypes attached to the Irish label, including *poor*. In an attempt to take charge of naming, and in order to subvert the process of "Othering" the newcomers, the Reverend McGregor wrote Massachusetts Governor Samuel Shute in 1720.[6] McGregor said that he and his group were surprised to hear themselves labeled Irish. According to McGregor, Irish were "papists" disloyal to the British Crown and the Government of Ireland.[7]

McGregor maintained that his group was made up of loyal people who had fought *against* the Irish *for* Crown and Country. (McGregor told people he had participated in the siege of Derry in 1688/89 at age 12.[8] Such support of Dutch Protestant William of Orange in opposition to his Catholic cousin James II, he hoped, might help create a bond between his people and the old-timers of Massachusetts.) *Irishness*, in McGregor's definition, was oppositional to the British Crown and Irish government in that it was Catholic. William of Orange became king of England and Ireland in 1689. Perhaps this was what McGregor was referring to—one people under a Protestant king. Or was McGregor implying that the 1707 Act of Union uniting England and Scotland put him and his co-religionists from the north of Ireland on equal footing with the English colonists already in Massachusetts? The Act of Union with Ireland, however, did not occur until 1801. McGregor's argument warrants further study.

McGregor did not define his group, which had appropriated Nutfield, New Hampshire, renaming it Londonderry, as *Scots*, nor did he use the term *Scots-* or *Scotch-Irish*.[9] That should not come as a surprise. Scotch-

Irish, in the centuries before the eighteenth, referred to migratory clans who moved among settlements in southern Scotland, the western isles, and Ulster, Ireland. These Gaelic-speaking people were organized politically into clans—and they were Catholic. In Ireland, they presented a problem to the newly established British Crown in that they were migratory and therefore not stationary in one political jurisdiction.[10] In Pennsylvania, however, James Logan stated the group of Ulster immigrants who had squatted at Conestoga Manor in 1731—land set aside by William Penn for the Conestoga people—had been labeled "Scotch-Irish" by old-timers in the area.[11]

McGregor intimated that he and his people had served the "Brittish Crown" [sic] cause, venturing their all in its service, and, therefore, deserved to be treated as British equals.[12] His equation seemed to be: Service to the British crown equaled Britishness. In post-colonial terms, McGregor was identifying his group as being identical with the colonizers. In other words, he was adopting Englishness (or Britishness) for himself and his people in order for them to be accepted by the locals in control.[13] In his letter, McGregor claimed that English settlers had joined the immigration venture, as they "really had a mind to Plant with us ... many of them are now incorporated with us."[14] His statement was blatantly untrue, if we compare the writings of others of the period. In the century that followed, descendants working on the Scotch-Irish foundation myth played up McGregor's presumed anathema toward the Irish yet downplayed any pro-British sentiment—especially after the Revolutionary War. In these post-Revolutionary texts, writers asserted that Nutfield settlers had actually held English settlers in contempt.[15] English settlers lived apart from Londonderry, New Hampshire's north-of-Ireland immigrants, on Westrunning Brook.[16]

McGregor's opposition to the Irish label and his attempt to meld Ulster origins with Britishness, however, mattered little. People from Ireland were still considered Irish. Two centuries later, Belfastian Mrs. J.C. Durham attempted the same argument in 1911, for example, in a book about the old houses of Belfast. No longer relying on a McGregor subtlety, she equated Belfast's original Ulster ancestry with Anglo-Saxon:

> To us these homes represent grandfathers and great-grandfathers, who were inspired by the quest of the ideal, unlike some races, content to sit in the sun and merely exist, ours were driven on by the irresistible desire of the Anglo Saxon race to be something and to have something, not merely for the having, but to have for the being. This spirit was back of our Scotch Irish ancestors.[17]

In Durham's definition Anglo-Saxon and Scotch-Irish were one and the same. Durham never used the term Irish, evidently preferring not to name names, merely referring to "some races, content to sit in the sun and merely exist," but we know of whom she spoke. After all, there were not many other options in Belfast from which to choose. The weight of historical evidence indicates that Ulster immigrants were not necessarily Anglophiles. While eighteenth-century immigrants from Ireland did join with the British, campaigning against the French on Cape Breton in 1745, for example, their loyalty to the English did not necessarily remain staunch. For example, Dr. Matthew Thornton, born in Limerick, Ireland, and practicing medicine in Londonderry, New Hampshire, participated in the attack on Cape Breton. Thirty years later, he signed the Declaration of Independence.[18] *Englishness* was not necessarily a preferred ethnicity in Londonderry, New Hampshire, especially after the American Revolution:

> The English churchmen were in a minority, and greatly maligned by the Scotch, who came as disaffected and aggrieved occupants of confiscated lands in the northern counties of Ireland, despising the Irish, whom they had displaced, for their obedience to a foreign religious potentate, and hating the English with a national rancor for having gained authority over them by the treachery and baseness of court favorites.[19]

What is clear, however, is that *descendants* of the original settlers continued to assert their right to self-label, especially beginning in the nineteenth century and even into the twentieth. This may have been a reaction to the stereotypes accompanying the Irish label which remained intact for centuries, and the fact that anti-Irish virulence reached a crescendo mid-nineteenth century amid the Know-Nothing Movement in the United States.

What is clear in Belfast's published histories is that the men who bought shares in Belfast came from an area encompassing several present-day New Hampshire towns: Derry, Londonderry, and parts of Auburn, Hudson, Windham, and Manchester.[20] Ten of the first twenty-five settlers came from Derry; others came from Windham and Chester; at least one was from Newburyport and two others from Boston, Massachusetts.[21]

What are we to make of the designation of Derry, as separate from Londonderry, New Hampshire? Are the town names political—and ethnic/religious—statements as they are in Ireland? (Londonderry, re-built by the City of London, after the Siege of Derry in 1689, can denote Unionist support.[22] Derry tends to be the name used by nationalist Irish, which in itself assumes a political, cultural, economic, and religious stance. To add to the confusion, unionists sometimes use Derry.) *Was* there a difference? We can draw inferences from settlers' actions in the American colonies. What is clear in the nineteenth-century productions is that, generally, the civil and religious divisions among Londonderry, New Hampshire's settlers were not often discussed.[23]

The earliest written material in Belfast, Maine, which worked to change Belfast's ethnicity from Irish to Scottish was produced by physician Herman Abbot, who didn't live to see his *History of Belfast from Its First Settlement to 1825* in print. He was forty-two when he died in 1825, leaving his manuscript unfinished.[24] His book remained in manuscript form until 1900, when it was serialized in the weekly *The Republican Journal* and later that same year was published in book form by Grace E. Burgess. While in manuscript form, however, it was shared with other local historians, such as William White, who used it in the preparation of *A History of Belfast with Introductory Remarks on Acadia*, published in Belfast in 1827.

Abbot's comments on Scots roots led those who came after him to seek materials from sources that supported a British and/or Scots origin creation myth; however, Abbot himself tried to have it both ways: "It was to be expected that they would bring with them the religion, manners, habits and customs of the places they had left. Twenty-seven out of thirty-two purchasers belonged to Londonderry or Windham [New Hampshire], whose inhabitants were principally of *Scottish or Irish descent.*"[25] He, thus, pointed out that the original settlers were of mixed ancestry.

Still, Abbot worked hard to create Scots origins for Belfast, defining the ethnicity of its founders through their language use: "The Scottish dialect was understood and spoken by several of them; and some traces of it are retained to the present day." Finally, he noted that they were, indeed, Scots because of their reading material: "Those of the first settlers who remain and their immediate descendants, read the poems of [Robert] Burns with a keen relish and are enthusiastic admirers of the language of the Scottish Bard."[26] He made no mention of how one would determine whether a settler were "Irish," nor did he specify what Irish settlers might read to show themselves Irish.

Abbot listed his sources and spelled out his intentions in his opening paragraph. He used records of the town's proprietors and town records and consulted "the aged inhabitants and the descendants of the proprietors and first settlers."[27] John Cochran, "the only surviving original proprietor resident in this town," gave Abbot access to the proprietors' deed and records.[28] He laid out his intentions for the book:

> [C]ollect and preserve a few facts relating to the early history and settlement of this town; the leading traits in the character of its first inhabitants, together with their privations and hardships; to notice our litary [sic] and religious institutions; our growing wealth and population; to mark the course of events and to describe the

improvements which have taken place here in the period of little more than half a century....[29]

He used town records and other legal documents and resorted to personal interviews with elderly residents and/or descendants of original settlers when he found the documentation uninspiring.[30] He began his story in 1768 with the men of Londonderry, New Hampshire, seeking to purchase the area that would become Belfast. Of course, given the time, he made no mention of the women who accompanied those men to the shores of Penobscot Bay, nor did he ascertain who had actually ventured to Belfast. The story that Abbot unfolded was this: The founder designation was given to John Mitchell Jr., who was five when his family left Ulster, part of a group of Presbyterians headed to Boston in 1718, even though he was not the surveyor of the Belfast site.[31] In the American colonies, Mitchell became a surveyor of some repute, and Massachusetts Governor Bernard sent him to survey portions of Maine "soon after the termination of the French war."[32] In his survey, Mitchell found an area for sale on Penobscot Bay, where the Passagassawakeag River empties into the bay. He told Londonderry, New Hampshire, friends about it, and so became one of the founders of Belfast, Maine.[33] The site chosen, Joseph Chadwick was sent to survey in 1768, and purchase money was paid for a warranty deed from the heirs of Brigadier General Samuel Waldo, who held the patent, in August 1769.[34] More than two dozen men joined Mitchell's scheme, agreeing to buy 15,000 acres on Penobscot Bay, creating fifty-one shares.[35]

Abbot, then, was the originator of the Scotch-Irish Presbyterian creation story of Belfast. His interview with John Cochran set the stage. Cochran maintained he had been part of the Boston Tea Party on 16 December 1773.[36] As he was in the Belfast area as of 1770, according to records of the time, and as the settlers did not decamp until 1779, this claim appears specious, or, perhaps, merely one remembered with advantages. Or, did Abbot confuse Cochran father and son? Perhaps he was drawing on Cochran's faulty recollections, for he spent time talking about Londonderry, New Hampshire's two Presbyterian societies, each with its own clergyman. While that may have been a reality in New Hampshire, it was never the case in Belfast.

Joseph Williamson Jr., author of a two-volume history of Belfast, noted that Dr. Abbot, a physician, arrived in Belfast sometime in 1810, from Wilton, New Hampshire. There is little biographical data available on the doctor: He served as town clerk for four years (until his death); was active in the choir at the Congregational church; and was drafted into the militia of Captain Thomas Cunningham (Belfast had an obligation of thirty-three men) should hostilities have required Maine's men-at-arms during the War of 1812.[37]

There are few other tidbits about Dr. Abbot: He helped organize the Belfast Fire Engine Company in 1823.[38] He was a member of "The Auxiliary Marine Bible Society," a branch of the American Bible Society.[39] He wrote an ode for the Fourth of July celebration in 1820, which was sung on that occasion.[40] Clearly, Dr. Abbot moved among the elite of society and was himself a "mover and shaker" in the small community—and he was active in a Congregationalist church, not Presbyterian.

Presbyterian or Congregationalist?

While Belfast did have "tithing men," officers who enforced Sabbath laws, from 1786 to 1830, the strength of the Presbyterian hold on the area between the Penobscot and Kennebec seems weak, as Belfast, as late as 1795, had the only church in the Waldo Patent.[41] Indeed, as early as 1785, a *Methodist* had preached in settler James Miller's house—Miller emigrated as a child from Belfast, Ireland.[42] By 1809, Methodists had become a corporate body; Baptists had incorporated their Society by 1811. Unitarians were visible in town by 1818.[43]

Because a river divided the town, Belfast began with at least two factions: west and east siders. When one group proposed building a church on the east side of the river, a group on the west side tried to get it moved to their side. The compromise was two churches, neither of which was built for more than twenty years after settlement. The east siders built a 50 foot by 40 foot unheated building in 1792, from which they had to decamp in cold months to the heated schoolhouse across the road. The west siders built a 40 foot by 40 foot building in 1794, which stood at the corner of High and Pearl streets in the village of Belfast.

Before the east/west schism over building a permanent structure, Belfast's Presbyterians had made use of itinerant or traveling ministers, such as the Reverend John Murray, who preached the first sermon in Belfast in 1770.[44] Generally, when a minister was traveling through, the group met in someone's barn.[45] This, however, was evidently a rare occurrence. For example, while the village budgeted 8 shillings a week for boarding a minister to Samuel Houston, it did so with the caveat that it would be paid out only "if one comes to preach this Summer."[46]

When Old World settlers made their way to the New, they brought with them old feuds, biases, and prejudices, not to mention ideas about religion, personal behavior, government, and so forth. Ostensibly, those world-views could have been handed on to descendants, but, given generational shifts, descendants could have just as easily shifted their viewpoints because of their American experiences. While it may have been true that some of "the early settlers of Belfast had been educated in [the Presbyterian] faith," how long they held on to those Old World connections is a matter for conjecture.[47] The majority of those who settled Belfast were primarily American born.

Assertions that the area between the Kennebec and the Penobscot rivers was "strongly imbued with Presbyterian principles ... from the circumstance that the Scotch immigrants from Ireland had taken possession of the prominent points of that territory" bear investigation.[48] While late nineteenth-century local historians argued that those educated in Presbyterian principles "slowly and reluctantly yielded" to Congregational forms of worship, what is evident is that religion as practiced was always contentious in Belfast.[49]

One hundred years after settlement, the Reverend George W. Field, Belfast native and well-known native son, commented in his centenary address at the celebrations for the First Congregational Church of Belfast that organizing a church in Belfast was an occupation filled with "conflict and storm."[50] He noted, with pointed humor, that ministers came and went on a regular basis for many years. The Reverend Price, the first minister, whose call in the 1790s was hotly contested, for example, lasted six years before he was fired. The Reverend Alfred Johnson, much acclaimed by later residents, lasted seven years, but had faced the ignominy of having his pay regularly decreased.

Field maintained the only reason Johnson was remembered fondly was because of his son, who entered the law and became a judge in Belfast.[51] In subsequent years, ministers lasted only two years. Field summed up the century of religious contention, suggesting both Scots *and* Irish racial inheritance as factors:

> The *"per fervidum ingenium"* which their earliest historian [Abbot] attributes to the Scotch, this heightened by the fiery and possibly somewhat contentious quality which the Irish element mingled with their blood, may have been somewhat responsible for it.[52]

Field collapsed popular conceptions of two separate identities into one and ignored the local trope that the original inhabitants were Scots only. In his estimation, Scots and Irish mingled before emigration. The old stereotype of being hot tempered, however, remained intact. Field was most circumspect in declaring the Scots hot headed—he used Latin to call names. The fact that the "Scotch" hot temper had to be labeled in Latin, while the "fiery and somewhat contentious quality" of the Irish remained in English, is a striking juxtaposition. Indeed, Field's collapsing of Irish with Scot was at odds with his predecessors (Abbot and those who followed him).

Writing History

After Abbot's death in the early nineteenth century, the administrator of his estate placed his manuscript history with William White, the author of *A History of Belfast with Introductory Remarks on Acadia*. He, in turn, fearing the loss of Abbot's manuscript, lodged it in the town clerk's office.[53] Like his predecessor, White spelled out his sources in his opening remarks: In addition to consulting Abbot's manuscript, he used "[t]he manuscripts of Chadwicke and of Mitchell, and the books of the proprietors of the township; the town records, and the records in the land office and the office of Secretary of State of Massachusetts."[54]

Using Abbot as a guide, and being pointed to Scotland as the place of origin, White chose to use a number of secondary sources, including Scottish economist Adam Anderson's multiple volume *Historical and Chronological Deduction of the Origin of Commerce from the Earliest Accounts to the Present Time*. He also used the work of American historians Jeremy Belknap and Thomas Prince.

What these nineteenth-century histories do not do is draw attention to the tenuousness of the supposed Scotch-Irish connection. Thirteen of the original corporation members, nearly 46 percent of the shareholders, never moved to the Penobscot Bay area. And, of the original purchasers of the fifty-one shares, only a handful traced their origins to either the 1718 Presbyterian ships from Ulster or to Londonderry, New Hampshire, proprietorships. And, given that Belfast settlement was nearly fifty years after Londonderry, New Hampshire's, in many families at least two generations had been born on the American side of the Atlantic. Any Presbyterian roots, therefore, had been weakened by time and acculturation.

The first settlers arrived on the Passagassawakeag River in 1769 and 1770. Thomas Steele and John Morrison, part of the "advance," drowned their first year in residence. Morrison was the *great-grandson* of an Ulster immigrant. Given that the majority of those who came to Belfast were American-born, those who were Irish-born stand out. Among those who purchased but did not settle in Belfast was Samuel Marsh, lot number forty, one hundred fourteen acres. While his *father* had been an early Londonderry settler, Marsh sold his lot to James Dunlap, who sold to Owen Callahan. There is confusion over the latter's name. An Irishman, supposedly named Owen *Kelleran*, opened Belfast's first tavern. Callahan/Kelleran later sold to Robert White, who didn't arrive until 1797.[55] The property purchased was where the erstwhile Kelleran's tavern had stood.[56] The upshot is that the first tavern in Belfast was owned by a man whom others described as Irish, not Scots.

Settlers spent the next few years clearing trees and building cabins and homesteads. Colonists were barely rooted when they found themselves confronted with the Revolutionary War and British troops on their doorsteps. By June 1779, the British were in control of Penobscot Bay at Bagaduce (modern Castine); the British required settlers around Penobscot Bay to sign oaths of allegiance to Great Britain.

American Irish

White, drawing on Abbot's history of Belfast, took pride in the anti-British fervor of settlers who set up a committee in 1777 to "lay before the General Court [the Massachusetts legislature] the misconduct of any person, by word or action against the [newly independent] United States."[57] Fifty years after McGregor's attempt to equate Ulster immigrants with the British, the Revolutionary War made Ulster settlers Americans in this version of events. Revolutionary fervor was what counted. When Belfast was abandoned to the British during the Revolution, White claimed all settlers left rather than sign loyalty oaths to the British:

> The spirit of freedom which had for so many generations warmed the blood of their ancestors was theirs by inheritance; and the profer [*sic*] [of protection] was rejected, and such intrepidity left them no choice; to the last man they abandoned their homes, leaving their flocks in the pastures and the corn in the fields ready for harvest.[58]

As evidenced by war service, a goodly portion of Belfast settlers did choose to identify with the new republic.[59] *After* the war, the implication was that *all* had embraced revolutionary ideals. Or so at least White would have us believe.

Joseph Williamson Jr., writing more than fifty years later in his own history of Belfast, debunked this patriotic hindsight, commenting that everyone involved with the committee reporting on anti-American rhetoric had, in fact, "been compelled to submit to an oath of allegiance." Ten of eighteen heads of families living in Belfast during the Revolution capitulated.[60] The majority, then, did not flee until *after* the failed Penobscot Expedition of 1779, which had made them fear for their safety. Colonials in Boston had formed a naval squadron and sailed for Penobscot Bay, hoping to retake Castine; however, they dawdled on their way, then saw Union Jacks to their rear, and decided to sail up the Penobscot River and scuttle their ships, rather than risk having them fall into British hands. It was the worst Continental naval loss of the war. Those locals who had signed loyalty oaths did not feel safe in the aftermath of the battle that never was. Settlers abandoned Belfast, seeking safety "beyond the reach of the enemy."[61] Most did not return until 1784.[62] The corporate structure of Belfast was dissolved and not reconstituted until 1785.[63]

Histories of Belfast, other than William White's in 1827, were not published until the latter third of the nineteenth century, by which time the Scotch-Irish foundation myth was firmly entrenched. The story of the Scotch-Irish in America unfolded in accordance with needs arising in the early nineteenth century and continuing into the twentieth. Story tellers claimed that some Scots colonists had resided in Ulster only a few decades, yet had to concede that others' families had been in Ulster nearly 100 years.[64] Even with a century of habitation in Ulster, these stories continued, such colonists resented being designated Irish.

Nineteenth-Century Needs

By the mid-nineteenth century, America was wracked by a number of major conflicts. Slavery and its abolition, of course, headed the list of contentious issues. Two severe economic depressions—the Panics of 1837 and 1857—caused widespread uncertainty. As Irish Famine refugees flooded the eastern seaboard, America moved into a rabid anti-immigrant phase—especially targeting Catholic Irish.[65] The movement to separate Scots from Irish—and even Scots from Gael—redoubled its efforts. These self-labeled, so-called Scotch-Irish, in an effort to sever themselves, their names, and their heritage from being the butt of anti-immigrant ugliness sweeping the country, spent a great deal of time and energy making their case.[66]

In their writings and speeches, these Ulster descendants argued, even though ancestors had made a brief stop in Ulster in a trek from Scotland to the English colonies in North America, those ancestors had not remained long enough in Ulster to become Irish. The Reverend Edward L. Parker, for example, in his *History of Londonderry: Comprising the Towns of Derry and Londonderry, New Hampshire*, published in 1851, asserted that, "Although they came to this land from Ireland, where their ancestors had a century before planted themselves, yet they retained unmixed the national Scotch character. Nothing sooner offended them, [*sic*] than to be called *Irish* [emphasis in the original]."[67]

How the Ulster immigrants differed from the Irish was thoroughly discussed 10 June 1869 by lawyer and politician Charles H. Bell of Exeter, New Hampshire. Bell participated in a day of celebration and speeches in honor of the hundred-fiftieth anniversary of the founding of Londonderry, New Hampshire. He acknowledged that the founders had come "from the north of Ireland."[68] He, however, chafed at the designation of Scotch-Irish if people were implying the two groups had mixed prior to emigration: ... for it is certain that there was no mixture of blood in the little band who cast their fortunes here; they were of Scottish lineage, pure and simple. They sprang from a colony of Scots, which had planted itself more than a century before, in the province of Ulster, in Ireland, and whose numbers had been increased, from time to time afterward, by fresh arrivals from the parent country.

Bell belabored the point throughout his oration. One can assume that, as there was no report that he was booed from the stage, his words were met with approbation. He was there to present—and help perpetuate—the mythology of the Scotch-Irish ancestors as it had been passed down.

He insisted that those ancestors had been "*among* the Irish, but not *of* them [emphasis in the original]."[69] He followed the nineteenth-century predilection for seeing the cultural and ethnic identity entwined with religious affiliation. He asserted that the "Scots were, to a man, Presbyterians of the straitest [*sic*] sect, while their neighbors were as uniformly Romanists."[70] He adamantly maintained there had never been any mingling of races, for throughout his speech he insisted that the difference between Scot and Irish was a racial divide, and assertions to the contrary were "simply chimerical."[71] Bell spent nearly a third of his speech defining "Scotchness" as "not Irish."

It was in the second third of the speech that Bell began to define the cultural norms that made a person Scottish. He did so by dropping "Scottishisms" into his speech, talking about lads and lasses, for example.[72] The cultural world of the early Scots in New Hampshire, according to Bell, revolved around annual fairs, sports, athletic exercises, funerals, and weddings.[73] He did not, however, show how such events would have differed for other Irish immigrants.

By the end of the nineteenth century, the story of the Reverend McGregor's five ships of Presbyterians that reached Massachusetts Bay 4 August 1718 was firmly ensconced as the origin tale of Scotch-Irish America.[74] The storytellers even reworked history of the mother country and the genesis of difference. In these versions of events, the Scots were not tribal, but the wild Irish were, with their own laws, dress, customs and manners.[75] In the Scotch-Irish creation myth, Scots destined for Ulster were not drawn from Gaelic-speaking regions, because the plantation was an attempt to break down the tribal/clan system. The stories went so far as to claim that the Gaelic clans in Scotland were hunted down, their leaders hanged.[76] (McGregor's family heritage, replete with clan, tartans galore, and coat of arms in Gaelic, evidently was ignored.) The story declared that primarily Lowland Scots, or non-Gaelic speakers, who were also Protestants, were settled in Ulster.[77] The "wild" Irish were described as raiders, pillagers, cattle-thieves, and murderers.[78] Chiefs and septs were seen as political units of unchecked ambition; the *kernes* and soldiers licentiously idle; the Brehon laws barbarous, as were Irish customs and apparel; their manners savage:

> ...the tribal system of Ireland with its state of chronic disorder was a remnant of the same barbarism against which Caesar fought in Gaul and Charlemagne in continental Europe. The planting of trusty colonies among uncivilized peoples as garrisons to check their insubordination and as centers from which culture could be diffused was a practice that went back to the times of the ancient Roman commonwealth ...[79]

All in all, the argument ran, Ireland was desolate and filled with an untamed people, a land needing reclamation via plantation of a new population.[80] The plantation of Ulster supposedly put an end to "wasting" land and colonists took the moral high ground, asserting that by making good "use" of the environment, wealth resulted, which somehow vindicated the seizures: "there can be no doubt of the success of the plantation. Ulster had been the most backward province of Ireland. It became the most populous and wealthy."[81] These same arguments were being used in the U.S. at the same time as the concept of Scotch-Irish was being created in America to explain away the aggression against Native nations and the seizures of their territory.

According to these Scotch-Irish foundation myths, Lowlanders (non-Gaels, speaking Lallans) from Scotland had backed the English throne and had been rewarded with land in Ireland, seized from the local peoples.[82] They maintained a culture separated from the local Irish peoples, usually with the aid of walled, fortified cities. These Ulster "Scots" did not see themselves as Irish, nor did the locals in Ireland perceive them as such, nor did they see Gaelic "Scots" as Scots, evidently. The *wild Irish* were put onto reservations much like the natives in the United States.[83] From an American perspective, Scots and Scotch-Irish were made equal to English—or nearly so:

> The matter of ethnic origins has been touched upon, because some writers upon the Scotch-Irish have placed the Picts, the Caledonians, and other early inhabitants of Scotland among the forebears of the Scottish settlers in Ulster. But as a matter of fact the settlers were almost as English in racial derivation as if they had come from the North of England.[84]

Again, the perpetrators of this version of Ulster immigrant culture ignored the western isles and highland clan histories of many of those who came to Londonderry, New Hampshire, and later, Belfast, Maine: For example, McGregor, McKeen, Houston, McCrillis, MacLaughlan, McIlvain, Gregg, not to mention Morrison.

These anti-clan, anti-tribe arguments reflect another harsh reality of life in the Americas. The American continent was filled with tribal peoples, against whom Americans of European descent were waging incessant aggression. The comparison of tribal cultures created an ethical dissonance. How could a young nation, which had declared all men created equal, morally justify seizing millions of acres of tribal lands from Native peoples, such as the Maliseet, Mi'kmaq, Passamaquoddy, or Penobscot, if its own roots were with tribal peoples on the other side of the Atlantic? The easiest way out of the moral morass was to rewrite history and deny any ancestral tribal affiliations.

Religion and Ethnicity

Academics have attempted to disentangle the mess, postulating that Ulster Presbyterians had a triple identity in the eighteenth century. Ulster immigrants to America were "Scottish in religion, local dialect, and specific culture; Irish by birth, polity, and local associations; and British by ultimate political allegiance and aspects of their wider culture (educated speech, legal and commercial procedures, etc.)."[85] This is a tidy presentation, but the fact that Gaelic-speaking Highlanders became Presbyterians confuses such neat categories. Irish history was convoluted and not a simple narrative. Dissenters—and that included Presbyterians—suffered under exclusionary laws which recognized only the Church of Ireland. In eighteenth-century Ireland, religious conversions, especially from Catholic to Protestant, were more common than scholars have acknowledged: Intermarriage and conversion were prevalent, especially among poorer immigrants.[86] Class and status, thus, played enormous roles in the drama.

Many colonists from Scotland had been several generations in Ulster, Ireland, before emigration to America—not to mention the original clans of Scots Irish traveled among the western isles, highlands, and northern Ireland. Some of those colonists in Ireland were descendants of Highland Scots. A goodly number of those who sailed in 1718 for America were Presbyterian. By 1720, Ulster Presbyterians were in trouble with the British Crown. Presbyterians, the largest bloc of Protestant dissent, were excluded from higher civic, state and military offices after 1704 and virtually barred from the land-owning class by 1720—*as were Catholics*.[87] While Ulster Presbyterians may have come to the new world for religious freedom, there were economic interests involved as well.[88] Members of the established church (Church of Ireland) gained economic security, status, and access to political power. Those outside the establishment were denied access—to everything (education, economic security, professions, land ownership, etc.). Those who had money to invest did so. Those who wanted to earn a living wage were drawn to where the money was invested:

> English and American economies offered far greater rewards to Irish labour, skills, capital and enterprise than Ireland could ever hope to do, and the entry into the labour markets of both these countries was relatively easy for the Irish man or woman and became easier as earlier emigrants paved the way and linguistic barriers fell.[89]

The descendants of the 1718 immigrants to Londonderry, New Hampshire, were reared in the American colonies. Families had been two or three generations in New Hampshire, before individuals ventured to Belfast. Their ties to Presbyterianism had weakened in the fifty years that had passed—many had affiliated with the Congregationalists, the established church of Massachusetts. Congregationalists, however, trace their roots through *English* settlement via the Puritans of Massachusetts Bay and the Separatists of Plymouth Colony.[90] Of the group that arrived in Belfast after the Revolutionary war, for example, were Samuel McKeen, John Gilmore, Jr., and John Tuft, all from Windham, New Hampshire.[91] All were Congregationalists, and all served as church deacons, as did Tolford Durham. The first minister called full time by the community in 1796, twenty years after settlement, was Congregationalist.[92] Although a fractious two dozen opposed the Reverend Ebenezer Price's call, they were accused of being more concerned about the acreage being set aside for him than worried about his religious persuasion.[93] Perhaps having dedicated space within a community, which is expensive, with a minister dedicated to that one community, which is even more expensive, is a sign of "making it." Belfast's early settlers did not have the wherewithal to set aside space dedicated only to church services, nor did they have the requisite finances to hire a full-time minister for at least two decades, not unlike a great number of late nineteenth-century Catholic congregations nationwide. Such dedicated spaces and hired spiritual leaders may be indicative of "settling in." In comparison, the Catholic population of Belfast was estimated to be only 150 as late as 1877.[94] The Catholics did not build a church until the 1890s. Can we extrapolate that Belfast's Presbyterians, too, never were a large group?

Until statehood in 1820, Maine was obliged to support Massachusetts' state-sanctioned Congregational churches financially. This irked many Mainers, especially in the years following the Revolution. State-supported religion, smacking as it did of Federalism, hierarchy, and a privileged establishment, did not fare well in the frontier hinterlands. Indeed, Bowdoin College in Brunswick, Maine, the private Congregational college serving the sons of privilege, became a focal point of resistance, especially as the sons of "dissenters" (in this case, Baptists and Methodists) were not often given access to the power that it represented.[95] But the categories were not so clear cut. The second minister called by Belfast's First Church (Congregational) was the Reverend Alfred Johnson. Johnson's Congregationalism was influenced by Presbyterianism, however, as he had studied with the Reverend John Murray. Adding further to the confusion is the fact that Johnson was one of the founders of Bowdoin College, which was a bastion of Congregationalism.[96]

From 1800 on, the "hated compulsory ministerial tax" was under attack by Democratic Republicans in Maine. While various mitigations were enacted legislatively, the judicial system negated them.[97] Finally, with a majority vote (4 to 1), the Toleration Act, a move toward religious equality, was passed by Massachusetts in 1811.[98] The Congregational Society of Belfast treasurer's report from 1823, three years after Maine became a state, separated from Federalist-controlled Massachusetts, and a decade after state-supported Congregationalism had ended, lists the surnames of those who

Figure 6.1 First Church in Belfast (Congregational). Courtesy of the Belfast Historical Society and Museum.

belonged to First Church (Congregational) in Belfast: Four surnames dating from the settler generation, the supposed Scotch-Irish generation—Davidson, Durham, Houston, and Patterson—demonstrate an affiliation with

Congregationalism and concomitant Federalism.[99] Belfast in 1807, however, was one of only three coastal towns that voted for separation from Massachusetts in the decades-long movement, meaning Belfast leaned politically toward Democratic Republicanism (Jeffersonian). Belfast's Congregationalism, and its close ties with the Federalist cause, therefore, strikes a dissonant note. By the time of statehood, achieved through severance from Massachusetts in 1820 as part of the Missouri Compromise, Baptists were the pre-eminent denomination in Maine.

Scotch-Irishness in Practice

It is impossible to equate religious affiliation with ethnicity and/or culture. People choose their religion, their ardor for that religion, their politics, and so forth. Memory is a tool in culture creation. It is not static; nor is it stable.[100] The past is not immutable. It must be continually "re-constructed" and "re-presented."[101] While self-identification is justified, do we accept at face value the claim that all those who emigrated from Ulster were Scotch-Irish—meaning Presbyterian-practicing, Lallans-speaking Lowlanders, and nearly English? Americans are confused by the term Scotch-Irish. It is used to mean Highland Scot in a great deal of modern America, such as at Maine's annual Highland Games or Belfast's Celtic Celebration, replete with caber tosses and bag pipe tattoos. Gaelic Scotland has merged with Scotch-Irish Lowland Scots in an American hodge-podge. Ulster immigrants' descendants worked very hard to separate their heritage from Ireland, especially in the nineteenth century when the Scotch-Irish were touted as nearly English.

Nineteenth-century American writers and orators from the middling classes working to separate their Ulster immigrant ancestors from Irishness (which was still defined by a great deal of stereotype) created categories of Scottish culture traits. Such lists, however, created further awkwardness around who was and was not Scottish.[102] By 1866, the categories used to establish the Scotch-Irish as a separate people were clear: (1) Language use; (2) behavior; (3) word play; (4) economic practices; (5) social customs; and (6) Presbyterianism. So, how *did* people *act* Scotch-Irish?

Evidently people were Scotch-Irish via "patterns of kin, kirk, spoken language, and song, as well as some farm practices, that had not been fixed in Ulster either."[103] New Hampshire speakers and writers remarked on fairs, horse races, and wakes. The Derry (New Hampshire) Fair, famous for its horse racing and manly sports, was also well lubricated by alcohol: "our pious ancestors sometimes became a little demoralized by the convivialities [sic] of the closing day."[104] In other words, people *performed* Scotch-Irishness, and, by extrapolation, Irishness—and, it would appear, either performance was not all that different. The Scotch-Irish, then, were fondly recalled as partyers, not averse to abusing alcohol on "closing day." *Convivial demoralization* sounds better than *drunk*. Why the cuteness around the subject? Was it too closely associated with Irishness?

Ulster immigrants' descendants avowed that their ancestors had spoken English and Scots (a Germanic language, not Gaelic), rarely Irish, and sometimes a *patois*.[105] (What then to make of modern Clan McGregor's Gaelic motto?)[106] The various writers with Londonderry, New Hampshire, ties pointed primarily to pronunciation differences of English among their Ulster ancestors. So language created a sense of unity among the immigrants, but, at the same time, set them apart from any other locals. Ulster immigrant pronunciation of English words was discussed: House/hoose; down/doun; and integrity/inteegrity.[107] Interestingly, descendants of Ulster immigrants took pains to show the difference of Scottish speech norms from mainstream English in a gentle, seemingly loving way; whereas, Irish difference was often used as a putdown by mainstream Anglo culture. Again, this tone may be the result of who controls the discussion. Generally, the pronunciation differences in Scotch-Irish were discussed by members of the "Othered" community. Irish pronunciations, however, were generally used by the old-timers to make fun of the "Othered." Anecdotes, related by the descendants of the Ulster immigrants, were used to show the "quaintness" of the language and yet denoted the astute cut-to-the-chase observations of the founding ancestors: "'There you are—gabble, gubble, gabble, and common-sensey maun sit a hin the door!'"[108]

In many an anecdote, too, the British—in works after the Revolutionary War—were treated with just a wee bit of ridicule. For example, during the "old" French war, the Reverend Matthew Clark of Londonderry, New Hampshire, remarked on a young British army officer who came to church bedecked in his scarlet uniform, and just stood there, drawing attention to himself: "'Ye are a brave lad, y ha'e a brave suit o' claithes, and we ha'e seen them; ye may sit doun.'" The young man sat.[109]

The list of cultural norms included thrift, followed by plain speaking and obstinately sticking to opinions.[110] Ulster immigrants had been plain, frugal, frank, rough, quick, social—not back biters or mean spirited—in every way the superiors of their southern (i.e., Irish) neighbors: The Scotch-Irish were confrontational, loud, erect, open, and fun-loving.[111] The Ulster immigrants, too, claimed to have given that quintessential Irish cultural marker—the potato—to New England.[112] Their keen wit, sense of the ludicrous, enjoyment of repartee, and their "ready tongue[s] for apt sayings" were duly noted.[113] In order to work a good joke into a long speech, that ready wit of the Scotch-Irish often came to the fore and was presented in Scots English.[114] For example, an old man in Ireland was reading Scripture regarding how Samson caught 300 foxes:

...when the old lady, his wife, interrupted him by saying, "John! I'm sure that canna' be true, for our Isaac was as good a fox-hunter as there ever was in the country, and he never caught but about twanty." "Hooh, Janet," replied the old gentleman, "ye mauna' always tak' the Scripture just as it reads. Perhaps in the three hundred, there might ha' been aughteen, or may be twanty that were raal foxes, the rest were all skunks and woodchucks."[115]

The Scots in Ulster had learned certain positive traits in Ireland (without, so it was maintained, intermingling with the other race):

the sternness of the Scotch Covenanter softened by a century's residence abroad, amid persecution and trial, wedded there to the comic humor and pathos of the Irish.... But what clung to them in Ireland, the disposition to humor, rioting, and laughter, was only on the surface.[116]

Good humor, joking, laughing were all well and good, evidently, but Americans needed to know the folks from Ulster were serious stock underneath it all. "Tainted" cultural observances, such as waking the dead and riotous marriage ceremonies, were blamed on the Irish.[117]

Public Rituals

Wedding and funerary customs, as celebrated in Londonderry, New Hampshire, by those early settlers, seem similar to "Irish" celebrations of such events. Weddings, for example, featured a "run for the bottle."[118] In the days leading up to the wedding, male guests fired guns near the couple's dwellings. After that, the sporting part of the event began. Guests were invited three days before the wedding day and formed two parties—the bride's and the groom's. The men of the bride's party met the men of the groom's at the halfway point between the homes of the couple. Each side chose a champion to run for the bottle, kept at the bride's house. The winner brought the bottle back to the "stag" gathering, offered a toast, drank to the groom's health, and passed the bottle round. The party then marched the groom to the bride's house, firing guns along the way. The best man fetched the bride. Dinner, dancing, and "other amusements" followed.[119]

Funerary customs were no less noisy affairs in the Ulster Presbyterian community of Londonderry, New Hampshire, and included the traditional wake.[120] When a community member died, people stopped working and gathered at the deceased's home to "observe a custom which they had brought with them from Ireland."[121] Such wakes included solemn moments, as well as a great deal of hilarity:

After the reading of the Scriptures and prayer, liquor would be handed round, and before dawn the joke and the laugh would break in upon the slumbers of the dead. There was always a large attendance at a funeral. Sermons were rarely delivered on the occasion, but before the prayer strong drink was served to the mourners and to the whole congregation. The same was done after the prayer and at the grave, as well as at the house after the burial. Many a family became seriously embarrassed in consequence of the heavy expenses incurred by the funeral services.[122]

The traditional wake followed settlers to Belfast, Maine. Alcohol was consumed at Belfast funerals, but, writing well after the institution of the 1851 Maine Law, which prohibited alcohol sales, William George Crosby assured his readers in his *Annals of Belfast* that such "refreshments in the form of wine and, sometimes, other kinds of liquor" were used judiciously: "There was no excess; a simple glass sufficed; there was no merriment, but everything was conducted with the solemnity befitting the occasion."[123] It appears that Crosby took great pains to separate early settlers' funerary customs from those "Other" Irish wakes that, evidently, some found indelicate. If wakes had not been considered a problem by the generations for whom he was writing in the 1870s, perhaps Crosby would not have dealt with funerary customs at all. And, frankly, the judge, methinks, protests a little too much.

Wakes gave way to staid funerals. Clothing, dance, music, art, manners, and so forth changed over time and from generation to generation. These truths make it difficult to define—or even discuss—anything to do with culture. Children might have been embarrassed by their parents and by the cultural stereotypes flung at them; however, not all those born in Ireland denied their Irishness—even if later descendants proclaimed them Scots. Henry Parkinson's parents, purported to have been natives of Scotland who immigrated to Londonderry, Ireland, eventually settled in Londonderry, New Hampshire. Parkinson evidently took pride in his Irish birth—and in his Latin prowess, as his grave marker proudly proclaims: "*Hibernia me genuit: America nutrivit: Nassau Hall educavit.* [Ireland birthed me: America nurtured me; Nassau Hall [i.e., Princeton] educated me.]"[124]

Notes

1 R. Stuart Wallace, "The Scotch-Irish of Provincial Maine: Purpooduck, Merrymeeting Bay, and Georgia," in *They Change Their Sky: The Irish in Maine*, ed. Michael C. Connolly (Orono: University of Maine Press, 2004), 56. Courtesy of University of Maine Press and R. Stuart Wallace.

2 Kevin Kenny, *Peaceable Kingdom Lost: The Paxton Boys and the Destruction of William Penn's Holy Experiment* (Oxford: Oxford University Press, 2009), 150.

3 Jens Brockmeier, "After the Archive: Remapping Memory: A Historical Perspective," *Culture and Psychology*, 16, no. 5 (2010), 22.

4 Homi Bhabha, "Unpacking My Library Again," *The Journal of the Midwest Modern Language Association*, 28, no. 1 (Spring 1995), 6.

5 George F. Willey, *Willey's Book of Nutfield: A History of that Part of New Hampshire Comprised within the Limits of the Old Township of Londonderry from its Settlement in 1719 to the Present Time* (Derry Depot, New Hampshire: Geo. F. Willey, 1895), 7.

6 Poor, however, was a reality. McGregor, who chafed at being labeled Irish by the colonial government, had not received salary for more than three years before leaving Ulster. His parishioners suffered the effects of crop failure, soaring provision prices, smallpox and livestock disease epidemics, and huge increases in land rents while living in Ulster, Ireland. Kerby A. Miller, Arnold Schrier, Bruce D. Boling, and David N. Doyle, *Irish Immigrants in the Land of Canaan: Letters and Memoirs from Colonial and Revolutionary America, 1675-1815* (Oxford: Oxford University Press, 2003), 436. Patrick Griffin, *The People with No Name: Ireland's Ulster Scots, America's Scots Irish, and the Creation of a British Atlantic World, 1689-1764* (Princeton: Princeton University Press, 2001), 438: "Mr. McGreggor [*sic*] had 'no certain lodging in the parish [of Aghadowey].'"

7 The Rev. James McGregor, Letter to Massachusetts Governor Samuel Shute, 27 February 1720, quoted in *Irish Immigrants in the Land of Canaan: Letters and Memoirs from Colonial and Revolutionary American, 1675-1815*, Miller, et al., 438.

8 Willey, 53.

9 Kerby A. Miller, *Ireland and Irish America: Culture, Class, and Transatlantic Migration* (Dublin: Field Day, 2008), 130.

10 Kerby A. Miller, "Ulster Presbyterians and the 'Two Traditions' in Ireland and America," in *Making the Irish American: History and Heritage of the Irish in the United States*, ed. J.J. Lee and Marion R. Casey (New York: New York University Press, 2006), 258.

11 Kenny, *Peaceable Kingdom*, 32.

12 "Rev. James McGregor letter to Gov. Samuel Shute." Humanities E-Book Images, Chapter 49, Petition 1, "Rev. James McGregor, Nutfield, New Hampshire, to Governor Samuel Shute, Boston, Massachusetts, 27 February 1720." University of Michigan Library Digital Collections. Accessed 4 March 2021.

13 Lois Tyson, "Postcolonial Criticism," in *Critical Theory Today: A User Friendly Guide*, 3rd ed. (Routledge, 2015), 421.

14 McGregor letter to Shute.

15 Willey, 7.

16 Willey, 9.

17 Mrs. J.C. Durham, *Old Houses of Belfast* (Belfast: Waldo County Herald, 1911), 11.

18 "Medical Signers of the Declaration of Independence," *Missouri Medical and Surgical Journal*, LXIX, no. 1 (1895), 61.

19 Willey, 9.

20 *Images of America: Londonderry* (Portsmouth, New Hampshire: Londonderry Historical Society, 2004), introduction.

21 Town of Belfast 1800 census.

22 For a brief discussion of the Siege of Derry and subsequent plantation, see T.W. Moody and F.X. Martin, *The Course of Irish History*, revised and enlarged edition (Dublin: Radio Telefís Éireann, 1984), 191, and Sean

McMahon, *A Short History of Ireland* (Chester Springs, PA: Dufour, 1996), 83.

23 Willey, 7.

24 Joseph Williamson, *The History of the City of Belfast, Maine*, Vol. 1 (Somersworth, New Hampshire: New England History Press, 1982), 413.

25 Williamson, Vol. 1, 232 (emphasis added).

26 Williamson, Vol. 1, 233.

27 Herman Abbot, "History from Belfast from its First Settlement to the Year 1825," in *Early Histories of Belfast, Maine*, ed. Alan Taylor (Camden, Maine: Picton Press, 1989), 231.

28 Abbot, 231.

29 Abbot, 231.

30 Abbot, 231.

31 Williamson, Vol. 1, 63.

32 Williamson, Vol. 1, 63. The French and Indian War ended in 1763.

33 Williamson, Vol. 1, 63–65.

34 Williamson, Vol. 1, 87.

35 Williamson, Vol. 1, 64.

36 Williamson, Vol. 1, 93.

37 Williamson, Vol. 1, 433.

38 Williamson, Vol. 1, 711.

39 Williamson, Vol. 1, 745.

40 Williamson, Vol. 1, 776.

41 Duc de Liancourt, quoted in Williamson, Vol. 1, 229. According to Williamson, de Liancourt was a French nobleman traveling with Gen. Henry Knox through Maine in 1795.

42 According to Williamson, James Miller's hymn book, *The Psalms of David in Metre, more Plain, Smooth, and Agreeable to the Text than any heretofore. Allowed by the General Assembly of the Kirk of Scotland, Glasgow, 1714*, was later owned by the Reverend John L. Locke, a Methodist.

43 Williamson, Vol. 1, 255–260.

44 Williamson, Vol. 1, 254. Williamson noted that the west side building was given to the town, with the deal that the building's proprietors would not have to pay "tithes" for ten years. The town sold it to the Baptists in 1822, and they used it until 1837. The structure was then moved and became a stable—a sort of return to Christian beginnings.

45 Williamson, Vol. 1, 224–227.

46 Williamson, Vol. 1, 224.

47 Williamson, Vol. 1, 235.

48 Williamson, Vol. 1, 235. Williamson quotes Willis, from the Collection of the Maine Historical Society, VI, 32.

49 Williamson, Vol. 1, 235.

50 George W. Field, D.D., *Celebration of the One Hundredth Anniversary of the Organization of the First Congregational Church (Now Called the North Church) at Belfast, Maine* (Belfast, Maine: The Belfast Age Publishing Co., 1897), 30.

51 Field, 28.

52 Field, 30. *Per fervidum ingenium*, the fever of the race (i.e., hot headedness).

53 William White, "A History of Belfast: With Introductory Remarks on Acadia," in *Early Histories of Belfast, Maine*, ed. Alan Tayler (Camden, Maine: Picton Press, 1989), 245. The White family traced its roots to Deacon William White, "who came from Ireland to Londonderry, in 1725." His son, Colonel William White, Chester, New Hampshire, was married

twice and had 16 children. Susannah, a daughter from his first marriage to
Mary Mills, married Belfastian Jonathan Quimby. Colonel White's second
wife was John Mitchell's daughter Elizabeth. They had nine children. His
sons William, (III) the amateur historian of Belfast, and James settled in
Belfast. According to Alan Taylor, in *Early Histories of Belfast, Maine*, 229,
William White III was born in Chester, New Hampshire in 1783. He
graduated from Dartmouth College in 1806, Phi Beta Kappa. He read law
with the Honorable Amos Kent of Chester and the Honorable John Wilson
of Belfast. The Honorable John Wilson was the son of an immigrant from
Ireland. William White, our historian, practiced law in Union, Maine, then
moved to Thomaston, then to Belfast in 1813. A third White son settled in
Montville, part of the Greene Plantation. Williamson, Vol. 1, 197.

54 White, "History," 245.
55 Williamson, Vol. 1, 98 and 589.
56 Williamson, Vol. 1, 98 and 589.
57 White, "History," 254.
58 White, "History," 255.
59 Patrick O'Sullivan, ed., *The Irish in the New Communities; The Irish World Wide: History, Heritage, Identity*, Vol. 2 (London: Leicester University Press, 1992), 10. O'Sullivan, who edited this volume, argued that "ethnic identity is a matter of personal choice, a matter of picking out the most attractive grandparents.... Individuals belong to social groups, they strive to maintain or enhance their self-esteem, they do this mainly by distinguishing their group from neighboring groups along some dimension which makes them feel superior" (10).
60 Williamson, Vol. 1, 172–173.
61 Williamson, Vol. 1, 134.
62 Williamson, Vol. 1, 134.
63 Williamson, Vol. 1, 224. Williamson offers various dates for reconstitution, offering 1784 as well. See page 134.
64 Williamson, Vol. 1, 7–8.
65 Eric Foner, *Free Soil: Free Labor: Free Men: The Ideology of the Republican Party before the Civil War* (New York: Oxford University Press, 1995), 226–260.
66 Foner, "Free Soil," 226–260.
67 The Reverend Edward L. Parker, *History of Londonderry: Comprising the Towns of Derry and Londonderry, New Hampshire* (Boston: Perkins and Whipple, 1851), 68.
68 The Honorable Charles H. Bell, "Oration," in *The Londonderry Celebration: Exercises on the 150th Anniversary of the Settlement of Old Nutfield, Comprising the towns of Londonderry, Derry, Windham, and Parts of Manchester, Hudson and Salem, N.H., June 10, 1869*, Robert C. Mack, compiler (Manchester: John B. Clarke, 1870), 16.
69 Bell, 17.
70 Bell, 17.
71 Bell, 17.
72 Bell, 22.
73 Bell, 23.
74 The Reverend Arthur Latham Perry, *Scotch-Irish in New England* (New York: Charles Scribner's Sons, 1896), 7.
75 Henry Jones Ford, *The Scotch-Irish in America* (Princeton: Princeton University Press, 1915), 21.
76 Henry Jones Ford, 82–85.

77 Henry Jones Ford, 90.
78 Henry Jones Ford, 90–91.
79 Henry Jones Ford, 5.
80 Henry Jones Ford, 2.
81 Henry Jones Ford, 40.
82 Henry Jones Ford, 37.
83 Henry Jones Ford, 35.
84 Henry Jones Ford, 82.
85 David Noel Doyle, "Scots Irish or Scotch-Irish," in *Making the Irish American: History and Heritage of the Irish in the United States*, ed. J.J. Lee and Marion R. Casey (New York: New York University Press, 2006), 152.
86 Miller, "Two Traditions," 255–270.
87 Miller, "Two Traditions," 157.
88 Griffin, *No Name*, 26.
89 Michael Drake, "Population Growth and the Irish Economy," in *The Formation of the Irish Economy*, ed. L.M. Cullen (Cork: The Mercier Press, 1968, reprinted 1976), 74.
90 Manfred Waldemar Kohl, *Congregationalism in America* (Oak Creek, Wisconsin: The Congregational Press, 1977), 9.
91 Williamson, Vol. 1, 94.
92 Williamson, Vol. 1, 236.
93 Williamson, Vol. 1, 239–243.
94 Williamson, Vol. 1, 316.
95 Ronald F. Banks, *Maine Becomes a State: The Movement to Separate Maine from Massachusetts, 1795-1820* (Somersworth: New Hampshire Publishing for the Maine Historical Society, 1973), 140–141.
96 Williamson, Vol. 1, 254.
97 Banks, 141.
98 Banks, 141.
99 First Church Congregational, unpublished treasurer's report housed at the Belfast Free Library. Published with permission from First Congregational Church, Belfast.
100 Brockmeier, "After the Archive," *Culture and Psychology,* 16, no. 5 (2010), 10.
101 Brockmeier, "After the Archive," *Culture and Psychology,* 16, no. 5 (2010), 11.
102 Brockmeier, "After the Archive," *Culture and Psychology,* 16, no. 5 (2010), 32.
103 Doyle, "Scots Irish or Scotch-Irish," 163.
104 The Honorable James W. Patterson, "Address," in *The Londonderry Celebration: Exercises on the 150th Anniversary of the Settlement of Old Nutfield, Comprising the towns of Londonderry, Derry, Windham, and Parts of Manchester, Hudson and Salem, N.H., June 10, 1869*, Robert C. Mack, compiler (Manchester: John B. Clarke, 1870), 45.
105 Michael Montgomery, "Presidential Address: Voices of My Ancestors: A Personal Search for the Language of the Scotch-Irish," *American Speech*, 80, no. 4 (Winter 2005), 342.
106 https://en.wikipedia.org/wiki/Clan_Gregor. Accessed 4 March 2021.
107 Bell, "Oration," and Patterson, "Address," in *Londonderry Celebration*: 25–27; 45 (respectively).
108 Patterson, 41.
109 Willey, 89.
110 Bell, 25.

111 The Reverend Edward L. Parker, *History of Londonderry: Comprising the Towns of Derry and Londonderry, New Hampshire* (Boston: Perkins and Whipple, 1851), 68–70.
112 Bell, 34.
113 Bell, 28.
114 Parker, 249.
115 Parker, 250.
116 Parker, 70–73.
117 Parker, 73.
118 Willey, 54.
119 Willey, 54.
120 Willey, 90.
121 Willey, 90.
122 Willey, 90.
123 Crosby, 29.
124 R. Parkinson, "Henry Parkinson," *The Granite Monthly: A Magazine of Literature, History and State Progress*, 5 (1881-82), 215. My Latin translation is: "Ireland birthed me; America nurtured me; Nassau Hall [i.e., Princeton] educated me."

7   Bridging Social Boundaries

The lecturers before the Lyceum this winter were as follows: ... Miss Lucy Stone, on Woman's Rights, and on The Political Disabilities of Women.[1]

Over the course of the nineteenth century, some American women worked for more political clout, a say in national life. The 1848 Seneca Falls Convention, in New York state, led by Elizabeth Cady Stanton and Lucretia Mott, raised initial interest, and the nation's newspapers discussed the issue, sometimes with a disparaging tone. The women who met at Seneca Falls had status, as well as leisure time and discretionary funds. Stanton, the wife of a railroad investor/speculator, and Lucretia Mott, a Society of Friends preacher, came to the Woman's Movement from the Abolitionist Movement. Their awakening to the need for political access came as a result of the 1840 World Anti-Slavery Congress held in London, England, when women were not allowed on the voting floor. These women were forced into the role of observers rather than participants. This may have been the "ah-ha" moment when they discovered that they had few more *legal* rights than the people they were trying to free.

Sojourner Truth, a former slave from New York state, had contested the logical fallacy that women spoke with one voice in her "Ain't I a Woman?" speech at a women's meeting in Ohio in 1851. It had been obvious to her that not all women were seen as equals, or even as women, the cultural definition of which applied primarily to middling-class white Protestant women of English extraction. While possibilities for some of these women may have seemed to open up as property, marriage, and divorce laws were amended, those possibilities hinged on class, status, and race.

In this era, being Irish was considered being part of a race, and, as has been discussed, the Irish were considered in many quarters "less than" African-American slaves. In some instances, class and status could overcome racial mistrust, but that was also gendered. For example, the

DOI: 10.4324/9781003187660-7

male Irish immigrant and merchant William Brannagan socialized with the elite of Belfast society at the breakfast table at the Field boarding house, beginning in the 1840s. The Irish working women, however, who cooked and served food, did dishes and laundry, and cleaned house, never got such opportunities to advance. *Most women* did not.

American colonists' wives and daughters had been active participants in the rural economy. In the eighteenth century, they raised chickens, milked cows, made butter and cheese, spun, and wove.[2] New England women, continuing the tradition imported from Ulster, Ireland, wove linen from homegrown flax and also worked with domestic woolens. They made the clothes for their families, as well as added to the family economy by "selling" the surplus.[3] Homemade textiles earned credit with merchants. For example, in Belfast, John Brown earned 3 pounds 10 shillings credit for his daughter's weaving; Alexander Clark, earned 7 pounds 2 shillings 6 pence in credit for his wife's spinning in 1776.[4]

Frontier Norms

Perhaps it was because Belfast, Maine, was still considered frontier (in relation to Boston) that its women did not face more restrictive roles. There was no mention of a weaker sex, for example, when women participated in fighting an 1821 fire—they *womaned* the bucket brigade, handing empty buckets down the line.[5] Women could also hold jobs integral to the proper functioning of the community—even if those jobs were not given a title, label, or wage. For example, the *de facto post mistress* (although that title was not conferred) in the early days of the community was Mrs. Waitstill Bishop Whittier. Her husband, Thomas, owned and operated Whittier's Tavern.[6]

Some of the "old values"—public affairs controlled by males—remained intact in pre-Irish Famine Belfast. Women did not deal directly with merchants—their fathers and husbands took in any products, such as spinning and weaving. Purchases were also made by men, even if acting upon women's requests. On 30 September 1826, for example, resident Peter West purchased 32 yards of shirting material, at a cost of $5.34 at Gammon's Store. That was about one-fifth of his credit. This was the largest single purchase of fabric by anyone giving custom to Gammon's Store—most purchases by others ranged from 1 yard of linen to 3¾ yards Caroline plaid to 9 yards furniture print. The only other shirting purchase, by a Benjamin Nickerson, was for 4 yards, which cost 50 cents. A pattern for vests, according to the Gammon's day book, cost $1.12. Perhaps Mrs. West was supplementing the family income by sewing clothing for others in the community (although, the entire yardage *could* have been used by the females in the West family). Gammon's day book shows that men did all purchasing—no woman had an account in the book.

Some women in Belfast, however, provided a similar kind of barter exchange as that found at Gammon's store. Abigail Davis Field, wife of Belfast's first lawyer, Bohan P. Field, kept day books detailing her business enterprises, starting in the 1840s. In the big Field house on High Street, built in 1807, working women of all strata interacted.[7] What becomes apparent here is that ethnicity was not as clear a demarcation of difference as were economic status and social class.

Women of Belfast were not as confined as urban women. Class structures in urban environments led to more strictures about expected public decorum. Like their big city cousins, "middling" women, or women with "middling" pretensions in nineteenth-century Belfast, followed some of the larger society's cultural norms.[8] They visited on Fridays or entertained in turn. They made appearances at public venues. Women's rights activist Lucy Stone lectured at Belfast's Lyceum in 1854. But, even if they were wives of privileged males, many women in Belfast ran their own businesses or worked alongside their husbands in mercantile establishments.

Women of Belfast who succeeded had been prepared for that success. Educated men married educated women. The children produced in such unions were also educated. In other words, literacy engendered literacy—and, thus, access to the prevailing white Anglo-Saxon Protestant culture. But, unlike urban women, Belfast women also moved into careers without drawing notice. They just did it. Belfast's cultural and gender norms help explain why.

Looking closely at the business of the Field boarding house, we learn money earned can be nuanced. In her earliest day book, Abigail outlined the day-to-day business transactions among women in Belfast. Just as among the men frequenting Gammon's Store, there seems to have been a great deal of bartering. Women's exchanges were generally for clothing fabrication, eggs, milk, cream, and butter. In September 1841, Abigail recorded a great number of transactions: 25 cents for two yards of checked fabric for aprons, 18 cents per yard for 12 yards of flannel, 40 cents for 4 scan(t)s yards at 10 cents a yard. She noted that Hannah had "bought 41 cents worth from the box" and that "Lucy Davis owes."[9] Some clothing production she purchased, paying $2.57 "to Mrs. Shepherd for making pelice [sic], ..., 6 cents for cotton, ... 75 cents for stockings settled paid paid [sic]."[10] She sold eggs regularly to Mrs. R.C. Johnson.[11]

Bartering and working deals kept the Belfast economy functioning—in male or female circuits. Catherine Craig came to work as a "girl" in the Field House, in exchange for Abigail paying her tuition at the Belfast Academy, run by Abigail's son George.[12] Abigail's day book also points out wives worked beside their husbands in shops. For example, she notes that for "Loaf Sugar. Green Tea. Black Tea. Butter. Cheese. Nutmeg," she paid Mr. [Samuel] Peirce $1.50, $1.95, and "Mrs. Peirce *nine*

Figure 7.1 The Field House was built in 1807. Abigail Davis Field began running a boarding house in the stately home in the 1840s. Courtesy of the Belfast Historical Society and Museum.

dollars—this 1st day of October [emphasis in original]."[13] She also let other women use her credit at area shops, letting "Mrs. Hewes take up on my account at Mr. [Samuel] Moulton's store 3 dollars and 34 cents to pay in the spring Rec'd nine shillings of the above."[14]

Women bought, sold, and traded products, but they also bartered or charged for services. Mr. Moulton, who ran a shop, sent his laundry to Abigail, who appeared to be operating as middle woman, as she sent her wash to Mrs. Bond just days later.[15] Moulton later took up permanent residence in Abigail's boarding house, upon his return to Belfast after a decade in Boston, living there until his death on 15 February 1867.[16]

Although husband Bohan P. Field Sr. had begun his working life as a lawyer, and was well-off financially, the fact remains that Abigail was supplementing his earnings.[17] Perhaps the effects of the 1837 depression lingered, as well as the fact that Field left his law practice in 1834 to take up the farmer's life.[18] Abigail began operating the boarding house as early as 1841, two years before her husband's death—at least that is when the records begin. Abigail never discussed in her day books the reason(s) she opened a boarding house. What *is* apparent is that the Field family suffered no loss of status when she did—all the best people stayed in the house, aptly located on High Street on Field Hill.[19] Abigail even noted in her day book that on 9 October 1841 she could afford to buy status gifts: "Purchased two silver spoons—one a present for [son] Franklin," who turned twenty-one the next day.[20]

A thorough investigation of the Field boarding house operations gives insight into Belfast's social norms and interactions from 1841 through 1877. Abigail's records continued until her death in 1863; there are gaps—nothing from the 1850s remains. There is no discussion in the day books of when Abigail's youngest son and his wife joined her in the boarding house business, but upon reaching adulthood (age twenty-one), Benjamin Franklin (Frank) Field was still at home. The boarding house responsibilities were shared between Frank's first wife Caroline (Carrie) Tobey Field and her mother-in-law Abigail. After Carrie's death, Frank's second wife (Carrie's sister Anna) began running the enterprise. While running a boarding house alone could be exhausting, Abigail and her daughter-in-law often did run it without help. Frank, however, was also an integral participant in running the boarding house, even though the census recorded him as a farmer.

In addition to running the boarding house, Abigail supplemented her income selling cream and milk from her cow.[21] In this, Abigail would not have appeared unusual by Irish working-class standards. In Ireland, women were in charge of milking cows and feeding cattle. Rural women of the Irish working class, especially those living closest to subsistence level, also did manual labor. In fact, it was Irish women's work to white wash the house and to paint house doors red.[22] They helped with reaping, setting seeds, collecting seaweed, and cutting turf.[23]

> In traditional Irish life, as in most peasant societies, the rigid distinction between domestic duties and other types of work did not exist and women engaged in a wide variety of duties. This lifestyle continued in many areas [in Ireland] until the end of the nineteenth century.[24]

Irish-American women, married and unmarried, worked for wages in America in the mid-nineteenth century. In Five Points, New York, 35 percent of married and 74 percent of unmarried women did paid work. Single Irish women faced tough economic times by emigrating from Ireland: "Usually unmarried and needing paid labor in the market place from the moment of their arrival, immigrant Irish women faced the same economic and physical challenges in the world of work as their male counterparts across the diaspora."[25] While 35 percent of married Irish woman continued to work after marriage in such urban centers as New York City, married women—not just recent Irish immigrant women—worked for wages after marriage in Belfast. And, a number of Belfast's working women were married to men in the professional and merchant class, so it was not just wives of day laborers—or widows—who participated in household economies. Abigail Davis Field, Waitstill Bishop Whittier, and Mrs.

[Samuel] Peirce demonstrate that Belfast women were integral participants in their household economies.

Studies of working women in urban areas have compared Irish statistics with those of other immigrant groups. Italian-American women, for example, rarely worked after marriage—only 7 percent—even though *half* of unmarried Italian-American women worked for wages.[26] The cultural norm for Italian-American women in New York was that they gave up work for wages upon marriage. There is no point of comparison in Belfast for the Italian-American working woman's experience, as there was only one male born in Italy living in the town in 1860. In fact, the number of individuals born elsewhere was minuscule in most cases: One person was Scottish-born, one from Norway. Four people had been born in England. The next largest group was made up of twenty-eight people born in Canada. (Some of those born in Canada may have had Irish-born parents.) One family provided the entire German-born population—the Rinks family.[27]

Irish immigrants to Belfast did not compete with African-American slaves. In 1820, there were only two individuals designated as free colored living in Belfast, both under age fourteen. One was female, the other male. Their names were not recorded—but then no names were given for anyone other than the male householder in the 1820 census. The female was in Benjamin Whittier's house, and the male was in Thomas Cunningham's house.[28] On 29 August 1825, the infant son of Charles Bowes, "col[ore]d," died in Belfast.[29] By 1830, James Cook and Lucius St__s [unreadable], both "free colored" men between the ages of twenty-four and thirty-six, lived in Belfast. According to the 1840 Belfast census taken by Samuel S. Burd, there were fourteen "Colored Persons" living in Belfast. The largest minority group to arrive and live in Belfast, then, was the Irish, which composed about 4 percent of the population, in 1850.

Rural Norms

Those Irish-born women who found their way to Belfast, Maine, mid-nineteenth century were working class. Most were illiterate, according to U.S. census records. They came with a work ethic that involved physical exertion from a culture that expected women to bring in wages to the household economy. Industrialization had not made inroads in Belfast, and women remained integral components of household economies, regardless of class and status. This was a reality that working-class Irish-born women would have appreciated. Belfast women continued to supplement household incomes well into the nineteenth century by selling milk, cream, and eggs, although pigs had moved to the male domain by the mid-nineteenth century.[30]

In the decades before the Irish Famine, industrialization in Britain severely limited female economic possibilities, gradually making hand spinning and weaving obsolete. The mills of New England were recent introductions, but their effects were similar on the New England farm economy. In addition, cooperative creameries in Ireland started using machinery, and men ran the machinery—women had always worked at making butter and cheese as part of the farm economy in Ireland. Females there thus lost that income stream as well.[31] Rural Maine and Irish farming economies, thus, were quite similar. Perhaps we can argue that farm economies have more in common worldwide than scholars have as yet discussed. "Rurality" may be more of a culture than ethnicity.

Many of the immigrant Irish families owned their own cattle and pigs.[32] By 1862 Belfast standards, pigs were decidedly men's responsibility, including those Irish immigrants whose wayward pigs led to interaction with local authorities.[33] While women in Ireland may have been used to white washing houses and painting doors red, the paradigm for male and female work in Belfast was slightly different. Abigail's son Frank painted rooms, or hired a male painter, wall-papered, and helped with cleaning.[34] Quite often Frank would get caught doing what he called "wimmin's work," which made him chafe, so perhaps this was not normative gender behavior in 1840-1860 Belfast either.[35] Rural cultures, as do all cultures, can also change.

Ascertaining how many women worked for wages in nineteenth-century Belfast is difficult. Published information about women's paid work in Belfast prior to the 1860 census is sporadic at best. Belfast's first newspaper began publication in 1820, and it is in these weekly issues, with their paid advertisements, that we get glimpses of the world of women's work in Belfast.

Belfast women did a lot of clothing fabrication—many for hire. While there were a number of male tailors in Belfast in the earliest years of the nineteenth century, at least one woman was advertising in the 1840s as a tailor. Two decades earlier, only Phoebe Sager advertised her ability to provide women's clothing. She offered millinery and dressmaking services in the late 1820s.[36] Printed advertisements in the weeklies show that clothing construction became more of a female occupation over the decades. In early 1840, *The Republican Journal* printed advertisements for millenary and tailoring. Miss E.B. Conner, situated at No. 8 Phoenix Row, reported that she had

> recently returned from Boston, with the very latest New York and Boston Fall and Winter Fashions for Cloaks, Pelisses, Dresses, Bonnets, Caps, etc., and is now prepared to cut and make the above named Garments in the very best manner, and at the lowest rates, all work entrusted to her care will be attended to by herself and warranted to give satisfaction.

She went on to state that she had "Constantly on hand and for sale, ready made Bonnets, Caps, and Head-dresses. Straw Bonnets Bleached and Repaired at short notice."[37] We note, too, that she traveled for her work to Boston and that she was promising, in print, not to "outsource" the work to anyone else in the Belfast community. Her surname would appear to be Irish, but she was not listed as being from Ireland in the 1850 census.[38] Another woman's advertisement immediately follows Miss Conner's. Mrs. Noyes sought tailoring work. Both women were members of the merchant class. Mrs. Noyes was widowed:

> Mrs. H. Noyes, informs her friends and others in want of Tailoring that she is prepared to execute that kind of work, in a workman-like manner and solicits a *share* of patronage.—Cutting and Repairing done at short notice and at prices that will not fail to suit reasonable customers. SHOP in the brick building, next below Furber & Bean's hatstore, [sic] up stairs in the end.[39]

Sometimes, women's vocations were mentioned as asides in publications. Belfast's Vital Statistics of 1850 noted the death of young Mary A. Dean in January. She had been a dressmaker.[40] As the creation of textiles and finished clothing remained primarily a female occupation—on both sides of the Atlantic—immigrant Irish women would have found many similarities between their traditional culture and Belfast regarding the construction of garments.

Home-based textile manufacturing had provided good incomes for females in the north of Ireland prior to the 1840s. In Ireland's famine decade of the 1840s, the number of women employed in textile work in Ireland was cut in half.[41] From 1841 to 1881, textile employment for females all but disappeared in Ireland: "In 1841 there were over half a million female textile workers, mainly outworkers, [sic] by 1881 textiles employed fewer than 100,000 women."[42] Outworkers did piece work; therefore, women could work out of their homes yet still receive payment for the finished piece.

By the 1840s, as textile mills became more prevalent in the United States, the fact that some women worked outside the home—and that mill work drew women away from the rural economy—may have been more generally perceived than acknowledged. Issues of *The Republican Journal* in 1843 *frequently* mentioned women and the world of work outside the home. For example, in the 21 April 1843 issue, in an aside, the paper alleged that in the economic downturn of 1819, 10,000 men in New York sought work daily, and, the writer of 1843 hypothesized, "adding the women, [there were] twenty thousand persons who desired something to do."[43] It would seem, then, that the idea of women being in the work force was considered normal by 1843 Belfast standards. On 5 May, the paper reported that factory girls were on strike in Allegheny

City, Pennsylvania.[44] The following week, the paper reported on the appalling wages in London:

> Seamstresses, in London it appears, are paid one penny and a half for making sailors' shirts. By working very hard "and finding her own needles," she may earn four and a half pennys [*sic*] a day. The price of the cheapest quartern loaf she can buy is five and a half pence. A loaf of bread is one penny dearer than her whole day's work.[45]

The same issue continued reportage on British milliners—evidently the London papers had arrived at the Belfast docks and the editor made good use of them. The London news, reprinted in *The Republican Journal*, claimed that an investigation into the welfare of girls working as milliners in England "revealed a great extent of mental and physical suffering, among the poor girls employed as milliners, which has resulted from an excess of labor to which a Congo black was never subjected by the most exacting of his masters."[46]

Working Women

After some contemplation, someone at *The Republican Journal* wrote a lengthy editorial on women working in manufacturing. Perhaps it was the unsigned work of Editor Benjamin Griffin. Given the fact that people in Maine were particularly interested in the brouhaha over the northern boundary of the United States and that all things British were suspect and foul, the writer took care to point out that Americans should not get too cocky. The editorialist dismissed the claim that the famed Lowell, Massachusetts, textile mills had elevated the masses:

> The factory girls have got the education to enable them to write, not in the factory towns, but in their fathers' homes, and they are chiefly the daughters of farmers; and thus far it is an argument for the superiority of agriculture, and not of manufactures. That they save from the pittance of wages they receive, enough to buy some few luxuries, and that they steal from their hours of rest time to write or read, is creditable to themselves, and not to the system.[47]

Later that summer, the paper noted that 6,275 of the 9,000 operators in Lowell were female.[48] In October, in other column filler, the paper reported that, according to the *Lowell Advertiser*, factory girls were earning 55 cents a week for 75 to 80 hours of work. The editor threw his support behind the working women of Lowell in the 27 October 1843 issue, reprinting material from the worker-edited *Lowell Offering* and suggesting that their argument that working women did themselves honor rather than losing status was admirable:

> WORKING FOR A LIVING—We find the following excellent article in the "Lowell Offering," edited by the factory girls in Lowell. It breathes the right spirit, and every mother and daughter and father and son, should read it:

> From whence originated the idea that it was derogatory to a lady's dignity, or a blot upon female character to labor, and who was the first to say sneeringly, "Oh! she works for a living!" Surely such ideas and expressions ought not to grow upon a republican soil. The time has been when ladies of the first rank were accustomed to busy themselves in some domestic employment. Homer tells of princesses who used to draw water from the springs and wash with their own hands, the finest linen of their respective families. The famous Lucretia used to spin in the midst of her attendants; and the wife of Ulysses, after the siege of Troy, employed herself in weaving until her husband returned from Ithica [sic].[49]

The women who wrote the *Lowell Offering* were urging that women should remain vital parts of household economies. The Lowell women sought to rebut the idea that, in order to be classified as ladies, women could not work for money.

In addition to work in clothing manufacture, Belfast females also found employment in domestic service. Evidence for hired household help arrived with the professional-class invasion at the turn-of-the-century. The first two-story house was not built until 1791; Belfast houses in 1820 were still modest.[50] Yet as early as 1821, some Belfast, Maine, householders sought girls to do housework and promised good money—if the girls could produce excellent recommendations.[51] Kitchen maids, especially those who understood cooking, were promised a liberal wage when Manasseh Sleeper advertised the fact that he had purchased a local tavern house.[52] Running a household was labor intensive—and cooking was considered a female activity.

Gender norms changed over the years. In the early years of the republic, gardening was a female occupation, as it was related to food preparation. While her husband ran a tavern in Belfast circa 1805, for example, Mrs. Waitstill Whittier, when her post office duties didn't intervene, cultivated an extensive flower and vegetable garden—although the garden plot itself was considered to belong to her husband, Thomas Whittier. (The Whittiers disappeared from Belfast's story shortly after the close of the War of 1812 by moving ten miles west to Searsmont, part of Greene Plantation, where he took up the lumbering trade and made more money than he had in the tavern business.)[53] Just twenty-five years later, maintaining gardens was more "manly."[54] Gardening was certainly a male affair at the Field House. Local Belfast women in the 1860s and 1870s put up the harvest, making preserves and canning tomatoes, for example. Men might help their wives with canning projects (at least Frank Field did), but that was the extent of male cooking, at least in the Field household.[55]

Comparing Frank's day books with those of his mother and first wife gives readers the opportunity to see housework from several viewpoints.[56] Frank ran the house alone after his first wife's death, with the aid of hired help. Within six weeks of her death, he complained in his day book that "housekeeping is Terrible Hard Business [emphasis in the original]."[57] Just eight months later, still deeply depressed and in mourning, Frank remarried Carrie's younger sister, Anna (Annie) Tobey. Occasionally, Frank discussed his garden. He sowed peas, beets, onions, sweet corn, pole beans, and potatoes in early spring. He also did not call himself a gardener—he was listed as "farmer" in the U.S. census. But, he had another responsibility in Belfast: He ran Belfast's Pound.

Social Leveling

The Belfast Pound gave Frank Field regular contact with the Irish community. In these interactions, recorded by Frank, we glimpse how old-timers in the community dealt with the newcomers. The Pound was a community leveler. Anyone who owned animals, or who suffered the depredations of others' animals, could seek justice in Frank's impound lot. All charges could be challenged and left to supposedly calmer, fairer-minded judgment. The fines for infractions could be stiff, but there were rewards.

The Irish-born newcomers, usually on the receiving end of law enforcement, found the Belfast Pound was the one place where newcomers received more equitable treatment from the Belfast legal apparatus. Animals that roamed—into other people's gardens and control—were subject to "arrest." The Irish immigrant newcomers quickly grasped how the system worked and used it in the same ways the locals did. The Pound impound, in a certain light, seems the equivalent of today's purchase of a lottery ticket. If the victims knew the owners of the wandering animals, and if they knew the status of said owners, some victims might set a high price on their personal property destruction, for example.

Frank Field made use of his Pound keeper notebooks to remark on life in Belfast and to note difference, clearly marking "John Collins (Irishman)" every time he had dealings with him. He also noted Thomas Lucius as Frenchman. Field, however, was not consistent with this. For example, he never recorded that Brian McCabe was Irish, even though he was. One explanation for this might be that McCabe had been in the area longer, perhaps even as early as 1840.[58] Closer inspection shows that several Irishmen did not earn Field's "Irishman" label: Patrick Sweeney, Daniel Sheehan, Cornelius Dorathey [*sic*], James Scanlin, Mikel [*sic*] Readen [Reardon], Pat Devaney, Andrew Bates, Michael Gannon, John Gannon, T. Owens, Thomas Logan, John Cunningham, and John Mahoney were never singled out as being Irish, even though they were. To keep confusion to a minimum, Frank Field noted when he hired [non Irish] John Collins, a painter, to paint two rooms and when he bought a cow of [Irish] John Collins for $20.[59] This supposed "Othering" Frank was guilty of, upon further inspection, might have been a simple mnemonic device, a way of remembering which John Collins he was talking about: John Collins, the painter; his son, John Collins, also a painter; and John Collins, the Irishman.[60]

The Pound record books, which Frank started keeping in 1853, also make clear that some of the Irish evidently had enough wealth that they owned several animals and that most of them could afford the repeated fines and fees associated with cows running amok.[61] Brian McCabe, for example, owned at least two cows—one with small horns and one large red one—and perhaps a pair of oxen.[62] As he lived in an "apartment" in a building that housed at least two other families, where he found pasturage is something of a mystery—although, his neighbors might quickly have pointed out, they were evidently expected to feed McCabe's animals.[63]

Animals brought old and new Belfast into close contact. Locals, too, could make the equivalent of a citizen's arrest of errant animals. A.L. Leighten impounded Bryant [Brian] McCabe's cow and demanded $5 in damages. McCabe objected. The job of the pound master was to find disinterested third parties as referees to assess the damages claimed, which also led to fees for the appraisers. The referees in this instance found in favor of McCabe, reducing the damages payable to Leighton to $1.[64] Patrick Sweeney, on the other hand, impounded a chestnut horse and demanded $5 in damages, which amount was paid.[65]

It was not just males who participated in impound roulette: Mrs. William Wells, for example, demanded $4 from Judge Alfred Johnson for the depredations perpetrated by his cows. (Judge Johnson was born in Belfast, the son of Belfast's first full-time minister.) The judge objected; Frank appraised damages at 50 cents.[66] Women also could be billed for damage caused by their cows: Mrs. Snell's cow did $10 worth of damage at William Salmond's place, and Charles Palmer demanded $10 for the damage caused by Mrs. Harper's cow.[67] Dr. Monroe demanded stiff penalties when he "arrested" cows. Evidently, the women in his neighborhood had cattle that liked his gardens. He demanded $10 for damage inflicted by oxen owned by Mrs. Peter Rowe. When Mrs. Rowe objected to Dr. Monroe's demand, Frank sent two well-known local men of equal status to Dr. Monroe to assess the damage. The assessors reduced the claim to $1.[68] Dr. Monroe also demanded $5 for damage caused by Mrs. Doty Blake's cow. Mrs. Blake actually made a personal appearance in Frank Field's pound records—the only woman to do so. When Mrs. Blake took her cow and refused to pay the fine, Frank remarked, "A hard cud shee."[69]

Impounding animals was a preoccupation for some people in Belfast, especially in the Puddle Dock area. In 1862, there were about eight cases of impounded cattle—the number of head is not easy to ascertain, as herds, ranging from three to seven cows, were recorded as often as single bovine incidents. Horses more rarely roamed free; pigs infrequently did so; upon occasion, entire sheep flocks were created—individual sheep being led astray by a wandering ewe or ram—only to be impounded. Once, a privately owned stag was taken prisoner.[70]

Irish women made their presence known in the world of "the impound." Ellen Reardon, for example, impounded J.D. Tucker's cow and demanded damages when her cabbages were allegedly stomped and/or chomped by Tucker's cow.[71] The Irish, like true Belfastians, regularly impounded one another's cattle, as well as those of old-timers.[72] Also, like the old-timers, they did not stint at breaking their beasts out of detention: "The cow with small horns belonged to Bryant [sic] McCabe. Said cow was taken out on the night of the 24th of June by the braking [sic] of the lock."[73]

What the Pound keeper's books seem to signify is that women did indeed tend milk cows. (Those women who impounded cows evidently were not frightened by the large animals, knew how to corral them, and were not hesitant to demand damages.) Men took responsibility for steers and oxen, and men (and their sons and male hired hands) were the primary contacts with the local authority. Men of status could generally get their animals out on faith, promising to send the money forthwith: "Dear Sir, Please let Mr. Carter have the steer Mr. Howes impounded and I will settle the bill with you. Yours Truly, William Crosby." Frank, of course, let *his uncle* have his steer. Before we level the charge of nepotism, we need to consider that Frank charged *his brother* full fees when he impounded his brother's cow on the Sabbath.[74] He also extended the courtesy of releasing an impounded cow upon promise of payment the next day to a Mr. Cunningham (perhaps the Irish Cunningham), but Frank was left waiting for the money.[75]

While the immigrants from Ireland regularly impounded one another's animals, they might also make good for one another. For example, Daniel Sweeney paid $1.50 for fines and 75 cents feeding fees on a "herd" of pigs owned by Pat Devaney. Evidently, not everyone was so circumspect about paying for impounded animals: "Sunday, Oct. 25 [1863] the above described black pig was owned by one P____ Moody of Belfast.—Pig was stolen on Saturday Night Oct. 24th, 1863. Due on the pig when stolen $2.50."[76]

Frank's log for Belfast's Pound shows that Irish immigrant women in Belfast had gardens.[77] While an immigrant Irish woman might grow cabbages and have other edibles in her garden, the only reference to gardening by any of the Field women had to do with flowers.[78] It would appear, then, that class and status dictated that field work was a male affair in Belfast by mid-century. Irish male immigrants, working for the local elite, also took over gardening duties. Charles Bellows Hazeltine made a fortune in the California gold fields, returned to Belfast, built a large home in the same neighborhood as the Fields, and built a hothouse. He then employed Irish immigrant Patrick Hanley for the next twenty-seven years as "his gardener and right hand man."[79] (Another wealthy local man, Captain Edwin Herriman, employed an Asian houseboy and an English gardener.)[80] It appears, then, that gardening was "Othered" in some ways over the course of the nineteenth century. The ability to pay someone to do the task somehow elevated the employer. Gardens had become symbolic of class.

Food Preparation

In addition to offering rooms to let, the Field House fed boarders throughout the 1840s to 1860s, so staff included cooks and servers. Abigail often had problems finding good help. She pointed out in her day book when a hired girl was too young, such as Lucy Davis and Elizabeth Cilly, who were both hired and fired in 1842.[81] Abigail did her own baking.[82] Her daughter-in-law Carrie "made sausages."[83] Girls were employed in various household tasks, especially washing clothes. In many references to laundry in Abigail Davis Field's day books, the laundress, in at least two instances, was a widow—and a recent Irish immigrant.[84] Sometimes the young hired girl would assist.[85] Other tasks included clothing manufacture, such as spinning sock yarn.[86] Most girls stayed only a few months in the Field house.[87] The difficulty, for the employer, was to find a girl who had been well schooled in household cleaning, clothing manufacture, including spinning and knitting, as well as sewing, and laundry. These old-fashioned skills evidently were hard to come by. The food served to the boarders at the Field House was basic, and, of course, drew on the area's larder. In April 1841, Abigail reported seven boarders. That June she bought salmon, sugar, eggs, coffee, crackers, "hallaboot [halibut]," salted fish, molasses, and raisins, presumably to serve her guests. By the twentieth of August, she reported "no boarders, save family."[88] In addition to growing many fruits and vegetables, locals made good use of what nature provided. In summer, Frank Field would take his children and any hired girls in residence berrying. The women of the house spent time making currant jelly, *putten* up raspberries, and canning tomatoes. The fall before he died, Frank helped Annie put up peaches, pears, and tomatoes.[89] The Fields kept detailed lists of food items and costs. In the first three months of 1873, when at least the regular boarders were at home, beef, veal, sausages, eggs, clams, chickens, fish, and cheese provided protein. Generally, the Fields did not buy vegetables, given that Frank had an extensive garden. His reports of what the "wimmin folk" put up each year indicated that they also served quite a bit of food from their extensive pantry. They did, however, purchase milk, butter, tea, and coffee, as well as gin, whiskey, and rum. Evidently, they no longer had their own cow for milk and butter. Meal, sugar, nutmeg, pepper, and molasses were bought periodically, as were oranges. They also occasionally bought corn.[90]

Abigail Davis Field hired Irish help off and on, starting with Mrs. Margaret Spinks in 1842. Carrie did, too.[91] Carrie was not especially taken with *a* Briget [sic], whom she dismissed for being "a worthless good for nothing *thief* [emphasis in original]."[92] Frank also employed women from the Irish immigrant community, including Mrs. Hawks [Haugh], possibly Bridget Haugh McCabe's stepmother.[93] On 7 August 1874, Frank reported that after a spate of no hired help, he had "Irish help. Wake in Earnest [sic]—."[94] He was not clear if that fact caused him to become the man of mourning; however, the entry does indicate that he was less than ecstatic with hiring Irish help.

Feminization of Education

Education was a sign of class difference in Belfast. While women who married men of status could read and write, education had been primarily a male affair in the early years of the nineteenth century in Maine. Immigrants from Ireland prior to mid-century would have found little different in that regard. The first academy in Belfast was a wooden structure near downtown. Opened in 1811, it operated off and on until mid-century, males serving as teachers. The teachers all boasted graduation from private colleges, such as Harvard, Bowdoin, Williams, or Middlebury. When the British occupied Belfast during the War of 1812, they housed troops in the building. It was sometimes used for church services until the Unitarians built their own structure, but from 1819 to 1836 it was abandoned. The building was refurbished in 1836, and 152 students enrolled.[95] Abigail's son George, a graduate of Bowdoin, taught at the rededicated facility from 1841 to 1842 and from 1846 to 1847.

By the time of the mid-century Irish Famine, however, teaching was primarily a female occupation in Maine. Indeed, the high school, grammar school, select school, intermediate school, and primary schools in Belfast in 1868 all had women principals and assistants.[96] Teaching was essentially the only "white collar" occupation available to Irish or Irish-American women. S.E. Gammons, twenty-three, and her nineteen-year-old sister Laura J., whose father had been born in Ireland, served as teachers. The feminization of teaching had begun in earnest in the 1840s. The *Third Report of the Board of Education of the State of Maine*, published in 1849, stated that in the Teacher Institutes offered in Belfast 24 October either 1847 (or 1848), one hundred and nine females attended, but only seventy-six males. The numbers varied for other institutes throughout the state, but women generally outnumbered men.[97] Even though the numbers of females in teaching quickly outnumbered those of males, female wages were dismal in comparison. In Waldo County, male teachers earned, on average, $17.67 per month, exclusive of board, while women earned, on average, $5.12 per month (or $1.28 per week), exclusive of board.[98] Female educators could be hired for less than a third of what it cost to employ a male teacher. Teachers were hired through a local agent, who was supposed to check on certifications and to work with local school committees. According to the published report, these two things rarely happened. Agents played favorites when hiring teachers, according to the report. In addition, agents were supposed to provide a list of all possible students, age four through twenty-one, each May. The budget was set up based on such lists; however, the report asserted that some agents lied; others gave total numbers of students, but didn't provide a list of names, with the result that it was nearly impossible to tell who was in school and who wasn't.[99] It cost 86 cents per student per year, or $14.62, for a complete education from age four through twenty-one, according to the report.[100]

The 1850 U.S. census recorded all those in a household twenty and older who were illiterate. It also kept track of who had been to school. Of the 133 Irish-born individuals in Belfast over age twenty, only sixteen were listed as illiterate. The number of illiterate immigrants *may* have been higher. Only a few had been to school, presumably in Ireland: Matilda McGuire, thirty, and her two children, Patrick, ten, and Michael, eight. It is not clear if the two boys were in school in Belfast.

Ellen and Michael Reardon had been in school the previous year. She was twenty-four and he thirty-two. Their two-year-old son had been born in Ireland. Anne Sullivan, twenty-six, too, had been in school during the previous year. Her husband, Daniel, worked as a laborer and was listed as illiterate. The Sullivans had four children, the two eldest, ages eight and six, had been born in Ireland. The five- and three-year-olds were both born in Maine. Obviously, if the three adults had been in school in the previous year, they would have had to have done so in the United States. Of the remaining twenty-eight Irish-born children between the ages of four and twenty-one, only four were in school and two of those were from the same family.

In eighteenth-century Ireland, girls' education was an afterthought, no matter what their socioeconomic class.[101] Women were not allowed to get university degrees until 1879.[102] Public primary education became available in Ireland as early as 1831, the first in the British Isles, although it came with a political price tag. The government, centered in London, sought to end traditional Irish culture and the school materials available emphasized British values: "School materials presented 'Paddy' and 'Bridey' as intellectually incompetent, violent, drunken, and slovenly, drifting into poverty because of early marriage and indiscriminate reproduction."[103] In other words, the cultural stereotypes of the eighteenth and nineteenth centuries were employed by British colonial authorities in Ireland. Literacy rates did not rise in Ireland until the late nineteenth century. As late as 1871, 37.5 percent of men who married and 45.2 percent of women who married marked marriage certificates with an "X." Those percentages dropped dramatically in the next thirty years, so that by 1901, only 13.2 percent of men and 10.7 percent of women signed their marriage certificates with "X." Irish census data from 1841 show that more than half of males fifteen through twenty-four could read and write and 75 percent of females could.[104] Irish girls, unable to find employment, devoted more time to their school work and shed illiteracy at a faster rate than Irish boys.[105] Girls' literacy allowed them to succeed in United States (and other countries') urban areas; however, while Irish-born women were not literate, their daughters raised in the United States were.[106] Rising literacy rates in Ireland came too late to aid the Irish women who found themselves in Belfast in 1860.

Rural Social Norms

For all the evidence that Irish immigrant women worked for wages— considered an anomaly, or deviant—in urban areas, there is no evidence to show that working women in Belfast were considered outside community norms. Irish immigrant women in Belfast would have found themselves among people who shared a great many of their cultural norms. A closer inspection of two representative women highlights subtle differences: We have already met both women—Abigail Davis Field and Bridget Haugh McCabe. While not of the same generation, they show us old-timer versus newcomer differences and similarities (or vice versa).

Bridget Haugh McCabe, the woman who inspired this study, is a measuring stick of sorts. In what ways was she different from Belfast contemporaries? In what ways was she similar? What set her apart as Irish? Was it simply a matter of her having been born in Ireland, or did she practice cultural norms that were different from those usually practiced in Belfast? If Bridget is to represent "Irish woman," who better to serve as her foil than Abigail Davis Field, a woman who lived in Belfast from the opening of the nineteenth century to the Civil War era?

Abigail Davis Field, born in Billerica, Massachusetts, moved to Belfast in 1807 upon her marriage at age twenty to a man thirteen years older than she. Unlike illiterate Bridget Haugh McCabe, she left behind day books and letters, so we have access to her thoughts on family, work, religion, and politics. Her husband, Bohan Prentice Field, was born in

Northfield, Massachusetts, moving to Maine in 1801 to become Belfast's first lawyer.[107] In fact, Abigail Davis met Field in Belfast when she visited her sister Sally, who had married Belfast's second lawyer, William Crosby, himself from Billerica; thus, we see friendship and family circles brought these people together in a place where they had chosen to live and to help create the character of a small city.[108] The frontier aspect is what drew the young lawyers, Field and Crosby, to the shores of Penobscot Bay. Here they hoped to make their fortunes. The migratory Davis sisters from Billerica evidently were adventuresome enough to join these men in the enterprise.

Forty or so years later, Bridget Haugh came to the area from Ireland. She was poor and illiterate. Evidently, she emigrated from Ireland to Maine with her father, Thomas Haugh. Her mother does not appear in any records. Either the mother died before the father and daughter arrived in Belfast, or the mother simply did not live long enough to be noted by statisticians. Once again, however, we see evidence of family circles at work: Thomas had a brother with a family in Belfast.

Bridget's Uncle Charles Haugh and his wife "Margarett [sic]" were born in Ireland; however, according to the U.S. census taker, their eldest son, John, age 18 in 1850, had been born in Maine, meaning Charles had either immigrated long before the Irish Famine, probably before 1832, or the census recorder misidentified John as Maine-born. Charles Haugh was not recorded as a resident of Belfast in the 1840 U.S. census. Ostensibly, Charles Haugh could have lived elsewhere in Maine before coming to Belfast.

Bridget's Uncle Charles was most likely in a second marriage, as his next eldest child was ten years younger than son John. While this is not irrefutable proof of a new marriage, the fact that six children were born in Belfast, all two or three years apart, seems to make that a plausible scenario. If Uncle Charles had indeed immigrated in the 1830s, that might explain why in 1850 he possessed real estate valued at $1,000 and lived in a detached home with his family and a twenty-year-old female named Mary Burke. (Burke may have been a relative and/or boarder, or even a live-in domestic.) By 1860, Charles Haugh had amassed $2,000 in real estate and $500 in personal wealth and had six children at home.[109]

While Charles Haugh appears to have achieved economic success in America, Bridget's father was not so fortunate. Thomas Haugh, given the Police Court evidence, had a drinking problem. Perhaps his later arrival or his difficulties with alcohol kept him economically impoverished, for he and his new wife lived in what might have been a boarding or apartment house for Irish immigrants, according to the 1850 census. Thomas Haugh owned nothing and possessed no personal wealth. He and his new wife lived in the same building as Henry and Sarah Gowan, both Irish-born, and their two small children who had been born in Maine.[110] Thomas Haugh and his new Belfast bride,

Bridget Dorson, twenty years his junior, formed a separate household in the same building.[111] Daughter Bridget, even though she did not marry Brian McCabe until 1853, is never mentioned in the census materials. So Bridget's arrival in Belfast is unclear. Perhaps she came separately. Or, perhaps when the census evaluator came through, she was living as a domestic elsewhere in town.

Both women—Abigail and Bridget—then, were embarked on an adventure when they moved into the area. Bridget was sixteen when she married; Abigail twenty. Both had family in the area. The differences, however, if ignoring ethnicity, started with status and its outward signs.

Bridget Haugh McCabe was illiterate and had earned no status upon marriage, for she married a widowed, Irish-born laborer with three stepchildren and a biological child. Brian McCabe had been single in 1849 when he married Irish immigrant widow Margaret Spinks, who had three children. He and the widow Spinks had one son together; then she died under mysterious circumstances. Shortly thereafter he married Bridget.[112]

Her father Thomas and his new wife, also named Bridget (nee Dorson), had two sons during the next decade, so Bridget Haugh McCabe had two half-brothers young enough to have been her own sons.[113] The men in her immediate family had no property or livelihood other than as laborers. In an era when women gained status from the men in their lives, Bridget Haugh McCabe gained nothing other than the fruits of a day laborer's wages. Brian McCabe had a reputation in Belfast by the 1850s—and not a good one. His name recurs throughout legal documents. Benjamin Brown accused him of "maletious trespass [sic]" before the Court of County Commissioners. McCabe wasn't prosecuted.[114] He was, however, fined a dollar and $5.04 in costs for drunkenness on 4 July 1853.[115] "Bridget Haugh," perhaps his wife, or his step-mother-in-law Bridget Dorson Haugh, had McCabe arrested for drunkenness. He was arraigned 13 January 1858. He pleaded not guilty and was acquitted.[116]

Ironically, comparisons of the two women show few differences besides the major one of status. Abigail married a man thirteen years her senior. She gave birth to nine children over a thirteen-year period, all but two of whom lived into adulthood. Her first child was born in 1809, two years after her marriage. From 1811 until 1815, she gave birth to five children. After a three-year gap, she gave birth to three more children—each two years apart.

Bridget was fifteen to sixteen years younger than Brian McCabe and only sixteen when she married.[117] They had three children during their nine-year marriage: The first child was born in 1854, one year after her marriage. There was a four-year gap before a second child was born in 1858. The third child was born in 1860. We do not know if there were other pregnancies. But, Bridget also had stepchildren, at least two of whom lived in the house. If not working created lady status—rather than status or longevity in a community—Bridget should have been considered higher on the social ladder: She apparently did not have to work for wages after marriage.[118]

If Abigail had looked out the windows of her large home toward Penobscot Bay, she would have had a panoramic view of Puddle Dock, where Bridget lived in rough quarters. Some of Bridget's extended family (Haugh is also spelled Hough, Hock(s), Huff, Hawkes, or Hawk) lived in Puddle Dock, a rough-and-tumble area near the docks, at the bottom of the hill, where wharf rats wandered up and effluvium of the wealthy ran down. Most of the Puddle Dock men were day laborers or sailors. While Abigail may have paused in her cooking, cleaning, and supervising of girls, the fact remains, she was hard at work earning revenue. As boss, the one paying the wages, Abigail had status; at the same time, however, there is no evidence that Bridget worked for money to supplement her husband's day-laborer income. (While her husband's first and fourth wives did work as laundresses, they did so while unmarried.)

Brian McCabe's first wife, Margaret Spinks, had worked for Abigail Davis Field. As the widow Spinks with three children, she needed work. Abigail hired her as a laundress in 1842. Nowhere in Abigail's day book does she discuss how long Mrs. Spinks worked for her, starting on 19 September 1842, but had she worked as laundress for any length of time, she probably stopped working outside the home upon her marriage to Brian McCabe in 1849.[119]

Another aspect of how "status" set the two women apart was their families' positions in regards to the law. Abigail's family enforced the laws, which gave the Fields positions of authority and status. Her husband had been a lawyer; one of her sons became one. Another ran the local Academy, later becoming a well-known minister. Bridget came from a family whose members were always in the Police Court dockets—on the receiving end of law enforcement. Bridget's father was frequently charged with assault and battery, drunkenness, and, at least once, with receiving stolen goods.[120] Other male relatives, including a nephew, were also regularly listed in the Police Court docket. These "evils" coalesced into a veritable universe of "Otherness" in Belfast, Maine, in the mid-nineteenth century, where not a century before, the recently arrived Ulster Irish, coming by way of Londonderry, New Hampshire, shared many of the same cultural traits. In fact, Abigail Davis Field's nephew, William George Crosby, regaled readers with his written *Annals of Belfast*, wherein he described the drunken mayhem in the Belfast of just fifty years earlier.

Even Bridget's Uncle Charles, with his real estate and personal wealth, had to contend with the locals and their laws. His eleven-year-old son Henry was found guilty of throwing stones on 30 April 1853, fined, and stayed in jail until 3 May 1853, when his father finally paid the $1 fine and $5.05 in costs. Henry had entered a guilty plea, but, Judge Williamson recorded, he could not pay the fine and costs. Keeping a child in jail for throwing stones seems harsh. Given the fact that Charles Haugh did not come up with $6.05 in cash for three days might indicate that cash was not readily at hand, real estate values to the contrary—or that he was teaching Henry a lesson. To put the fine into context, the cost for public drunkenness ranged from $1 to $10, plus costs.

In comparison, in another juvenile court case from just five years earlier, boys from the judge's own social class stole tar barrels, which they intended to light for a bonfire on the Fourth of July. What was their punishment? They were ordered to post bonds and to stay away from tar barrels for a year. No one was incarcerated, even though the boys had feared that eventuality. Evidently, their families had no difficulty covering the fines and costs.[121] Women, too, appeared in the Police Court. In fact, the court found Bridget Haugh McCabe guilty of assault and fined her $3 plus $5.64 in costs when Ann Welch, another Irish immigrant, accused her.[122]

The house where Bridget lived contained three families: The Widow Sweeney and two teenage children; Bridget and her family (husband and five children); and building owners Levi and Mary Butler.[123] The Butlers were locals. The house and its inhabitants would have been well known to authorities, given that Levi Butler and his tenants were involved in the Police Court Docket thirty-nine times out of nearly two thousand cases.

Levi Butler himself had been convicted of assault, violation of liquor laws, and drunkenness. His first liquor law violation got him a $20 fine and time in jail.[124] Levi's wife, Mary, was also convicted of "selling intoxicating liquor" and fined $20 and costs.[125] The building was searched and the liquor confiscated 15 January 1859.[126] Levi was convicted and sentenced for "violation of liquor law" 12 November 1860.[127] He was sentenced a second time for another infraction and fined another $20.[128] Spending $60 in fines and about $15 in fees in a little over one year, and lost work time spent in jail, should have been incredibly prohibitive. Levi and Mary Butler continued the operation, indicating the rewards far outweighed the cost of the deterrents.

Butler, and perhaps his tenants, was involved in the liquor trade in the 1850s, which was illegal in Maine from 1851 to 1856, the first state to ban liquor sales. One indication that the tenants may have been involved was Mrs. Sweeney, who had been a widow for years, did not work outside the home (at least, not work that was recorded), nor did her two teenage children. How could they afford this? How did Brian McCabe make enough money as a day laborer to support his household and pay a number of fines and court costs over the years? Or, did his money come from an illegal source, such as manufacturing liquor? In 1856, even though the Maine Law had been repealed, only licensed liquor purveyors were allowed to sell spirits. The Butlers, obviously, were not licensed.

Abigail and Bridget were Christians. Abigail Davis Field attended church regularly, overseeing a Sabbath school and ensuring that her children were brought up in the church:

> The thought of my heart then was—I will never seak [sic] great things for my children—I will cherish no anxieties to see them rich and honoured and elivated [sic] to the high places of Earth, but all that I will ask will be to see them the subdued and regenerated children of God—to see them set in Heavenly places in Christ Jesus fitted for humble usefulness and numbered with the saints in glory everlasting.[129]

Abigail's Christian practice was a daily activity, and her children were dutifully inculcated in Protestant tenets. In fact, her son George became a well-known minister.[130]

Bridget was Catholic, as evidenced by the fact that her first-born son with Brian McCabe was baptized by Father Bixio, S.J.[131] There are no written records that her other children were baptized. Her daughter, still a toddler when Bridget died, evidently self-identified as Catholic, however. In 1877, there was a flurry of activity when the Catholic hierarchy feared a lack of priests would lead to a lack of faith. So, two years after the Most Reverend James Augustus Healy, D.C., became bishop of the Portland diocese, one of his first acts was to create the parish of Winterport-Bucksport-Belfast.[132] The parish's first resident priest, the Reverend Jeremiah McCarthy, conducted a number of infant baptisms in Belfast that year. The new parents, many of whom had not been confirmed, became a project for the new bishop. In his first visit to Belfast as Bishop, he presided over the confirmations of six dozen people.[133] Those adults included Thomas Haugh, most likely Bridget Haugh McCabe's cousin, born in 1854, as well as Bridget's daughter Margaret Anne McCabe, who in 1877 would have been between seventeen and eighteen years old.[134] Ever active in support of the Catholic church, merchant William Brannagan served as sponsor, as did a [Mary] Clarence. At least two were adult converts: Nineteen-year-old Joseph Robert Jennings and twenty-five-year-old Mary M. Clark.[135] Why were these adults not baptized as children? Perhaps, given the fact that Belfast had no full-time priest in residence until the 1890s, it would have been too difficult; however, the area was served regularly by priests from better established parishes. Brannagan always offered one of his properties for Mass, beginning in the 1840s, so the difficulty factor seems specious.[136] Bridget, on the other hand, did not seem to mark her Irishness by any obvious Catholic observance.[137] This, too, would not have been unusual in Ireland, as generally less than half of all Irish Catholics attended Mass regularly in 1834—the percentages were even lower in the west of Ireland.[138]

Yankee Abigail Davis Field and Irishwoman Bridget Haugh McCabe were not that different from one another. Each was young when she married. Each married a man substantially older than she. Each had several children. Field moved north from Massachusetts; McCabe emigrated from Ireland. We could argue that *both* women were migrants to Belfast.

When Bridget died on 4 January 1861, she made her mark on the public consciousness of Belfast. Her death under mysterious circumstances garnered her a place in the public histories, but that fame—or notoriety—was fleeting. There is no recorded grave for Bridget Haugh McCabe in Belfast's Grove Cemetery. (Her widower, Brian McCabe, however, was buried in the plot owned by James/Jamie, one of his sons with Bridget.) While Brian did not receive a grave marker, his remains are noted as being in the plot, Lot 10, in the "new" part of the cemetery. Abigail Davis Field, on the other hand, was buried with pomp in the "old" family plot in 1863. She is surrounded by her children, including Frank and his two wives.

The obvious distinction between the two was the status of the men they married. Field's husband was an educated professional; McCabe married an illiterate day laborer. Field could read and write; McCabe could not. Field was Protestant; McCabe, Catholic. Those categories, however, did not have as much influence over their social spheres as did class and status, which might have dictated their religious affiliation, education, marriage, and career options. Both women helped create Belfast.

Notes

1 William George Crosby, "Annals of Belfast for Half a Century," in *Early Histories of Belfast, Maine*, ed. Alan Taylor (Camden, Maine: Picton Press, 1989), 191.
2 Bruchey, Stuart, *Enterprise: The Dynamic Economy of a Free People* (Cambridge: Harvard University Press, 1990), 48.
3 Joseph Williamson, *The History of the City of Belfast, Maine*, Vol. 1 (Somersworth, New Hampshire: New England History Press, 1982), 682.
4 Williamson, Vol. 1, 682, note 1.
5 Crosby, 47.
6 Crosby, 15.
7 Joseph Williamson and Alfred Johnson, *The History of the City of Belfast, Maine*, Vol. 2 (Somersworth, New Hampshire: New England History Press, 1983), 129.
8 Barbara Welter, "The Cult of True Womanhood: 1820-1860," *American Quarterly*, 18, no. 2 Part 1 (Summer 1966): 151-174. Downloaded from JSTOR, 10 June 2020.
9 Abigail Davis Field Day Book, 2 September 1841 (unpublished), courtesy of the Belfast Historical Society and Museum.
10 Abigail Davis Field Day Book, September 1841.
11 Abigail Davis Field Day Book. The eggs were purchased sometime between February and April 1842—Abigail Davis Field's dating was not consistent.
12 Abigail Davis Field Day Book, 1 October 1842, "Catherine Craig worked

for me to pay her tuition at the academy. Three dollars and sixty-seven cents." Craig had worked at the house in 1841 as well, "Settled with Catherine Craig this 28th of June 1841 due Catherine 36 cents," "[Catherine] commenced work from 22nd [of July through the] 26th of August 1841—4.59 4.52."

13 Abigail Davis Field Day Book. The $1.50 and $1.95 payments are undated.
14 Abigail Davis Field Day Book, 12 September 1841.
15 Abigail Davis Field Day Book, May 1841, "Commenced doing Mr. Moulton's washing the last week in May 1841...1 June 1841 Sent my washing to Mrs. Bond."
16 Samuel Moulton arrived in Belfast after the War of 1812 (1822), when there was an influx of young professional men into the then-village. He and a partner, William I. Cross, opened Cross & Moulton, a tin plate and sheet-iron works, in 1823, on Main Street. That business lasted one year. By 1836 he was involved in the launch of Belfast Bank, which managed to survive, and seemingly flourish even through the financial crisis of 1837. See Williamson, Vol. 1, 568 and 702.
17 Abigail Davis Field Day Book, 15 April 1841, "Mr. Felch came here to board. 16th 7 boarders."
18 Williamson, Vol. 1, 385.
19 Boarders—many of whom came year after year—were drawn from the worlds of politics, legal system, and commerce. For example, a regular was Hugh Johnston Anderson, former Member of Congress (1837–1841) and three-time former governor of Maine in the 1840s. The boarding house was the focal point of Anderson's extended family—his widowed mother, some of his adult children joined him and his wife there, for example. Their comings and goings were all recorded by Field in his day books. For Anderson biography, see Williamson, Vol. 1, 203–204 and Vol. 2, 408.
20 Abigail Davis Field Day Book, 9 October 1841.
21 Abigail Davis Field Day Book. Abigail Davis Field sold cream and milk to Mrs. Johnson.
22 Margaret Lynch-Brennan, *The Irish Bridget: Irish Immigrant Women in Domestic Service in America, 1840–1930* (Syracuse: Syracuse University Press, 2009), 4.
23 Gearóid Ó Tuathaigh, "The Role of Women in Ireland under the New English Order," in *Women in Irish Society: The Historical Dimension*, ed. Margaret MacCurtain and Donncha Ó Corráin (Westport, Connecticut: Greenwood Press, 1979), 28.
24 Mary E. Daly, "Women, Work and Trade Unionism," in *Women in Irish Society: The Historical Dimension*, ed. Margaret MacCurtain and Donncha Ó Corráin (Westport, Connecticut: Greenwood Press, 1979), 71.
25 Janet Nolan, "Woman's Place in the History of the Irish Diaspora: A Snapshot," in *Journal of American Ethnic History*, 28, no. 4 (Summer 2009), 79.
26 Hasia Diner, *Erin's Daughters in America: Irish Immigrant Women in the Nineteenth Century* (Baltimore: The Johns Hopkins University Press, 1983), 377.
27 1860 U.S. census.
28 1820 Belfast census.
29 Belfast Vital Statistics, volume 2.
30 Abigail Davis Field Day Book. Abigail kept track of the eggs she sold to Mrs. R.C. Johnson in 1842, as well as the 1 pint of cream: 30 April 1842. Benjamin Franklin Field Day Book, 8 March 1866. Frank took care of the pigs.

31 Timothy W. Guinnane, *The Vanishing Irish: Households, Migration, and the Rural Economy in Ireland, 1850-1914* (Princeton: Princeton University Press, 1997), 37 and 54.

32 Benjamin Franklin (Frank) Field Pound Keeper Day Book, unpublished (courtesy of Belfast Historical Society and Museum). While Frank's Day Book cannot possibly account for all animals in Belfast, it does make clear that the Irish owned cattle: John Collins (Irishman) owned a "greyish cow," a red heifer with white flanks, and a white heifer; Charles Haugh owned a hornless red and white cow and a buffalo; Pat Devaney owned pigs; T. Owens owned a red cow; Michael Gannon owned a dark brindle cow and two bright red cows; John Gannon owned a red cow; Thomas Logan had a cow; John Cunningham owned a gray heifer and a red cow; John Mahoney owned a red heifer; Bryant [*sic*] McCabe owned a cow with small horns, a large red cow, and a pair of dark red oxen.

33 Benjamin Franklin Field, Pound Keepers Day Book. A number of pigs were impounded 6 September 1862. The pigs belonged to Pat Devaney. Frank Field promised to waive charges and agreed to feed the pigs; all Devaney had to do was pay the forfeiture. Daniel Sweeney paid the bill, $1.50 forfeiture and 75 cents for feeding the pigs twice that day.

34 Abigail Davis Field Day Book, 14 February 1863, "Mr. Collins painting two rooms."

35 For example, Annie Tobey Field gave birth to a baby girl in January 1871 at the age of 41. She took three weeks to recuperate before "taken [*sic*] up [her] family duty." In May of that year, Frank helped the "wimmin" redecorate, which he found onerous, recording the days he spent doing women's work: 13 May 1871 "Painted the Dining Room"; 15 May 1871 "Paper the Dining Room"; 16 May 1871 "Papered the East room up stairs [*sic*]"; 17 May 1871 "Making myself useful to the wimmin"; 18 May 1871 "Still helping the wife clean house"; 19 May 1871 "Putting down carpets, curtains, etc."; 21 May 1871 "household duties kept me from church"; 23 May 1871 "Sowed my late peas" Finished House Cleaning [emphasis in original]. He papered the kitchen 1 July that year, too.

36 Crosby, 70 and 78. Phoebe Sager was a milliner and dressmaker before 1827. She published notification she was leaving town in 1829. Her husband was later convicted and hanged for her murder in 1834.

37 *The Republican Journal*, 22 October 1840, 3.

38 Miss Conner may have been the daughter of William H. Conner, a merchant from Sandwich, New Hampshire, who died in 1827. Williamson, Vol. 1, 538.

39 *The Republican Journal*, 22 October 1840, 3.

40 1850 census.

41 Nolan, 31.

42 Daly, "Women, Work and Trade Unionism," 71.

43 *The Republican Journal*, 21 April 1843, 1, column 4.

44 *The Republican Journal*, 5 May 1843, 3, column 3.

45 *The Republican Journal*, 12 May 1843, 1, column 2, bottom.

46 *The Republican Journal*, 12 May 1843, 2, column 3.

47 *The Republican Journal*, 6 June 1843, 2, columns 1 and 2.

48 *The Republican Journal*, 7 July 1843, 2, column 6.

49 *The Republican Journal*, 27 October 1843, 1, column 6.

50 Crosby, 7.

51 *Hancock Gazette and Penobscot Patriot*, 1, no. 32, 8 February 1821, and II, no. 33, 13 February 1822.

52 *Hancock Gazette and Penobscot Patriot*, II, no. 2, 4 July 1821.
53 Crosby, 7.
54 Field family day books.
55 Field family day books.
56 Caroline Tobey Field Day Books. Anna (also called Annie), the second wife, was not a diarist. In the year after Frank's death, she attempted to keep up his day book, but entire months would elapse with only one or two entries. Frank originally had taken over the day book of his first wife to work out his grief and mourning after her death. Carrie had taken over the books from her mother-in-law Abigail. Annie noted boarders and events sporadically—there are a handful of entries about her two biological children and her stepchildren.
57 Benjamin Franklin (Frank) Field Day Book, 5 August 1864. Emphasis in the original.
58 This is conjecture, but the U.S. census lists a William McCabe as head of household in the 1840 census. There is another unnamed male in the house in 1840 and the approximate age would be appropriate. The last bit of evidence is that Brian McCabe named his first-born son William A. McCabe.
59 Abigail Davis Field Day Book, 14 February 1862, "Mr. Collins painting two rooms"; Benjamin Franklin Field Day Book: 17 November 1871, "Bought a cow of Irishman Collins pd 20"; Abigail Davis Field Day Book. In 1862 Frank had paid $35 for a cow, which his mother remarked upon, 22 May 1862. The difference in cost may have been tied to the war economy, or Collins may have decided that constantly paying fines and fees for one of his cows that, evidently, could not be kept out of people's property was too expensive.
60 J.E. "Eyebrook" or "Ibrook" Collins, painter, appears in the 1850 U.S. census for Belfast. John Collins, Irishman, appears in the 1860 U.S. census for Belfast.
61 Belfast Pound Records, unpublished, courtesy of Belfast Historical Society and Museum.
62 Belfast Pound Records: both cows were impounded repeatedly—24 June 1853; 2 July 1853; 17 August 1853; and 19 September 1853. The first three incidents cost McCabe 75 cents each time. The September incident led to A.L. Leighten demanding $5 damages. McCabe objected. Field appointed referees who appraised Leighten's claimed damage and recommended $1. The pair of oxen damaged three different home owners' property—D.L. Harmon, $5; L.D. Haraden, $5; and E. Loud, $3. The pound fee was $1. The total of $14 "was paid by Bryant McCabe."
63 The U.S. census collector notes the house number and lists three separate households, with three separate numbers, in the same building.
64 Pound Keeper's Book, 19 September 1853.
65 Pound Keeper's Book, 19 July 1853.
66 Pound Keeper's Book, 10 October 1853.
67 Pound Keeper's Book, 119 and 131.
68 Frank Field tried out different ways of keeping records. The brouhaha with Dr. Monroe appears as case 113, 25 August 1854. Dr. Monroe impounded seven head. A Mr. Ephraim Swett, acting for Mrs. Rowe, took out the cows and left the team of oxen as security. It took seven days to resolve the dispute, which ended up costing $17.94 total, even with the reduced damages: $5.25 (pound costs for impound); $2.82 (fees for appraisers); 50 cents (warrant); $5 (feeding and watering oxen for 7 days); $1

(damages); $3 (fees on cows); 37 cents (watering cows). Herbert Rowe paid all charges.

69 Belfast Pound Books for 1853, 131.

70 The totals are taken from the Belfast Pound Keeper's Books.

71 Belfast Pound Keeper's Book, 20 October 1862. Tucker objected and did his own appraisal, which was generally not allowed: "I have called on the Irish madam that impounded my cow. She said I could have my cow by paying your bill for impounding. You said it was 50 cents—I send the amount by the bearer of this note. You will please deliver him the cow. I examined the *not* injured cabbages. She had not injured her property one cent. The tub stove in by the mill is good as new. Yours respectfully, J.D. Tucker."

72 Pound Keeper's Book. John Collins (Irishman) and John Cunningham, also from Ireland, took turns incarcerating one another's animals in 1863. In 1853, Daniel Sheehan impounded cows owned by Mr. E. Burgess and Mr. John Lane. Sheehan demanded $10 in damages. Cornelius Dorathey [*sic*] demanded 25 cents for damage caused by Nehemiah Abbott's cow.

73 Pound Keeper's Book. Breaking the lock was a local pastime: E. Wilson was charged with breaking it 21 August 1853. Not even a month later, on 13 September 1853, Herbert Pitcher, the son of William Pitcher, owner of "said cows" busted out his dad's cows. The lock was broken and two cows taken yet again in late September. The lock was broken three more times before year's end: 10 October, 14 October, and 17 December.

74 Brother Bohan Field Jr., fearing he would be late for church, left the cow roaming. Frank wryly remarked that he hoped his brother had gotten his money's worth of preaching.

75 Pound Keeper's Book, 131. Frank did not make clear if this Mr. Cunningham was one of the two men recently emigrated from Ireland of that name, or a member of the Cunningham family that had been in the community for decades, arriving as early as 1820.

76 Pound Keeper's Book, 24 September 1863.

77 J.D. Tucker sent a note to Pound Keeper Frank Field 20 October 1862, obviously upset that the "Irish madam" had impounded his cow.

78 Caroline Tobey Field's Day Book entry, 4 June 1864, "Mary Field came for geranium leaves."

79 Megan Pinette, "The Gardeners of Old Belfast," *Belfast Historical Society & Museum News*, 5, no. 1 (Summer 2016), 1.

80 Pinette, "Gardeners," 1.

81 Abigail Davis Field Day Book. Lucy Davis lasted only one day: "Lucy Davis came here to do my work Quit [*sic*] to [*sic*] yong [*sic*]," Elizabeth Cilly made it three days in the house: 2 January 1842, "Elizabeth Cilly came to live with me." Abigail marked her leaving 5 January 1842 with "My Cilly girl gone home. Not old enough to do any work." "The last hired girl *stole a water proof*," [emphasis in original] declared an outraged Frank Field 20 November 1866.

82 Abigail Davis Field Day Book, 3 April 1841, "Did not bake as usual a very windy unpleasant day."

83 Caroline W. (Tobey) Field, 15 January 1864 (unpublished), courtesy of the Belfast Historical Society and Museum.

84 Abigail Davis Field Day Book. Widow Margaret Spinks did laundry for Mrs. Field at least once, 19 September 1842. Caroline W. (Tobey) Field Day Book. Twenty-two years later, 15 May 1864, Carrie reports that "Mrs. Haney washing."

85 Abigail Davis Field Day Book, 21 September 1841, "Mrs. Felch and Hannah [Ratliff] washing."

86 Abigail Davis Field Day Book, 21 October 1841, "Hannah [Ratliff] spinning stocking yarn."

87 Abigail Davis Field Day Book. Hannah Ratliff started work at the Field House 13 September. By 27 December 1841, Mrs. Field reports that "Hannah gone to live somewhere else."

88 Abigail Davis Field Day Book.

89 Benjamin Franklin (Frank) Field Day Book. Frank died in early 1877.

90 Benjamin Franklin (Frank) Field Day Book, "House Expenses for 1873."

91 Carolyn Tobey Field Day Book, 16 May 1864 (unpublished), courtesy of the Belfast Historical Society and Museum.

92 Abigail Davis Field Day Book, 18 May 1863.

93 Benjamin Franklin Field Day Book, 21 February and 26 April 1872. "Mrs. Hawks supersedes Miss Greer," yet by 26 April, Miss Greer is back, doing the washing.

94 Benjamin Franklin Field Day Book, 7 August 1874.

95 Williamson, Vol. 1, 331–332.

96 Belfast Directory, published in 1868.

97 *Third Report of the Board of Education of the State of Maine* (Augusta: William T. Johnson, printer to the State, 1849), 29.

98 *Third Report of the Board of Education*, 37.

99 *Third Report of the Board of Education*, 18 and 64–66.

100 *Third Report of the Board of Education*, 6.

101 O'Tuathaigh, 31.

102 O'Tuathaigh, 35.

103 Nolan, 38.

104 Guinnane, 65.

105 Nolan, 39.

106 David M. Katzman, *Seven Days a Week: Women and Domestic Service in Industrializing America* (New York: Oxford University Press, 1978), 231.

107 Williamson, Vol. 1, 385.

108 Maine did not become a separate state until 1820, as part of the Missouri Compromise.

109 U.S. census for 1850 and 1860.

110 Janet A. Nolan, *Ourselves Alone: Women's Emigration from Ireland 1885–1920* (Lexington: University of Kentucky Press, 1989), 79. Estimates are that 15 percent of Irish-American households had at least two lodgers in 1900.

111 1850 U.S. census.

112 Brian McCabe married Margaret Spinks, widow, 16 June 1849; however, Spinks had been resident in Belfast since at least 1842, for Abigail Davis Field hired her to do laundry 19 September of that year (Abigail Davis Field, Day Book). McCabe married Bridget Haugh 16 October 1853.

113 1860 U.S. census.

114 Court of County Commissioners, March term AD 1854, Book B set, State v Bryan McCabe, Case #361.

115 Police Court Docket.

116 Police Court Docket, Case #318.

117 Bryan [*sic*] McCabe became a naturalized U.S. citizen on 15 May 1868. His records indicate he was born in 1822 in Co. Cavan, Ireland, arriving in the United States via Eastport, Maine in 1839. James Moorhead and Michael Casey served as his witnesses. When he married Bridget Haugh 16 October

1853, he was 31 and she 16. Superior Judicial Court, Belfast, Waldo County records.

118 Nolan, *Ourselves Alone*, 80. Married women were frowned upon in the work force as they were seen as taking jobs from men and single girls.

119 Abigail Davis Field Day Book, 19 September 1842.

120 Police Court Docket, Cases #224, #284, #295, #381, #504, #602, #901, #950, and #959.

121 Crosby, 161.

122 Police Court Docket, Case #507.

123 Williamson, Vol. II, 179-182 and the 1860 census.

124 Police Court Docket, Cases #326, #609, and #594.

125 Police Court Docket, Case #424.

126 Police Court Docket, Case #425.

127 Police Court Docket, Case #554.

128 Police Court Docket, Case #609.

129 Abigail Davis Field Day Book, 1841.

130 George Warren Field served a church in Bangor. Abigail Davis Field made multiple commentaries on family, friends, and acquaintances who were dying and speculated whether they, to use the vernacular of our time, were right with Jesus.

131 Personal email from Richard D. Kelly, Jr., 19 October 2006.

132 Baptismal Records August 23, 1877-September 19, 1908: Winterport-Bucksport-Belfast (unpublished). Jeremiah McCarthy was the first resident priest (courtesy St. Brendan the Navigator Catholic Church, Camden, Maine). Winterport is the second largest town in Waldo County, Belfast being the largest. Bucksport is located across the Penobscot River in Hancock County.

133 William Leo Lucey, S.J., *The Catholic Church in Maine* (Francestown, New Hampshire: Marshall Jones, 1957), 210.

134 Baptismal Records August 23, 1877-September 19, 1908: Winterport-Bucksport-Belfast (unpublished). These records are kept at St. Brendan the Navigator Catholic Church in Camden, Maine. The frontspiece declares that there are a total of 73: 30 males and 43 females; however, actual count shows 28 male and 42 female names. At least one of those may have been a convert, as Joseph Robert Jennings was baptized as well as confirmed that day. Males confirmed: Thomas Buldoc, James Casey (1), James Casey (2), Thomas Crowell, William Cunningham, Michael Fahey, Michael Fogerty [sic], Patrick Haney, James Haney, John Hanley, Patrick Hanley, Thomas Haugh, John Hill, Francis Joseph Hogan, John Hogan, Joseph Robert Jennings, Michael Kane, James Noonan, Thomas Noonan, Charles O'Connell, Michael O'Connell, Michael O'Leary, Thomas O'Leary, Charles Owens, Daniel Sheehan, John Ward, Michael Ward, and Peter Ward; females confirmed: Catherine Francis [sic], Mary, and Sarah Jane Boyle; Ellen Callinan; Frances Maria, Margaret Ellen, Mary, and Mary Agnes Casey; Johanna Collins; Margaret [Higgins?] Dilworth; Mary, Sarah, and Sarah Ann Fogarty; Mary Agnes Gammon; Mary Hanley; Bridget and Mary Ann Hershian; Ellen and Jane Hogan; Catherine Mary and Mary Kane; Sarah Laura Kelley; Mary Ann Lynsky; Annate [Annette?] Lyons; Margaret Anne McCabe [Bridget Haugh McCabe's daughter]; Bridget Agnes Morriss/Norris; Hanorah O'Connell; Margaret Gabrielle, Mary, and Mary Ellen Owens; Catherine Preston; Annie Evilena, Mary Mathilda, and Susan Russell; Hanorah and Ellen Sheehan; Ellen Nora Strong; Catherine Frances, Julia Agnes, and Margaret Mary Sullivan; Rosaline Sylvester; and Celia Ward.

135 "Jennings 1877 October 7th Joseph Robert Jennings born at Belfast July 4th 1858 of Joseph Jennings and Elizabeth Robbins his wife was baptized at Belfast by Rev. John W. Murphy of Bangor, Me. Sponsors James Casey and Mary A. Noonan" and "Clark. 1879 Feb 23rd I baptized Mary M. Clark aged about 25 years daughter of Ira and Sarah Clark. Sponsors Patrick Brogan and Ellen Sheehan. J McCarthy." Clark was baptized, not confirmed. Baptismal Records August 23, 1877–September 19, 1908: Winterport-Bucksport-Belfast (unpublished). These records are kept at St. Brendan the Navigator Catholic Church in Camden, Maine.

136 Williamson and Johnson, Vol. II, 58-61. There is no discussion of a Catholic community or church in Williamson's first volume of Belfast history, which he wrote alone. Alfred Johnson finished the second volume after Williamson's death. The three-page history of Catholics and Brannagan are contained in Volume II.

137 Neither Bridget Haugh McCabe's birth family nor Brian McCabe left any records that they supported the Catholic congregation in Belfast; although Brian's fourth marriage to widow Bridget Hanrahan was solemnized by Father Richard W. Phelan: "Dispensations from Banns having been obtained I married Brian McCabe, son of Patrick and Bridget McCabe to Bridget Hanrahan daughter of Michael and Honor White in presence of Patrick Noughton and Margaret McCabe [Brian and Bridget Haugh McCabe's daughter]" 24 January 1883. John, the son that Bridget and Brian McCabe had baptized Catholic, also continued at least a nominal relationship with the ——Catholic Church. His marriage to Margaret Ryder was conducted by a priest in 1882. Marriage Records 1877–1908, Winterport-Bucksport-Belfast, St. Brendan the Navigator Parish.

138 Janet A. Nolan, *Ourselves Alone*, 29.

8   Making It Through the War

Intelligence of the surrender of Fort Sumter reached Belfast on the morning of Monday, April 15, 1861. No longer did any hope of averting civil war remain.[1]

Bridget Haugh McCabe died just three months before Fort Sumter fell and the Civil War began. Her story faded quickly as war took over public consciousness. As the war progressed and volunteers became scarcer, Belfast, a city of modest numbers, was required by the Lincoln administration to send many men between the ages of eighteen and forty-five to serve the Union cause. Local finances were also hit hard by the war, which, given the economics of the post-1857 Panic, must have been difficult. The two Belfast banks put up "one-fourth of their capital to the State, as a loan for war purposes."[2] Some Belfast-area businesses issued printed checks, which were used for currency in 1862–1863, until the government banned their use.[3] The city also appropriated funds to aid the families of those who enlisted to serve.[4]

In some respects, the war was a leveler in the Belfast community. It sent 31 percent of its males to the war; 858 men either volunteered, were drafted, or were hired as substitutes or representatives to go to the Civil War. One hundred Belfast men died as a result of service, including first-generation Americans Henry Haugh and Charles Spinks. (Henry was Bridget Haugh McCabe's cousin and Charles Spinks was her stepson.) This was the only time in Williamson's *History of Belfast* that Irish immigrants were given acknowledgment as sons of Belfast—each of the war dead garnered a brief obituary in "Sketches of Deceased Soldiers."[5]

The Belfast-enlisted companies joined the Fourth Maine Infantry Regiment at Rockland and left for Washington, D.C., in June 1861, each man having agreed to serve for three years. This regiment suffered severe losses: Nearly half were killed, wounded, or missing after the Battle of Fredericksburg (Maryland) in 1863.[6] In the first year of the war, Belfast had nine recruiting stations. Not many of Belfast's would-be soldiers signed up for the regular army, most choosing to serve with "home

DOI: 10.4324/9781003187660-8

boys."[7] In 1862, Belfast was required to find an additional sixty-one men, either through volunteerism or, that failing, a draft, to serve for three years. In order to stave off a draft, Belfast city council members recommended an additional $55 bounty for each volunteer, making the advance pay $150 for each man. In addition, leading citizens put up additional rewards. For example, John W. White offered a $100 signing bonus to the first man to enlist.[8]

That autumn, President Lincoln's administration put out a call for an additional 300,000 men to serve for nine months. These men were to be procured through volunteers. Again, Belfast sought to buy volunteers: An additional $100 was added to the then-current bounties offered. These bounties were divided between the man and his family: $20 to the volunteer and $80 to his family.[9]

By 1863, the Union turned to desperate measures, putting conscription into practice. All able-bodied men between the ages of twenty and forty-five were put on notice. Any males between twenty and forty-five could be drafted: Anyone between twenty and thirty-five, as well as any un-married men between the ages of thirty-five and forty-five, constituted the first class. A second class was to be put on notice: These were the married men between thirty-five and forty-five.

Draftees could buy their way out by providing $300. Sons of Belfast elites, as well as sons of the Irish immigrants, were drafted. Hugh J. Anderson Jr., second-generation American, son of the former governor, paid the $300. Some men, such as William Crosby, provided substitutes. Crosby paid substitute Eugene Ryder. Nearly 100 men provided sub-stitutes, men willing to fight in their stead; twenty-four Belfast men paid $300 in lieu of going to war. While money provided an out for some, substitution was also a way for older married men in the community to help out the war effort—basically paying someone to represent them in the war. A smattering of Irish-sounding surnames appears in the sub-stitution lists: Cornelius W. Meade, George A. Gallagher, George F. Cary, Mark O'Brien, Daniel Lehehan, Thomas Dolan, George Patrick, S.H. Higgins, and G.E. Hennessey. Also on the conscription lists, how-ever, were sons of more recent Irish immigrants, such as Andrew Bates, the Gannon brothers, James Gowen, Henry Haugh, (Bridget Haugh McCabe's cousin), Patrick Sheehan, John Sweeney, and James Whalen, among others.

Yet another call to arms sounded in autumn 1863. Belfast was re-quired to find another seventy-six volunteers/draftees by January 1864. This time, the city voted a $300 bounty for every enlistee. Those men on the conscription list paid money into this bounty fund.[10] A number of men too old, or otherwise deferred, also provided private funds for "representative recruits" to "represent" them on the battlefield.[11] By 1865, it was becoming harder to make the required quotas, so bounties rose. Belfast's mayor at the time, A.G. Jewett, noted that every volunteer's family would be taken care of: The city would pay $300 for one year of service; the state $100; the federal government $100; and each man would receive a monthly salary estimated at $20.[12] Indeed, from 1862 to war's end, 397 Belfast families, or 969 people, received $16,665.32.[13]

The rolls also revealed how Belfast's citizens had migrated westward yet retained contacts at home: Two former Belfast men served in California units; four were in Massachusetts; two in New York state; three in Illinois; one in Louisiana; one in Washington, D.C.; and one in Iowa. The majority who served were culled from area farms; dozens of seamen, sailors, and fishermen served in the Navy. Painters, students, barkeepers, clerks, laborers, hostlers, blacksmiths, millers, harness and saddle makers, tailors, mechanics, axe makers, joiners, carpenters, as well as merchants and ship masters headed off to war.

Economic Cycles

In the years leading up to the war, Bridget Haugh McCabe would have noticed that wages were clearly depressed for both males and females.[14] A catastrophic 1860 cut in male (and female) wages might have resulted from slow regrowth in Belfast after the national 1857 financial panic.[15] Belfast had not proven immune to periodic economic downswings in the past. Just twenty years earlier, the Panic of 1837 had hit Belfast's first-generation Irish-Americans hard, especially those members of the merchant class: Hugh Johnston Anderson and fellow Irish-American Nathaniel Lowney had been investors in the failed railroad corporation backed by the leading men of Belfast. The corporation members had intended to build a railroad from Belfast to Quebec. News of the plan had fueled real estate speculation.[16] Prices rose, then crashed.

The Panic of 1857 repeated the 1837 boom-and-bust cycle. Perhaps low wages for day labor might have been caused by a labor glut; however, that is not the whole case. The reality is that economic panic in 1857 caused upheaval in the United States' economy in the years preceding the Civil War and well into the war years. While the effects of the Panic in places like New York City seemed to heal rapidly, smaller, rural economies did not spring back so quickly. In some cases, mills stopped running. There were 5,000 business failures in 1857, partly a reaction to the collapse of land speculation. Shipping went down. Some textile mills tried to keep their workers by reducing hours. Unemployment was massive. Even domestic servants were laid off as people were forced to downsize.[17]

The answers as to what caused the 1857 Panic are many and varied. While U.S. grain markets were glutted in the early 1850s by overproduction, that was mitigated when U.S. grain producers found a market in Britain, involved in the Crimean War. That war ended in 1856.[18] In the meantime, land speculation, as it had in 1837, had overheated the U.S. economy. In addition, there had been overspeculation in railroad stock and overconfidence in railroad expansion. While 20,000 miles of railroad track had been laid in the early 1850s, most probably by quite a few Irish day laborers, only 2,500 miles of track were laid in 1857.[19] There was also political turmoil aroused by the Abolition debate, angst spurred by the Supreme Court's Dred Scott decision in the spring of that year, and the failure of Ohio Life Insurance and Trust, which led to runs on some banks.[20] In the aftermath of the Panic, gold prices rose to the point that small change was out of circulation.[21]

Belfast's labor costs, as presented in day books and household accounts, had rarely wavered over the course of the previous years, so 1860s' realities must have made it seem like the end times were at hand—or, for old-timers, more like nothing-ever-changes. The Gammon's Store day book, dating from 1826, showed a barter economy in full operation. Dollars were scarce, and men were paid in credit for their labor and goods, such as lumber or cords of wood.[22] While Belfast wages appear to have lagged, given statistics from 1845 New York, for example, we need to remember that the urban centers had higher cost-of-living expenses. So while inexperienced all-purpose maids could earn up to $4 a month in 1845 New York; and an experienced maid could make between $5 and $6 a month; and cooks, nannies, and ladies maids could command nearly twice that, given urban costs, wage earners would not have been "ahead."[23]

Belfast's male farm labor wages, which had remained stable for most of the century, plunged from $20 a month with room and board to $14 by 1860.[24] Nationally, from 1830 through 1850, the U.S. economy suffered from deflation (–0.56 percent per year from 1830–1840 and –1.09 from

Figure 8.1 Simpson's Wharf in 1870 Belfast. Courtesy of the Belfast Historical Society and Museum.

1840–1850). Prices (and a subsequent rise in buying power) were 5.34 percent lower in 1840 than they had been in 1830. That doubled in the next decade: Prices were 10.3 percent lower in 1850 than they had been in 1840. From 1850 to 1860, the national economy entered into an era of inflation. Prices rose to the point of being 6.4 percent higher in 1860 than they had been in 1850 (or 0.62 percent per year).

Why Women Worked

What this meant in Belfast was that more women worked outside the home. More females *had* to work (and did) in 1860 to offset low male wages. Harrison Hayford, Belfast census taker in 1860, reported that 2,757 females and 2,763 males made up the citizenry.[25] The 1860 U.S. census, the first to record women's paid work, showed 418 females, or 15 percent of Belfast's total female population, worked for wages. (The percentage would be much higher if female infants, toddlers, and schoolchildren were taken out of the mix.) Belfast women worked legally as schoolteachers, tailoresses, domestics, milliners, dressmakers, or seamstresses, or they ran boarding houses. Clothing and apparel provided the next largest group (seventy-four women) with wages. In a complete turnaround from two decades prior, all teaching jobs in Belfast were held by women: Fifty taught school.

More than half of Belfast's working women were employed in domestic service. Belfast households employed 266 Maine-born women as domestic servants in 1860, but only twenty-five Irish-born females. That means Irish domestics were only 9.39 percent of the total number of women working as domestics; however, when looking only at the Irish community, domestic service takes on greater importance. There were 162 men, women, and children born in Ireland living in Belfast in 1860 (just under 3 percent of Belfast's total population). Within the Irish community, however, 15.43 percent worked as domestic servants, which might mean that service had a great deal more influence within the Irish community than the other way around. The youngest Irish female working as a domestic was fourteen and the oldest fifty.

As a group, Belfast's domestics were not always single and not all "lived in." Of the 291 women (and one man) who worked in domestic service in 1860, for example, nearly 16 percent were married with children. Ninety percent of working women worked because of economic need.[26] A single immigrant generally worked as a day laborer or domestic, so did local young people. For example, two single Irish women with the same surname worked as domestics. Bridget and Harriett Brien were twenty and thirty, respectively. Harriett worked as a live-in domestic in lawyer Nathaniel Lowney's house. His real estate wealth was listed as $6,000. Bridget Brien, perhaps Harriett's sister, worked in the home of land agent James W. Webster, whose real estate holdings were valued as $11,000. Yet, in a different social class, Mary Burke, age twenty, lived in Charles and Margarett [*sic*] Hocks' house, Bridget Haugh McCabe's aunt and uncle. (Hocks is a misspelling for Haugh, but that tells us how the name was pronounced locally.) Both Charles and Margarett were Irish-born. Charles' real estate holdings were valued at $1,000 in 1850, a good deal less than first-generation Lowney. In addition to Charles and Margarett, three children—and Mary Burke—lived in the house. Were Bridget Haugh McCabe's uncle and aunt, too, taking in boarders? Was Burke family? Was she, perhaps, the hired help?

Research shows that native-born domestics were most numerous in small cities and rural areas, especially in those places where the foreign-born or African-American populations were quite small. Rural families often placed girls in town, which saved the family money and brought some in.[27] Belfast, decidedly, fell into those categories. While some scholars have argued that "servants 'were socially the equal of their employers, especially in New England and in the smaller towns'" in the years *before* the Civil War, the fact that Belfastians referred to domestics as hired "girls" (and the girls really were quite young) seems to rebut that notion.[28] There was also an apparent two-tiered approach to domestic service. For example, when boarding house owner Frank Field's wife Carrie became ill and could no longer perform her household chores, she was still dealing with "girl" problems in one of her last day book entries: "June, Thursday 2 The girl went home another expected tomorrow. Friday 3 Evelina Nickerson came to work. Blessed are people who can do their <u>own</u> work."[29] Girls were different—and more transient—from more mature domestic servants. For example, Carrie performed her final chore on 5 June 1864, washing Mrs. McLellan's curtains, evidently in preparation for Mrs. McLellan taking over as paid housekeeper on 12 June.[30] In addition to employing the professional housekeeper, the Fields employed two nurses for Carrie—Miss Smith, temporarily, and Mrs. Wentworth, who came on 19 June and remained in the house for nine days, seeing the family through the funeral and interment.[31] Amid the turmoil from Carrie's death, domestic Miss Johnson gave her one-day notice.[32] The young, single domestics were not dependable, at least according to comments in the Field day books. They were flightier than the more mature, more professional domestic help. Some were simply too young to be of any help. Over the years, Frank Field's mother, Abigail Davis Field, the original owner of the boarding house—and original keeper of the day books—commented continually on the help or the lack thereof. When she had no help, Abigail and her daughter-in-law had to do it all: "Carrie and self doing our work without <u>help</u>."[33]

In the 1860s, Belfast's old-timers and newcomers might have been drawn closer together by sacrifice; however, as the town's elites could buy their sons an "out" from war service, but the laboring class could not, that seems unlikely. Even though the war caused major upheaval in the community, what becomes apparent is that family organization for old-timers and newcomers was similar. War service, or lack of service, did not seem to call into question elite males' "manliness" in public venues. William George Crosby did not suffer a loss of status for buying his way out, for example.

Male Gender Norms

A good number of gender norms for males were shared across class and status lines. Men were viewed as unable, perhaps even incompetent, at single parenting, especially of small children in the Belfast of this era. This underlying norm may have been responsible for Brian McCabe's rather hurried marriage to Bridget Haugh in 1853, coming as it did closely after the death of his first wife, Margaret Spinks. McCabe had married Spinks in 1849. She had three children from her previous marriage, and she and McCabe had a son together. McCabe had three stepchildren and a biological son when Margaret Spinks McCabe died. A woman in the house was a necessity. In this need, Brian McCabe was not alone.

Because McCabe was illiterate, we do not know what, if any, turmoil the death of a wife and mother caused the family. (There is also no written proof that he was responsible for her demise, other than the accusations and innuendo raised at the inquest looking into Bridget Haugh McCabe's mysterious death.) We do gain some insight into the male viewpoint, however, because of the records Frank Field left. When Caroline (Carrie) Tobey Field, his first wife, died on 22 June 1864, he fell into an abyss of depression and grief. Frank lost not only his helpmate but also his children.

Carrie died on a Wednesday evening, was buried on that Friday in Grove Cemetery, in the Field family plot, and on Saturday Frank reported in his day book that the women went through Carrie's clothes.[34] On Monday, he wrote that women were picking up the children's clothes. Just a week after Carrie died, her younger sister, Anna (Annie) Tobey, arrived. She spent the next day "fixing the children's clothing." By 8 July, Annie Tobey and the two elder children left for Farmington, seventy-two miles away, where Carrie and Annie's mother and the children's grandmother lived. A toddler, Ben, stayed with his father, and Frank's old nurse, Annie Frost, came to stay. Frank then hired a Mrs. Wentworth, who had been Carrie's nurse, to run the boarding house. On 15 July, he wrote sadly, "Home no home to me."[35]

Throughout this traumatic time, Frank went through several hired girls: Just six days after Carrie died, "Miss Johnson poor help left," and a month later, "Miss Maria Warren discharged worse than no help."[36] He had to rely on written word to get any news about his children living in Farmington, which, according to his reports, did not come until the first of September. In the meanwhile, he keenly felt the losses, noting that all were "gorn," and even though the weather was pleasant, the day was "a gloomy one to me."[37] He sadly noted his absent son Frank's fifth birthday, which he could not celebrate with him. He wrote on 18 September 1864, "how long oh how long enough two do but no head to do it with."[38] The comment seems almost incomprehensible, but on 26 September he writes, "Same fool—Mrs. Wentworth took good care of me." He also reported on 9 October 1864, "No friction in the family," and on 18 September he left for Farmington. What was causing the friction prior to there being "no friction" is not clear, but the evidence is suggestive, especially when he reported on 14 October, "Tempest in the teapot. Sarah Raynolds left." He wrote on 19 October 1864, "Noticed by a Lady <u>took one glass brandy</u> [emphasis in the original]."

Two days later, Frank wrote in very dark ink when he reported that his hired housekeeper Mrs. Wentworth left his employ while he was in Farmington. The ink may have been an accident of quill rather than an emotional outburst, as Mrs. Wentworth returned as housekeeper on 11 January 1871—six years later.[39] (Perhaps any dispute had been resolved in the interval.) When he returned from Farmington on 25 October, he brought son Frank home. At that point, he had both boys in Belfast, while his daughter Annie stayed in Farmington with her grandmother. His old nurse, Annie Frost, continued to stay on as housekeeper. In January 1865, he spent a week in Farmington. On 2 March he traveled to Farmington again and wrote rather tersely in his day book on 5 March, "Married by Rev. I. Rogers."

He never explained in his day book that he had married his former sister-in-law, Carrie's sister. His only reference to the new bride was to her role in the family: "*Mother* attending the funeral of Pres. Lincoln [emphasis added]."[40] He talked about the two eldest children going to school and getting the chicken pox. He also remarked, "One year to day since dear Carrie died."[41] As the months progressed, he still did not comment on his new wife; however, he noted sadly the anniversary of his mother's passing and his first wedding anniversary—to Carrie: "Seven years ago to day [*sic*] I was married."[42] He was also quite concerned when his childhood nurse Annie Frost became quite ill.[43] In another rare reference to the new wife, he reported that "Mother gorn down street. Christmas presents."[44]

Mother's—Anna Tobey Field's—birthday arrived on 11 January 1866, but, so he reported, Frank had no present for her. Two days later, "Mother" was poor. By 25 January, he took "Mother" and the three children to Farmington, stayed a few days, and then left the entire family there. He did not return to Farmington until 16 February, stayed a few days, and brought the two boys back to Belfast on 20 February. Evidently, the separation helped Frank sort his priorities. By 5 March 1866, he commented that he was married one year (to Annie). He left for

Farmington on 9 March and returned to Belfast with "Mother" and his daughter, Annie.[45] Most likely, the second marriage was difficult, especially in the first year. By the autumn of 1866, Frank reported that he and "Mother" were beginning to act as a couple in Belfast. They went calling, or "went to the Bluff."[46] Perhaps the trip to the Bluff helped clear the air. Although it took another two weeks, after nearly two years of marriage, Frank finally called his wife by her first name: "Annie preparing to go to Bangor in the morning."[47] She traveled with Mrs. Davis and her son and Frank's brother George. Frank was very unhappy "keeping house without a woman."[48] He reported on 12 November that "Annie returned home and we are glad."[49] By the time Annie Tobey Field's birthday arrived on 11 January 1867, Frank could report that all was well: "My wife's birthday. All pleasant."[50] Evidently, he had learned his lesson. As their marriage lasted, he continued to note his mother's and Carrie's death dates, his wedding anniversary with Carrie, but he added Annie's dates, too: "Seven years to day since I was married haven't repented of it yet."[51] It appears it took nearly two years before this former in-law could form any kind of personal emotional bond with Annie. Over the years of the marriage, the children rotated back and forth to their grandmother in Farmington, often staying weeks, months, and sometimes years until her death in July 1874.

His friend and neighbor, Judge Joseph Williamson, Belfast's amateur historian, never recovered his children after his wife died. When Ada Hortense Peirce Williamson grew ill in the late winter of 1872, the entire family took up residence in the Field House as boarders. Hired nurses tended to her there. She died on 19 March. By early April, Joseph Williamson took up permanent residence in the Field House, closing out his Belfast house; his daughters Ada and Fannie, and son William he sent to live with relatives. His two girls visited occasionally, but he was free to continue his law practice, which required frequent travel to Portland, Boston, Chicago, and New York. Joseph Williamson never remarried. He died in 1902.

Family Circles

Keeping a family circle intact was difficult but remained the goal for many, regardless of social class or status, Joseph Williamson to the contrary. Frank Field was not alone in remarrying quickly after his first wife's death. Laborer Brian McCabe married Bridget Haugh McCabe after the death of his first wife, Margaret Spinks McCabe. There were small children in the house. Indeed, he married a third time in 1864 just three years after Bridget Haugh McCabe's mysterious death. His third wife was a childless widow, Margaret Handerhan. McCabe still had several small children at home. He and the second Margaret remained together until her death of consumption in 1882. He married a fourth time just months later, another childless widow, Bridget Hanrahan. He had adult sons living with him at the time, but he moved in with Bridget Hanrahan, who had been working as a laundress since her husband died. Brian died a year and a half later at age seventy-seven.[52]

Irish immigrants traveled to Belfast as family groups, according to the 1860 census. Fifty-one Irish *families* lived in Belfast, twenty-three of those families having been in residence since the 1850 census. The original Belfast settlement of 1770 comprised fifty-three *people* of both

Figure 8.2 Belfast found wealth after the Civil War. The business community was thriving, according to this 1875 map. Courtesy of the Osher Map Library, University of Southern Maine. Map of Belfast, Waldo County, Maine. https://oshermaps.org/map/50364.0001

sexes and all ages; the impetus for Belfast's post-Revolutionary rebirth in 1784 was led by a mere fourteen families, joined by another eight from the area around Londonderry, New Hampshire. The size of the Irish community, then, was more than double that of the original settlers of 1770 and 1784.

The majority of Belfast's Irish immigrant households were headed by men aged forty and older (twenty-eight families); nineteen were headed by individuals between the ages of thirty and thirty-nine; only four were headed by twenty-somethings. Thirty individuals were single; however, one or two of those people were young adults who had moved out of the parental home.[53]

After the war, Belfast's economy changed. There is no clearer sign of that change than the number of women working in domestic service in Belfast. While some scholars have argued that American women did not want to serve, feeling it beneath them, and surmised that Irish women were happy to do so, the statistics in Belfast do not support this. Wages and the wages of the males in their lives seem to have driven women's choice of labor. Irish females had a great deal of competition from local females for the slots available in domestic service in Belfast. Local wages rebounded after the Civil War. One reason 1870 wages were robust is that the war had depleted the local labor supply. After 1865, Belfast's population had dropped by 241. This may have been caused by the enumerator failing to count people who were temporarily absent.[54] However, that fact doesn't explain why the 1870 census records the number of females working for wages had also declined—by nearly half. There were more jobs available in the hospitality industry in 1870—hotel work for laundresses, wait staff, maid, and cooks—but even the number of women holding teaching jobs was reduced by more than half. In 1860, fifty women had worked as teachers; by 1870, only twenty did. After domestic service, the largest category of employment was still clothing/apparel in 1870, which occupied fifty-two women.

Single Irish women living in as domestics in the middle- and upper-middle-class homes in big cities have been represented as the norm. In New York City's Five Points neighborhood, for example, 25 percent of women lived in as domestics.[55] It was by watching the mores of the middle class from their vantage point as domestics that Irish-born women supposedly learned how to comport themselves and thus paved the way for the acceptance of the Irish into American society more readily.[56] Prior to 1880, only 15 percent of the U.S. population lived in the fifty largest cities. Middle-class people in these cities were the employers of 32 percent of all servants and 49 percent of all laundresses.[57] What was clear was that middle-class urban women lived in houses too big for them to run by themselves. However, the amount of female work in any family was overwhelming: "[A woman] with a large family found it hard to manage even a respectable working-class dwelling by herself."[58] Domestic servants were a necessity and, for some, a status symbol. While American middle-class women may have used domestic servants to free themselves from domestic drudgery and with their "new found domestic freedom from chores" worked to get themselves the right to vote, rural women needed help to keep their enterprises running and meet family responsibilities, including food preservation.[59]

While Irish-born females provided 60 percent of Portland, Maine's, servant class, not to mention the majority of servants in Boston, Cambridge, Hartford, Lowell, New Haven, Providence, and Springfield, in Belfast they had competition from the locals.[60] Studies of urban Irish women immigrants have remarked on the service tradition in Ireland, where domestic labor had been the single largest employer of women. In Ireland, most domestics were single, and in the United States Irish women tended to marry at a later age than other women. Irish immigrants also knew English. As a consequence, they entered household labor and probably continued to work longer at it than other white women. To work a lifetime in an employer's family without marrying was an accepted custom in Ireland.[61] While Irish women in cities had little competition, except from African-American women, Belfast did not follow the urban norms.[62] Supposedly, domestic service was a low-status occupation that "tended to be shunned by the native-born, and thus, it was work performed disproportionately by immigrants and blacks."[63] The work was grueling and required that females be available to their employers seven very long days a week, but in 1860 Belfast domestic work drew many women—not just immigrants.

Most domestics' days began at 5 or 6 a.m. and ended as late as 10 p.m., especially on wash days.[64] As late as 1910, domestics in Maine worked an average of just under 10 hours a day.[65] By 1900, 54 percent of Irish-born women were domestics in the United States, compared to 21.9 percent of English- and Welsh-born, 27.5 percent of Scottish-born, and 9.1 percent of Italian-born.[66] If laundresses are included, then nationally 60.5 percent of Irish women worked as domestics by 1900.[67]

Statistics from 1870 Belfast belie the idea that Irish women stayed in domestic service longer than other white women. By 1870, those females choosing to work in domestic service could demand much higher wages; however, given the large decline in female wage earners in 1870, it seems fewer females felt the need to work for wages—period. Perhaps we should be looking at what was happening to male wages nationwide. Very few Irish-born women worked as domestics in Belfast compared with those who had in 1860. By 1870, male day laborer wages had risen even higher than 1850 rates.

In 1870, there were 2,163 females living in Belfast.[68] Not all worked. "Keeping house," according to the 1870 United States census, was the largest occupation for Belfast women—945 women did unpaid work in their own households. (One woman was not listed in any category, which may simply have been a census taker oversight. One woman was in jail.) A number of unmarried women (322) were "at home," presumably helping their mothers or the woman of the house with domestic chores after leaving school and/or before their own marriages, but who did not receive wages for any work. A third group of women were categorized by census takers as having "no occupation." These eighty-five women were generally elderly or infirm. The only other group of females who were not paid for work was the 529 girls enrolled in school.

In the post–Civil War decade, the number of women working outside the home had fallen by a little over half: 228 women, or 8.4 percent of *all* females, worked for wages, based on the incomplete United States census data. The numbers employed in domestic positions had been more than halved. Where 291 women had worked as domestics in 1860, only 134 women were serving Belfast households in 1870. As we have seen, there was a demand for domestic servants—evidenced by the rise in pay from 1850s' $1.75 per week, to the low point of 1860s' $1 per week, to the heights of 1870s' $2.50 per week. Although the largest employment group was domestic service, women born in Ireland or whose parents were born in Ireland were a very small proportion of the domestic servants of Belfast in 1870—only five women—which means under 4 percent (3.73 percent) of the domestic servants in Belfast were Irish immigrants or first-generation Irish-American. A few Maine-born women with Irish-sounding surnames worked as domestics, but they were not listed as being from Ireland or as having Irish-born parents—Melvina and Elvina Mahoney, Julia Condon, Eliza Higgins, Georgianna Kelley, Fannie J. Donnell, Mary Grady (her parents were simply noted as being "foreign-born"), and Catherine Casey. If we consider these "maybes," possibly 9.7 percent of domestics were Irish or of Irish extraction. What is apparent is that there were more options to choose from for female work, but fewer women were working for wages outside the home. What seems clear when comparing the numbers of females engaged in domestic service in 1860 and 1870 Belfast is that, like their Yankee sisters, Irish women left domestic service as soon as the men in their lives earned adequate wages.

The Field boarding house, which catered to people of status, needed competent help.[69] By the 1860s and 1870s, Frank Field had to travel a good many miles to find hired girls—Searsport (7 miles east), Bucksport (24 miles east), Frankfort (20 miles north), Swanville (8 miles north), and Winterport (24 miles north) were all mentioned in his day book entries. After the "boys" returned from war in 1866, Frank grumbled that all the good help was getting married.[70] Yet, even in the robust economy of 1870 Belfast, when fewer women worked, a short-hand term for domestics was still the ubiquitous "Bridget."[71]

The inability to keep girls employed in the Field house may have been caused by the Fields' unwillingness to pay more than $1 per week after wages rebounded after the Civil War, a fact which did not escape Frank's notice. Evidently, the turn in wages occurred sometime between 1863 and 1866. For example, Caroline Tobey Field, Frank's first wife, paid

Mary Byrnes $1 per week for a seven-week period from 18 July through 5 September 1863.[72] By 1866, Frank ruminated whether it were better to "Pay or be select. That is the question."[73] Given the comments Frank made in his day book, by the end of the Civil War, costs for help had risen. Putting up hay in summer 1865, for example, had cost him $40. It was a sizable enough figure that he made mention of it in his day book.[74] He also noted that he paid Annie Frost, his childhood nurse who had come to his rescue after wife Carrie's death, $50. She had remained for several months. After he paid Annie Frost, he went to his mother-in-law's home in Farmington and retrieved his new wife and his daughter from his first marriage, and, upon their return, his new wife "paid [Annie Frost] for the last year." He did not, however, give the amount.[75]

Post-War Wealth

Another reason for fewer working women might have been the result of the cost of the war in Belfast. Perhaps people could not afford hired help; however, the fact is that even with inflation at 4.67 percent per year by 1870, it was only *after* the Civil War that Belfast residents saw their personal wealth grow dramatically. Although most of the downtown was destroyed by fire in 1865, by 1874 the number of men paying taxes of more than $100 had grown to 217. (In 1851, only nineteen men had paid taxes of $100 or more.)[76] Obviously, the war period initiated a period of growth for some.

After the Civil War, wealth found Belfast. Two banks were in operation: Belfast National Bank and the Bank of Commerce. The first had $150,000 in capital. James P. White served as president. His family had long roots in the community, and he had been born there at the beginning of the century. White made his fortune as a merchant and then as shipbuilder. When he retired, his personal fortune was worth $50,000 and his real estate was listed as $10,000 in the 1870 census. This, however, was a far cry from the 1860 census report of his wealth, which listed $20,000 in real estate and $150,000 in personal wealth. The decade before the war, however, his real estate was worth only $12,000. Obviously, the decade of the 1860s brought great changes to Belfast. The surnames of the bank's directors would have been familiar to anyone who knew Joseph Dolliff's "The Greene Indian War." (The directors included White, Reuben Libby, Prescott Hazeltine, Daniel Haraden, and Joseph Williamson.) Dolliff had taunted in his verses John Haraden, Daniel's father, a merchant, as well as White.[77] Hazeltine, born in Massachusetts, managed to accrue a sizable fortune by 1860 as a merchant in Belfast. (His son, Charles Bellows Hazeltine, went off and made a fortune in the California gold fields, supposedly, and came back to build a huge house in Belfast.) Neither he nor Williamson was treated to Dolliff's scorn, but their names had been a long time in the community.

Belfast's second bank was run by Asa Faunce, the builder of the *Suliotte*, which had sailed to San Francisco in 1849. The Bank of Commerce had only $75,000 in capital. The only name harkening to early settlers was Nathan Houston, one of the Bank of Commerce's directors.

Belfast boasted two newspapers—*The Republican Journal* with its Democratic leanings was challenged by *The Progressive Age*. There were two telegraph offices, the International and Western Union. The operators of both were female. Twenty-six wharves ranged along the harbor, and six different ship yards provided many opportunities for employment. Mills—lumber and grist—were employed along the Passagassawakeag. There were paper and straw manufactories in town, as well as axe factories, barrel makers, carriage makers and painters. Six men worked as shoemakers. There was a gas and light works. Dry goods and groceries abounded, and there were at least two saloons.

There were more than half a dozen lawyers in town. Baptists, Universalists, Unitarians, Methodists, and Congregationalists employed full-time ministers. The Catholics were still being served by a circuit priest. Of the six schools in town—high school, grammar school, select school, intermediate school, and two primary schools—five had women principals and assistants. Two of those women were widows.

After the war, Frank Field's boarding house was in for some competition from more than a dozen widows, more married women supplementing their husband's incomes, and two hotels all renting out rooms.

Figure 8.3 St. Francis of Assisi Catholic Church was paid for by William S. Brannagan in the 1890s. Courtesy of the Belfast Historical Society and Museum.

Unmarried adult children who worked continued to live in parental households, perhaps helping defray costs. A number of clerks lived with the merchants who employed them (or their establishments). There were two jewelers in town.[78]

The Irishmen of 1850 and 1860 were still listed in the town directory of 1868. Most still worked as laborers. John Handerhan worked for McGilvery's Shipyard, living nearby, as did a number of other Irish immigrants. (Handerhan's widow Margaret was Brian McCabe's third wife.) Patrick Hanley was firmly ensconced as gardener at Charles Bellows Hazeltine's. Bridget's widowed aunt lived on Front Street (Puddle Dock). Others had moved south of the downtown.

After the Civil War, male farm labor wages with room and board rebounded to $25 per month.[79] Pay for general male day laborers without board was $1.25 a day in 1850, 67 cents in 1860, and $1.25 in 1870; with board, the rates for males were $1.00 a day in 1850, 50 cents in 1860, and $1.25 in 1870.[80] Female domestics, with board, earned $1.75 a week in 1850, $1.00 in 1860, and $2.50 in 1870.[81] By 1870, prices were 57.83 percent higher than they had been in 1860, and inflation was 4.67 percent per year.[82]

By 1870, the steady trickle of Irish immigrants to Belfast had also stopped. The upheavals of the Civil War subsided, and Belfast was reborn. The Irish immigrants of the 1850s were firmly established in the community, some building houses on Bayside or Union streets, on the south side of town. Their children had married and had children of their own. Many remained nearby, if not in Belfast proper. Future censuses made no mention of influxes of newcomers from Ireland.

Notes

1 Joseph Williamson, *The History of the City of Belfast, Maine*, Vol. 1 (Somersworth, New Hampshire: New England History Press, 1982), 464.
2 Williamson, Vol. 1, 465.
3 Williamson, Vol. 1, 475.
4 Williamson, Vol. 1, 465.
5 Williamson, Vol. 1, 506 and 514.
6 Williamson, Vol. 1, 475.
7 Williamson, Vol. 1, 470.
8 Williamson, Vol. 1, 473.
9 Williamson, Vol. 1, 474.
10 Williamson, Vol. 1, 487.
11 Williamson, Vol. 1, 491.
12 Williamson, Vol. 1, 494.
13 Williamson, Vol. 1, 498.
14 Stanley Lebergott, "Wage Trends, 1800–1900," in *Trends in the American Economy in the Nineteenth Century* (Princeton: UP, 1960), 456; accessed online 20 June 2016 at www.nber.org/chapters/c2486.pdf.

15 Charles W. Calomiris and Larry Schweikart, "The Panic of 1857: Origins, Transmission, and Containment," *The Journal of Economic History*, 51, no. 4 (December 1991), 807–834.
16 Williamson, Vol. 1, 668.
17 Kenneth M. Stampp, *America in 1857: A Nation on the Brink* (Oxford University Press, 1992), 151, 219, and 226.
18 James L. Huston, *The Panic of 1857 and the Coming of the Civil War* (Baton Rouge: Louisiana State University Press, 1987), 5 and 6.
19 Stampp, 215.
20 Calomiris and Schweikart, "The Panic of 1857," 808.
21 Williamson, Vol. 1, 475.
22 Day Book of the Gammons Store at City Point: 1826-__, Belfast, September 18, 1826. (Courtesy Belfast Free Library Archives. Given by Mrs. Fred Holmes, a cousin of Maud Gammons.)
23 Margaret Lynch-Brennan, *The Irish Bridget: Irish Immigrant Women in Domestic Service in America, 1840-1930* (Syracuse: Syracuse University Press, 2009), 91.
24 Williamson, Vol. 1, 845.
25 Williamson, Vol. 1, 844.
26 David M. Katzman, *Seven Days a Week: Women and Domestic Service in Industrializing America* (New York: Oxford University Press, 1978), 82.
27 Hasia Diner, *Erin's Daughters in America: Irish Immigrant Women in the Nineteenth Century* (Baltimore: The Johns Hopkins University Press, 1983), 63–64 and 151–152.
28 Katzman, 98.
29 Carolyn Tobey Field Day Book: 2 and 3 June 1864, Mrs. McLellan evidently was hired by the end of May, but did not take up her duties immediately. (Courtesy of Belfast Historical Society and Museum.)
30 Abigail Davis Field Day Book. Mrs. McLellan and her husband "commenced boarding together" at the Field house February 1863. (Courtesy of Belfast Historical Society and Museum.)
31 Frank Field took over his wife's day book sometime after the first week of June 1864. (Courtesy of Belfast Historical Society and Museum.)
32 Carolyn Tobey Field—now Benjamin Franklin "Frank" Field—Day Book: 28 June 1864.
33 Abigail Davis Field Day Book, November 1862. Carrie was eight months pregnant at the time.
34 Benjamin Franklin (Frank) Field Day Book.
35 Benjamin Franklin (Frank) Field Day Book.
36 Benjamin Franklin (Frank) Field Day Book, 22 July 1864.
37 Benjamin Franklin (Frank) Field Day Book, 8 and 17 July 1864. Gorn is dialectical, meaning gone.
38 Benjamin Franklin (Frank) Field Day Book, 18 September 1864.
39 Benjamin Franklin (Frank) Field Day Book, 10 January 1871. Mrs. Wentworth took over as housekeeper when Annie Tobey Field gave birth to daughter Caroline, 10 January 1871.
40 Benjamin Franklin (Frank) Field Day Book, 19 April 1865. Towns throughout America conducted funerals for assassinated President Lincoln.
41 Benjamin Franklin (Frank) Field Day Book, 22 June 1865.
42 Benjamin Franklin (Frank) Field Day Book, 25 November 1865.
43 Benjamin Franklin (Frank) Field Day Book, 4, 5, 14, 15, 18 December 1865.
44 Benjamin Franklin (Frank) Field Day Book, 20 December 1865.
45 Benjamin Franklin (Frank) Field Day Book, March 1866.

46 Benjamin Franklin (Frank) Field Day Book, 20 October 1866.

47 Benjamin Franklin (Frank) Field Day Book, 7 November 1866.

48 Benjamin Franklin (Frank) Field Day Book, 9 November 1866.

49 Benjamin Franklin (Frank) Field Day Book, 12 November 1866.

50 Benjamin Franklin (Frank) Field Day Book, 11 January 1867.

51 Benjamin Franklin (Frank) Field Day Book, 5 March 1872.

52 Maine Historical Society, *Belfast, Maine, Vital Records to the Year 1892, Vol. II, Marriages and Deaths* (Boston: Wright and Potter Printing Co., 1919), 262 and 584.

53 Patrick Sweeney's son Dennis is listed in both his father's household, as well as the home of his employer, N.P. Monroe.

54 Williamson, Vol. 1, 845.

55 Tyler Anbinder, *Five Points: The Nineteenth Century New York City Neighborhood that Invented Tap Dance, Stole Elections, and Became the World's Most Notorious Slum* (New York: The Free Press, 2001), 126.

56 Katzman, 70; Lynch-Brennan, xxii; Nolan, 94.

57 Katzman, 59.

58 Katzman, 148–149.

59 Lynch-Brennan, 68.

60 Lynch-Brennan, 65–66.

61 Lynch-Brennan, 69.

62 Diner, 71–72.

63 Katzman, 44.

64 Katzman, 110–111.

65 Katzman, 112.

66 Janet Nolan, *Ourselves Alone: Women's Emigration from Ireland 1885–1920* (Lexington: University of Kentucky Press, 1989), 68.

67 Katzman, 49.

68 My head count differs from Williamson, who estimates 2,710 females.

69 Abigail Davis Field, Carolyn Tobey Field, and Benjamin Franklin ("Frank") Field Day Books, 1841–1876. "Girls" could be defined as very young, perhaps even pre-teen: "Lucy Davis came here to do my work Quit [*sic*] to [*sic*] yong [*sic*]," 26 August 1841, Abigail Davis Field. Some of the "girls," however, who worked for Mrs. Field were married women, such as Mrs. Hannah Prince, who helped Mrs. Field cut carpets, 27 April 1841, Abigail Davis Field Day Book.

70 Frank Field Day Book: "14/15 November 1866 From early in the spring to late in the fall our hired help has done nothing but to get married."

71 Crosby, "Annals of Belfast," 50.

72 Caroline Tobey Field Day Book.

73 Frank Field Day Book, 17 August 1866.

74 Frank Field Day Book, 10 July 1865.

75 Frank Field Day Book, 21 February and 20 March 1866.

76 Williamson, Vol. 1, 847.

77 Williamson, Vol. 1, 431.

78 1868 Directory of Belfast, Maine.

79 Williamson, Vol. 1, 845.

80 Williamson, Vol. 1, 845.

81 Williamson, Vol. 1, 845.

82 "Inflation Calculator." U.S. Official Inflation Data, Alioth Finance, 11 Mar. 2020, https://www.officialdata.org/.

Epilogue

Irish immigrants and their descendants who made their way to Belfast, Maine, between 1770 and 1870 found that acceptance by old-timers was based on gender, class, and status; all newcomers, however, faced the same stereotypes. Bridget Haugh McCabe and William S. Brannagan show how gender, class, and status, in addition to stereotype, influenced old-timers' views of newcomers in Belfast mid-nineteenth century. McCabe was part of the last big group of Irish immigrants to arrive in Belfast, arriving within a few years of the Irish Famine. By 1850, Irish immigrants comprised 4 percent of Belfast's population. Immigrant Irish came as families with a few single people in tow—working-class people, most of whom were illiterate, as was McCabe. Her father was a day laborer with a drinking problem, who never "made it" in America. Her uncle Charles Haugh, however, also listed as a day laborer in census materials, had, by the time of his death, accrued property.

McCabe and Brannagan may have seemed to fit nineteenth-century stereotype in that both Irish newcomers were Catholic. Yet Catholicism was not the onus in Belfast it might have been elsewhere, nor were all nineteenth-century Irish immigrants Catholic. And, while a number of the newcomers of 1850 may have been Catholic, not all maintained even minimal obligations, as evidenced by the fact that a large number of children born in the Irish community in Belfast were adults with children of their own before they were ever baptized. McCabe saw to it her first-born child was baptized by a Jesuit who traveled through Belfast, but her daughter who was a toddler when McCabe died was not baptized until she was an adult. There are no records for her second son. Perhaps it was Brian McCabe who was the nominal Catholic who failed to have his youngest child baptized. On the other hand, Brannagan was an active Catholic, providing property and buildings for church services for decades before agreeing to donate land and to pay for construction of Saint Francis of Assisi Church in Belfast in the 1890s. He was also an astute businessman who worked "a deal" with the Catholic hierarchy to live in the rectory in his old age, in exchange for the donations. Brannagan's reception by old-timers, however, was quite different from that met by

DOI: 10.4324/9781003187660-102

the McCabes. He came via mercantile channels to Belfast. While Brannagan may have begun his American journey as a day laborer, he quickly moved into the merchant class, where he stayed the rest of his life. As a male merchant, Brannagan moved in completely different circles than Bridget Haugh McCabe. Brannagan, unlike the Haugh and McCabe families, was literate. As he was of the preferred gender, class, and status, he achieved acceptance by old-timers much more readily than a working-class, illiterate female, such as McCabe--or her day-laborer husband.

Brannagan, who arrived in the early 1840s, was merely one in a string of professional males who rewrote the history of Belfast. After the Revolutionary War, professional men moved into the area. The merchants, such as Francis Anderson from County Down, worked to create infrastructure, so that frontier goods could move to retail hubs such as Boston more easily. Later, his nephew Hugh Johnston Anderson took over Francis' mercantile enterprises. Hugh used the merchant class—and his affiliation with other first-generation Americans—to become involved in Democratic politics. So, from the merchant class, he achieved the backing to serve three one-year terms as Maine governor. With his Democratic ties, he also moved into federal positions and traveled to Washington, D.C., and even San Francisco, only returning to Belfast for summer vacations. At the end of his career, he retired to Portland, Maine, but was interred at Grove Cemetery, Belfast, when he died. The merchants who began arriving in the 1790s required the expertise of lawyers as well as teachers for their sons. The lawyers helped the merchants chase outstanding debts, accrued by members from the original settlement and their descendants. Among the first three lawyers in Belfast was John Wilson, the son of an Irish immigrant to Massachusetts. The sons of the elite also received education—many ultimately graduating from colleges and universities, such as Bowdoin and Harvard. The need for teachers drew William Lowney, who claimed to have graduated from Dublin College, and his son Nathaniel, who had been born in Maine. Nathaniel read law in Belfast and moved into Democratic politics as well. He served in a number of positions, including being Collector of the Port in Winterport, Maine. The sons of the elite had access to education because of their social class—in other words, their fathers could afford to have them educated. Religious affiliation was part of access. After the Revolutionary War, Congregationalism became associated with Federalism (or strong centralized government). The majority of Belfastians with religious affiliations, however, were more supportive of Baptists and Methodists.

Both old-timers and newcomers navigated via stereotypes. Diaries from the era indicate that being openly Catholic in the 1820s might have been scary, but that had changed by the 1840s in Belfast—even amid the national Know-Nothing Movement. Local newspaper editors in the early years of the nineteenth century looked askance at the newcomers. In the early years of the century, the Irish—and Irishness—were treated with disdain, and the papers' editors ran many stories about Irish tendencies toward violence and crime; however, by the 1840s, first-generation Americans were helping bankroll papers such as *The Republican Journal,* and its editorial "tone" shifted ever so slightly. The stories from Ireland were extensive and the coverage positive: The British, on the other hand, were shown in a negative light. While the paper continued to run "Pat and Mike" jokes, and the Irish were the perpetual butts of those jokes, the tone seemed to indicate the jokes were now "owned" by Irish Americans. Stories of Irishmen celebrating the Fourth of July were given a great deal of play. The Irish seemed to be quintessential American republicans (with a little *r*). Irish stereotypes were consistent from the early eighteenth throughout the nineteenth centuries: The Irish drank too much, fought too much, had too many children, and were poor. The irony in Belfast, however, is that many of those applying the stereotypes in the nineteenth century were themselves descended from immigrants from Ireland.

American society was always on the move. Transition was the only constant. The Irish in Belfast, as well as Boston, however, seemed more content to stay where they landed. One reason why may have been that they could find employment. Work that did not require massive outlays of money and/or education drew the Irish.

The group of male professionals who came after the Revolution and before the War of 1812, however, sought to separate Belfast's history from its Irishness, perpetuating a creation story whereby the original settlers were Scotch-Irish. This began early in the nineteenth century, so it cannot be laid at the feet of the Know-Nothing Movement. Belfast's early amateur historians worked hard to claim Scots' ancestry for the area. A number of investors, albeit hailing from Londonderry, New Hampshire, which had been settled by a group of Ulster Presbyterians, never traveled to Belfast. Their influence in the community, therefore, was limited. In addition, most of those who did settle in Belfast had been born in America—some the grandsons of the original settlers of Londonderry. That would mean, then, that most of those who settled in Belfast were Americanized, including two who had been born in Ireland. James Miller and John Mitchell had been small children when their families emigrated. They, too, had been enculturated in America. While the newcomers of 1718 had been Presbyterian, no Presbyterian minister was ever hired full time in Belfast. The first full-time minister was Congregationalist. Congregationalism, with its concomitant ties to Anglicanism and the British Crown, seems antithetical to Presbyterian "dissenter" status. The received histories of the nineteenth century, then, must be re-evaluated.

Class and status had more to do with acceptance in Belfast than immigrant status. Even the first generation of settlers in 1770, with their subsistence farming existence, did not garner much approbation. The professional class that invaded rewrote Belfast's history. "Making it" was measured in the property bequeathed to heirs. For example, Abigail Davis Field ran a boarding house for more than 20 years; her son helped her, and he inherited the house and the business upon her death. She had property to bequeath; however, because she was female, Field did not merit mention in any of the nineteenth-century histories; thus, gender also played a huge role in acceptance. Even though Bridget Haugh McCabe did not work outside the home after her marriage to Brian McCabe, her class and status were at the bottom when compared to Field, who had married Belfast's first lawyer. Ultimately, the question of whether McCabe was murdered rests on her class and status. She may well have died as a result of being a member of the laboring class. She and her husband lived in a house wherein a *shebeen*, an illegal liquor operation, was being run. Doctors, symbols of old-timer authority, probably would not have been called. Perhaps this explains why even Bridget's father testified at the inquest that nothing untoward had happened. We still note, however, no one intervened when they heard her screams. Just three decades earlier, however, a group of Belfast men had interceded when a drunken man beat his wife. For some reason, the old-timer community did not investigate until *after* Bridget's death. This could have been the result of prejudice; however, that prejudice may have been against the working class, not necessarily the Irish. In this, Belfast would not have been alone. On the national level, for example, abolitionist Lydia Maria Child had decided opinions on laborers, people who owned nothing and lived on a wage earned from others through the expenditure of sweat.[1] The majority of the Irish, in her estimation, were in this class. She forgave herself for her flagrant dislike of the laboring class, noting that no racial group wanted to be a member of it either: "Even the Irish shop-keeper, or provision-dealer, considers it a mésalliance to marry an Irish cook, or chambermaid. And as for the colored people, their *'fust* families,' carry matters with a high hand."[2] In other words, she didn't consider herself prejudiced on race matters, only on class—and that, she argued, was forgivable. Bridget's widower married two more times before he died. Did that mean the Irish women of Belfast did not fear him? It could.

The Civil War brought new wealth to Belfast for the elite; the working class found wages rebounded after the war. While many Belfast women in 1860 worked outside the home for wages, it appears they did so because male wages had been virtually cut in half and buying power was even less, perhaps as a result of fallout from the Panic of 1857. Given the low wages at the war's outset, sons of the Irish enlisted. Signing bonuses were most likely quite a draw. While the sons of the elite could buy their way out of going to war, the sons of day laborers had no such options.

Unlike urban areas, no separate Irish brigade was set up. The sons of Belfast served with the young men with whom they had grown up—in the Fourth Regiment, Maine Infantry. Contrary to assertions about Irish women in urban areas, Irish women in Belfast left domestic service—and most other jobs—as soon as the men in their lives made a living wage. After the war, wages shot up higher than they had ever been before. The numbers of women working outside the home was cut in half—but that was not because the work was not there.

Belfast, Maine, has no nineteenth-century record of a July 12th Orange Day celebration—nor a March 17th Saint Patrick's Day celebration, with the influx of Irish Catholics after the Famine. (At best, these kinds of events were remarked as taking place in other localities.)[3] These two Irish holidays of unity and opposition (depending on perspective) were ignored in Belfast. It was as though these people chose to weed out all public demonstrations rooted in Ireland and its politics. The first public celebrations—and, indeed, the only regular celebrations for most of Belfast's history—centered on the Fourth of July and the birth and death days of American founders (Washington, Adams, Jefferson). Nearly a century later, even the Famine Irish immigrants celebrated Independence Day with a great deal of hoopla, as demonstrated by the number of drunk and disorderly arrests taking place around the Fourth of July.[4] Perhaps, Mr. Dooley was right: "Whin an Irishman is four miles out at sea he is as much an American as Presarved Fish."[5]

Timing of immigration had an effect. Cultural traits are created by groups and change based on generational cohorts.[6] By the end of the nineteenth century, Irishness had undergone yet another permutation. When Belfast's Nellie Burkett became engaged, for example, she and her intended had to file information with the Belfast Catholic diocese. When the groom, Thomas O'Shea (his father, Denis, used Shea) filled out his information, he noted his father and mother were both from Ireland, living in Cambridge, Massachusetts. His father was a laborer. Young O'Shea, however, was an actor. He was marrying up: Nellie's father was a merchant. When the form asked for the groom's race under the euphemism of "color," he wrote, "Green."[7] Given the flippancy of his comment, O'Shea embraced his Irishness. After all, he was not afraid to irritate the priest in filling out the marriage license information with such blatant disregard of decorum. Times, it seems, had changed.

Notes

1 Child: 544.
2 Child: 544.
3 "[Orangemen in Liverpool] Riot" [Belfast, Maine] *Hancock Gazette and Penobscot Patriot*, Vol. 1, No. 9 (31 August 1820); St. Patrick's Day celebration notifications and coverage of the events in Bangor, Maine, sponsored by the Bangor Catholic Temperance Society *Whig and Courier* (16 March

1841, 15 March 1842, 18 March 1842, 14 March 1843, 15 March 1843, 16 March 1843, 18 March 1843). The [Belfast, Maine] *Republican Journal* ran information about St. Patrick's events in other cities and articles of interest to Irish readers in the days leading up to 17 March. (See "CONCERT," 5 March 1847, "Something about Ireland," 12 March 1847; a note on the Bangor celebration 28 March 1851; "Death of Moore, the Irish Poet," 26 March 1852; "Some Irishmen Wound up St. Patrick's Day in East Boston with a Fight," 23 March 1855; "Saint Patrick's Day in New York," 22 March 1867.)

4 Police Court Docket: City of Belfast, Commencing at the First Term of Said Court. March. 1853. John Doran, Brian McCabe, James Clark, George Stevens, Josiah Wood, Antony Mally, Ava Burgin, and Lewis L. Ryan were all brought before the Police Court on July 4 and 5, 1853. All, save George Stevens, were fined. Wood was acquitted on one charge but found guilty of intoxication and becoming quarrelsome. He was sentenced to 30 days in jail plus costs; however, he didn't serve any jail time. The Fourth must have been more sedate in 1854—only one appearance before the Police Court: Charles Johnson. Only John Doar appeared before the Police Court in 1855, on July 5.

5 Finley Peter Dunn, *Observations by Mr. Dooley* (New York: R.H. Russell, 1902): 84.

6 Meagher, *Inventing*: 71.

7 *Record of Marriage: For the Use of Ministers of the Gospel, Justices of the Peace and Others Who Are Authorized to Solemnize Marriages* (Portland: Thomas B. Mosher, 1892): 5. St. Brendan the Navigator Parish Records, Camden, Maine.

Bibliography

Primary Sources:

Abbot, Herman. "History from Belfast from its First Settlement to the Year 1825." In *Early Histories of Belfast, Maine*, edited by Alan Taylor. Camden, ME: Picton Press, 1989.

Account Current with the Charitable Irish Society, Membership Account Book, 1837–1861, Vol. 12. Unpublished. Massachusetts Historical Society.

Adams, John. "Adams' Argument for the Defense: 3–4 December 1770." *Founders Online*, National Archives, https://founders.archives.gov/documents/Adams/05-03-02-0001-0004-0016. [Original source: Wroth, L. Kinvin, and Hiller B. Zobel, eds. *The Adams Papers, Legal Papers of John Adams*, Vol. 3, *Cases 63 and 64: The Boston Massacre Trials*, 242–270. Cambridge, Massachusetts: Harvard University Press, 1965.]

Annual Report of the Maine Temperance Society (23 January 1833), Belfast, Maine.

"Belfast Directory." *The Rockland, Belfast, Camden, and Thomaston Directory for 1868*, 63–108. Boston: Langford and Chase, 1868.

Belfast, Town of. Census 1800.

Belfast, Town of. Census 1810.

Belfast, Town of. Census 1820.

Belfast, Town of. Census 1830.

Belfast, Town of. Census 1840.

Belfast, Maine, Vital Records to the Year 1892, Vol. II.

Belfast Probate Court, Case #1673.

Bell, Hon. Charles H., of Exeter, New Hampshire, "Oration." In *The Londonderry Celebration: Exercises on the 150th Anniversary of the Settlement of Old Nutfield, Comprising the towns of Londonderry, Derry, Windham, and Parts of Manchester, Hudson and Salem, N.H., June 10, 1869*, 15–37. Compiled by Robert C. Mack. Manchester: John B. Clarke, 1870.

Brackett, George. *The Republican Journal* 33, no. 2 (11 January 1861): 3, col. 1.

Brackett, George. *The Republican Journal* 33, no. 6 (8 February 1861): 2, col. 7.

Bungay, George Washington. *The Maine Law Museum; and Temperance Anecdotes: Original and Selected*, 61. Boston: Stacey and Richardson, 1852.

Burn, James. "James Burn Describes Irish and German Immigrants in New York City, 1850." In *Major Problems in American Immigration and Ethnic History*, edited by Jon Gjerde. New York: Houghton Mifflin, 1998.

Burtchaell, George Dames, and Thomas Ulick Sadlier, eds. *Alumni Dublinenses: A Register of the Students, Graduates, Professors, and Provosts of Trinity College, in the University of Dublin 1593–1860.* London: Williams and Norgate, 1924; 2nd ed. (Dublin: Alex Thom and Co., Ltd., 1933).

Charitable Irish Society. *(Account Current with the) Membership Account Book, 1837–1861,* 12. Unpublished. Massachusetts Historical Society.

Charitable Irish Society. *Constitution, By-laws and History of the Charitable Irish Society of Boston: Instituted 1737.* Boston: James F. Cotter & Co., n.d.

Child, Lydia Maria. *Lydia Maria Child: Selected Letters, 1817–1880,* edited by Milton Meltzer, Patricia G. Holland, and Francine Krasno. Amherst: University of Massachusetts Press, 1982.

<cemetery.cityofbelfast.org> (accessed 6 March 2014).

Constitution, By-laws and History of the Charitable Irish Society of Boston: Instituted 1737. Boston: James F. Cotter & Co., n.d.

Court of County Commissioners, March Term AD 1854, Book B Set, State v Bryan McCabe, case #361.

Criminal Docket. Police Court. Belfast. Commencing May 23, 1858, continued from book no. 2, cases #424 and #425.

Criminal Docket. Police Court. Belfast. Commenced May 25, 1863, continued from book no. 3, cases #979, #981, #984, #985, #1050, #1401, #1405, and #1863.

Crosby, William George. "Annals of Belfast for Half a Century." In *Early Histories of Belfast, Maine,* edited by Alan Taylor. Camden, Maine: Picton Press, 1989.

Death Records: 1877-: Winterport-Belfast, Searsport, Bucksport. Unpublished records. St. Brendan the Navigator Catholic Church, Camden, Maine.

Diary of Esther Orcutt. LB93.164. Unpublished. Penobscot Marine Museum.

Durham, Mrs. J.C. *Old Houses of Belfast.* Belfast: Waldo County Herald, 1911.

"Eighteenth Century Ulster Emigration to North America," Public Record Office of Northern Ireland: Education Facsimiles, Number 134.

Fenwick, S.J. Benedict, Second Bishop of Boston. *Memoirs to Serve for the Future: Ecclesiastical History of the Diocese of Boston.* Yonkers, New York: U.S. Catholic Historical Society, 1978.

Field, Abigail Davis. Unpublished Day Books. Field Papers. Belfast Historical Society and Museum. Belfast, Maine.

Field, Anna (Annie) Tobey. Unpublished Day Books. Field Papers. Belfast Historical Society and Museum. Belfast, Maine.

Field, Caroline Tobey. Unpublished Day Books. Field Papers. Belfast Historical Society and Museum. Belfast, Maine.

Field, Benjamin Franklin. Unpublished Day Books. Field Papers. Belfast Historical Society and Museum. Belfast, Maine.

Field, Benjamin Franklin. Unpublished Pound Papers. Field Papers. Belfast Historical Society and Museum. Belfast, Maine.

Field, George W., D.D., *Celebration of the One Hundreth Anniversary of the Organization of the First Congregational Church (Now Called the North Church) at Belfast, Maine.* Belfast, Maine: The Belfast Age Publishing Co., 1897.

First Church Congregational, unpublished treasurer's report housed at the Belfast Free Library.

Franklin, Benjamin. "From Benjamin Franklin to William Strahan, September 1, 1764." *Founders Online*, National Archives, https://founders.archives.gov/documents/Franklin/01-11-02-0092. [Original source: *The Papers of Benjamin Franklin* 11 (January 1, through December 31, 1753), edited by Labaree, Leonard W., 331–334. New Haven and London: Yale University Press, 1967.]

Franklin, Benjamin. "An Address to the Good People of Ireland, on Behalf of America, 4 October 1778." In *Winnowings in American History: Revolutionary Broadsides*, No. II, edited by Paul Leicester Ford. Brooklyn, New York: Historical Printing Club, 1891.

Franklin, Benjamin. "From Benjamin Franklin to Baron Francis Maseres, June 26, 1785." In *The Writings of Benjamin Franklin: Collected and Edited with a Life and Introduction*, edited by Albert Henry Smyth. IX. Norwood, Massachusetts: J. S. Cushing and Company, n.d.

Franklin, Benjamin. In "Letter to William Strahan, Passy, Augt 19th 1784." In *The Writings of Benjamin Franklin: Collected and Edited with a Life and Introduction*, edited by Albert Henry Smyth. IX. Norwood, Massachusetts: J. S. Cushing and Company, n.d.

Franklin, Benjamin. "A Narrative of the Late Massacres." In *The Heath Anthology of American Literature*, 1, edited by Paul Lauter, Richard Yarborough, Jackson Bryer, Anne Goodwyn Jones, Wendy Martin, Charles Molesworth, Raymund Paredes, et al., 733–744. New York: Houghton, Mifflin, 1998.

Gammons Store at City Point Day Book: 1826-__, Belfast, September 18, 1826, Belfast Free Library Archives. Given by Mrs. Fred Holmes, a cousin of Maud Gammons.

Hancock Gazette and Penobscot Patriot I, no. 16 (19 October 1820).

Hancock Gazette and Penobscot Patriot I, no. 24 (14 December 1820): 1.

Hancock Gazette and Penobscot Patriot I, no. 32 (8 February 1821).

Hancock Gazette and Penobscot Patriot I, no. 37 (15 March 1821): 4.

Hancock Gazette and Penobscot Patriot II, no. 2 (4 July 1821).

Hancock Gazette and Penobscot Patriot II, no. 2 (11 July 1821).

Hancock Gazette and Penobscot Patriot II, no. 3 (18 July 1821).

Hancock Gazette and Penobscot Patriot II, no. 5 (1 August 1821).

Hancock Gazette and Penobscot Patriot 11, no. 9 (29 August 1821).

Hancock Gazette and Penobscot Patriot II, no. 10 (5 September 1821).

Hancock Gazette and Penobscot Patriot II, no. 30 (30 January 1822).

Hancock Gazette and Penobscot Patriot II, no. 32 (6 February 1822).

Hancock Gazette and Penobscot Patriot II, no. 33 (13 February 1822).

Images of America: Londonderry. Portsmouth, NH: Londonderry Historical Society, 2004.

Journal of the Executive Proceedings of the Senate of the United States of America from December 1, 1845, to August 14, 1848, inclusive, VII. (8 August 1846). Washington, D.C.: GPO, 1887.

Knights of Columbus. "Council History." https://www.kofc3942.org/council.history. Downloaded 3 December 2020.

Lechmere, Thomas. Letter to His Brother-in-law John Winthrop, 4 August 1718. Collections of the Massachusetts Historical Society, 6th ser. V. Boston: Massachusetts Historical Society, 1892, 387 footnote. Accessed from Google eBooks, 13 August 2013.

Marriage Records 1877–1908: Winterport-Bucksport-Belfast. Unpublished records. St. Brendan the Navigator Catholic Church, Camden, Maine.

Massachusetts (Colony) General Court: Journals of the House of Representatives of Massachusetts 1718–1720, Vol. 2. Boston: Massachusetts Historical Society, 1921. Accessed from Google eBooks, 13 August 2013.

Maycock, Dr. Thomas. Personal Communication. Undated (circa 2010).

New Jersey Episcopal Diocese of Newark, New Jersey, Sunday, 27 March 1892, cert. #1096. (Ancestry Library-downloaded 27 July 2017.)

Parkinson, R. "Henry Parkinson." *The Granite Monthly: A Magazine of Literature, History and State Progress* 5 (1881–82): 215–219.

Parker, The Rev. Edward L. *History of Londonderry: Comprising the Towns of Derry and Londonderry, New Hampshire.* Boston: Perkins and Whipple, 1851.

Patterson, Hon James W. "Address." In *The Londonderry Celebration: Exercises on the 150th Anniversary of the Settlement of Old Nutfield, Comprising the towns of Londonderry, Derry, Windham, and Parts of Manchester, Hudson and Salem, N.H., June 10, 1869.* Compiled by Robert C. Mack, 25–27. Manchester: John B. Clarke, 1870.

Pendleton, Florence Ferguson. PMM 39 Pendleton Collection, Penobscot Marine Museum, Searsport, Maine.

Police Court (Docket of the): City of Belfast. Commencing at the First Term of Said Court. March. 1853. Criminal Docket ends. Aug. 1855 [cq]. Carried to Another Book. Cases: #6, #33½, #89, #113, #224, #284, #295, #326, #381, #424, #425, #504, #507, #554, #594, #602, #609, #901, #950, and #959.

Probate records, Middlesex County, Massachusetts, 20 September 1853. (Ancestry Library-downloaded 27 July 2017.)

Public Record Office of Northern Ireland: Education Facsimiles 121–140: "18th Century Ulster Emigration to North America," no. 134.

Record of Marriage: For the Use of Ministers of the Gospel, Justices of the Peace and Others Who Are Authorized to Solemnize Marriages (Portland: Thomas B. Mosher, 1892). St. Brendan the Navigator Parish Records, Camden, Maine.

Rules and Regulations of the Scots Charitable Society: Instituted at Boston a.d. 1684 and Reconstituted 1786. Unpublished. Massachusetts Historical Society.

Shute, Samuel. *Massachusetts (Colony) General Court: Journals of the House of Representatives of Massachusetts 1718–1720,* 2 (31 Oct. 1718). Accessed from Google eBooks, 13 August 2013.

Staples, Miles. [Belfast, Maine] Coroner's Report, "Inquest on the Body of Bridgett McCabe," 5 January 1861.

Superior Judicial Court, Belfast, Waldo County records, Naturalizing Records.

"The Case of Nathaniel M. Lowney, Collector of Belfast," unsigned pamphlet no. 1364, Maine Historical Society, n.d.

The Progressive Age 7, no. 18 (10 January 1861): 3.

The Progressive Age 9, no. 37 (25 June 1863).

The Republican Journal 5, no. 11 (18 April 1833).

The Republican Journal 5, no. 13 (2 May 1833).

The Republican Journal 5, no. 24 (18 July 1833): 3, col. 3.

The Republican Journal 12, no. 31 (3 September 1840): 1, col. 5.

The Republican Journal 12 (10 September 1840).

The Republican Journal 12, no. 38 (22 October 1840): 3.

The Republican Journal 12, no. 49 (7 January 1841).

The Republican Journal 12, no. 50 (14 January 1841).

The Republican Journal 13, no. 2 (11 February 1841).

The Republican Journal 13, no. 3 (18 February 1841): 1.

The Republican Journal 15, no. 11 (14 April 1843).

The Republican Journal 15, no. 12 (21 April 1843): 1, col. 4.

The Republican Journal 15, no. 14 (5 May 1843): 3, col. 3.

The Republican Journal 15, no. 15 (12 May 1843): 1, col. 2, bottom.

The Republican Journal 15, no. 16 (19 May 1843): 3, col. 2.

The Republican Journal 15, no. 19 (6 June 1843): 2, cols 1 and 2.

The Republican Journal 15, no. 12 (7 July 1843): 2, col. 6.

The Republican Journal 15, no. 24 (14 July 1843): 2.

The Republican Journal 15, no. 27 (4 August 1843).

The Republican Journal 15, no. 28 (11 August 1843): 1, col. 4.

The Republican Journal 15, no. 34 (22 September 1843).

The Republican Journal 15, no. 38 (20 October 1843).

The Republican Journal 15, no. 39 (27 October 1843): 1, col. 6.

The Republican Journal 15, no. 40 (3 November 1843): 3, col. 5.

The Republican Journal 19, no. 6 (5 March 1847): 3.

The Republican Journal 19 (5 March 1847): 2, col. 4.

The Republican Journal 19 (5 March 1847): 2, col. 6.

The Republican Journal 22, no. 14 (26 April 1850): 3.

The Republican Journal 22, no. 24 (5 July 1850): 3.

The Republican Journal 22, no. 27 (26 July 1850): 3.

The Republican Journal 24, no. 10 (26 March 1852): 3.

The Republican Journal 33, no. 3 (18 January 1861): 3, col. 2.

The Republican Journal 43, no. 50 (19 June 1873): 3, col. 2.

The Republican Journal 44, no. 20 (20 November 1873).

The Republican Journal 53, no. 22 (2 June 1881): 2.

The Republican Journal 73, no. 3 (17 January 1901).

The Republican Journal 73, no. 4 (24 January 1901): 1.

The Weekly Recorder VIII, no. 38 (19 March 1874): 3.

The Williamson Family Papers: 1: The College Years, 1844–1852. Rockport, Maine: Picton Press, 2003.

Third Report of the Board of Education of the State of Maine. Augusta: William T. Johnson, printer to the State, 1849.

Typed MS from hand-written original. July 5, 1896, July 12, 1896. Pendleton-Park Papers, Penobscot Marine Museum.

U.S. Census for Belfast, Maine 1850.

U.S. Census for Belfast, Maine 1860.

U.S. Census for Belfast, Maine 1870.

U.S. Census for Belfast, Maine 1880.

U.S. Census Bureau, American FactFinder. "Measuring America: People, Places, and Our Economy," factfinder2.census.gov. Downloaded 3 March 2014.

U.S. Congress. Senate. XX Congress, X sess., 29 December 1845. *Journal of the Executive Proceedings of the Senate of the United States of America, from December 1, 1845 to August 14, 1848, Inclusive*, Vol. VII. Washington: GPO, 1887.

White, William. "A History of Belfast: With Introductory Remarks on Acadia." In *Early Histories of Belfast, Maine*, edited by Alan Tayler, 245–279. Camden: Picton Press, 1989.

Willey, George F. *Willey's Book of Nutfield: A History of that Part of New Hampshire Comprised within the Limits of the Old Township of Londonderry from its Settlement in 1719 to the Present Time*. Derry Depot, New Hampshire: Geo. F. Willey, 1895.

Williamson, Joseph. *The History of the City of Belfast, Maine*, 1. Somersworth, New Hampshire: New England History Press, 1982.

Williamson, Joseph, and Alfred Johnson. *The History of the City of Belfast, Maine*, 2. Somersworth, New Hampshire: New England History Press, 1983.

Secondary Sources:

Akenson, Donald Harman. "The Historiography of the Irish in the United States of America." In *The Irish in New Communities, Volume 2 in the Series, The Irish World Wide: History, Heritage, Identity*, edited by Patrick O'Sullivan. London: Leicester University Press, 1992.

Akenson, Donald Harman. *Diaspora: A Primer*. Belfast: Institute of Irish Studies, 1996.

Amireh, Amal. *The Factory Girl and the Seamstress: Imagining Gender and Class in Nineteenth Century Fiction*. New York: Garland Publishing Inc., 2000.

Anbinder, Tyler. *Five Points: The Nineteenth Century New York City Neighborhood that Invented Tap Dance, Stole Elections, and Became the World's Most Notorious Slum*. New York: The Free Press, 2001.

Banks, Ronald F. *Maine Becomes a State: The Movement to Separate Maine from Massachusetts, 1795–1820*. Somersworth: New Hampshire Publishing for the Maine Historical Society, 1973.

Barclay, Katie. "Stereotypes as Political Resistance: The Irish Police Court Columns, c. 1820-1845." *Social History* 42, no. 2 (2017): 257–280.

Bauman, John F. *Gateway to Vacationland: The Making of Portland, Maine*. Amherst: University Press of Massachusetts, 2012.

Bhabha, Homi. "Unpacking My Library Again." *The Journal of the Midwest Modern Language Association* 28, no. 1 (Spring 1995): 5–18.

Bolton, Charles Knowles. *Scotch Irish Pioneers in Ulster and America*. Boston: Bacon and Brown, 1910.

Boskin, Joseph, and Joseph Dorinson. "Ethnic Humor: Subversion and Survival." *American Quarterly* 37, no. 1 (1985): 81–97.

Bric, Maurice J. "Patterns of Irish Emigration to America, 1783–1800." *Eire/Ireland* 36, nos. 1-2 (Spring-Summer 2001): 10–28.

Brockmeier, Jens. "After the Archive: Remapping Memory: A Historical Perspective." *Culture and Psychology* 16, no. 5 (2010): 5–35.

Bruchey, Stuart. *Enterprise: The Dynamic Economy of a Free People*. Cambridge, MA: Harvard University Press, 1990.

Calomiris, Charles W., and Larry Schweikart. "The Panic of 1857: Origins, Transmission, and Containment." *The Journal of Economic History* 51, no. 4 (December 1991): 807–834.

Campbell, Malcolm. *Ireland's New Worlds: Immigrants, Politics, and Society in the United States and Australia, 1815–1822.* Madison: University of Wisconsin Press, 2008.

Capizzi, Joseph E. "For What Shall We Repent? Reflections on the American Bishops, Their Teaching, and Slavery in the United States, 1838-1861." *Theological Studies* 65, no. 4 (December 2004). Gale Academic OneFile, downloaded 15 June 2020.

Carroll, Michael P. "How the Irish Became Protestant in America." *Religion and American Culture: A Journal of Interpretation* 16, no. 1 (Winter 2006): 25–54.

Clark, Dennis J. "Intrepid Men: Three Philadelphia Irish Leaders, 1880-1920." In *From Paddy to Studs: Irish-American Communities in the Turn of the Century era, 1880–1920: Contributions in Ethnic Studies, No. 13*, edited by Timothy J. Meagher, 93–115. Westport, Connecticut: Greenwood Press, 1986.

Connolly, Michael C., ed. *They Change Their Sky: The Irish in Maine.* Orono: University of Maine Press, 2004.

Cullen, L.M. *The Emergence of Modern Ireland: 1600–1900.* New York: Homes and Meier Publishers, 1981.

Curtis, Lewis P. Jr. *Apes and Angels: The Irishman in Victorian Culture.* Newton Abbot, Devon, England: David and Charles, 1971.

Daly, Mary E. "Women, Work and Trade Unionism." In *Women in Irish Society: The Historical Dimension*, edited by Margaret MacCurtain and Donncha Ó Corráin. Westport, Connecticut: Greenwood Press, 1979.

Danaher, Nessan. "Irish Studies: A Historical Survey across the Irish Diaspora." In *The Irish World Wide: History, Heritage, Identity* series, Vol. 2, *The Irish in the New Communities*, edited by Patrick O'Sullivan, 226–256. Leicester and London: Leicester University Press, 1992.

Denzin, Norman K. *Performance Ethnography: Critical Pedagogy and the Politics of Culture.* Thousand Oaks, Calif.: Sage Publications, Inc., 2003.

Diner, Hasia. *Erin's Daughters in America: Irish Immigrant Women in the Nineteenth Century.* Baltimore: The Johns Hopkins University Press, 1983.

Doyle, David Noel. "Scots Irish or Scotch-Irish." In *Making the Irish American: History and Heritage of the Irish in the United States*, edited by J.J. Lee and Marion R. Casey. New York: New York University Press, 2006.

Drake, Michael. "Population Growth and the Irish Economy." In *The Formation of the Irish Economy*, edited by L.M. Cullen. Cork: The Mercier Press, 1968, reprinted 1976: 65–76.

Eckstein, Susan. "On Deconstructing and Reconstructing the Meaning of Immigrant Generations." In *The Changing Face of Home: The Transnational Lives of the Second Generation*, edited byPeggy Levitt and Mary C. Waters, 211–215. New York: Russell Sage Foundation, 2002.

Ell, Paul S. et al., "No Spatial Watershed: Religious Geographies of Ireland Pre- and Post-Famine." In *Global Legacies of the Great Irish Famine:*

Transnational and Interdisciplinary Perspectives, edited by Marguerite Corporaal, et al., 197–224. New York: Peter Lang, 2014.

Fegan, Melissa. "Waking the Bones: The Return of the Famine Dead in Contemporary Irish Literature." In *Global Legacies of the Great Irish Famine: Transnational and Interdisciplinary Perspectives*, edited by Marguerite Corporaal, et al., 157–174. New York: Peter Lang, 2014.

Foner, Eric. *Free Soil: Free Labor: Free Men: The Ideology of the Republican Part before the Civil War*. New York: Oxford University Press, 1995.

Ford, Henry Jones. *The Scotch-Irish in America*. Princeton: Princeton University Press, 1915.

Gimbutas, Marija. *The Civilization of the Goddess*. San Francisco: HarperSanFrancisco, 1991.

Gjerde, Jon, ed. *Major Problems in American Immigration and Ethnic History*. New York: Houghton Mifflin, 1998.

Gleeson, David T. "Failing to 'Unite with the Abolitionists': The Irish Nationalist Press and U.S. Emancipation." *Slavery & Abolition: A Journal of Slave and Post-Slave Studies* 37, no. 3 (2016): 622–637. DOI: 10.1080/0144039X.201 6.1208911, 10.1080/0144039X.2015.1208911.

Graham, Colin, and Richard, Kirkland, eds. *Ireland and Cultural Theory: The Mechanics of Authenticity*. London: Macmillian Press Ltd., 1999.

Graham, Colin, and Kirkland, Richard. "Maybe That's Just Blarney': Irish Culture and the Persistence of Authenticity." In *Ireland and Cultural Theory: The Mechanics of Authenticity*, 7–28. London: Macmillian Press Ltd., 1999.

Griffin, Patrick. *The People with No Name: Ireland's Ulster Scots, America's Scots Irish, and the Creation of a British Atlantic World, 1689–1764*. Princeton: Princeton University Press, 2001.

Griffin, William D. *A Portrait of the Irish in America*. Dublin: The Academy Press, 1981.

Guinnane, Timothy W. *The Vanishing Irish: Households, Migration, and the Rural Economy in Ireland, 1850-1914*. Princeton: Princeton University Press, 1997.

Handlin, Oscar. *Boston's Immigrants: A Study in Acculturation*. Boston: Belknap Press of Harvard University Press, 1959.

Harvey, David C., et al. *Celtic Geographies: Old Culture, New Times*. London: Routledge, 2002.

Hoerder, Dirk. "Review: Recent Methodological and Conceptual Approaches to Migration: Comparing the Globe or the North Atlantic World?" *Journal of American Ethnic History* 29, no. 2 (Winter 2010): 79–84.

Huston, James L. *The Panic of 1857 and the Coming of the Civil War*. Baton Rouge: Louisiana State University Press, 1987.

Ignatiev, Noel. *How the Irish Became White*. New York: Routledge, 1995.

"Inflation Calculator." U.S. Official Inflation Data, Alioth Finance, 11 Mar. 2020, https://www.officialdata.org/.

Janis, Ely M. "Petticoat Revolutionaries: Gender, Ethnic Nationalism, and the Irish Ladies' Land League in the United States." *Journal of American Ethnic History* 27, no. 2 (Winter 2008): 5–27.

Jenkins, William. "Remapping 'Irish America': Circuits, Places, Performances." *Journal of American Ethnic History* 28, no. 4 (Summer 2009).

Judd, Richard W. "The Aroostook War, 1828–42." In *Maine: The Pine Tree State from Prehistory to the Present*, edited by Richard W. Judd, Edwin A. Churchill, and Joel W. Eastman. Orono: University of Maine Press, 1995.

Katzman, David M. *Seven Days a Week: Women and Domestic Service in Industrializing America*. New York: Oxford University Press, 1978.

Kenny, Kevin. *The American Irish: A History*. New York: Pearson Education, Inc., 2000.

Kenny, Kevin. "Diaspora and Comparison: The Global Irish as a Case Study." *The Journal of American History* 90, no. 1 (June 2003): 134–162. Downloaded from http://jah.oxfordjournals.org/ by guest on February 4, 2016.

Kenny, Kevin. *Diaspora: A Very Short Introduction*. Oxford: Oxford University Press, 2013.

Kenny, Kevin. *Making Sense of the Molly Maguires*. Oxford: Oxford University Press, 1998.

Kenny, Kevin. *Peaceable Kingdom Lost: The Paxton Boys and the Destruction of William Penn's Holy Experiment*. Oxford: Oxford University Press, 2009.

Kenny, Kevin. "Twenty Years of Irish American Historiography." *Journal of American Ethnic History* 28, no. 4 (Summer 2009): 67–75.

Kenny, Kevin. *The Great Irish Famine: Impact, Ideology and Rebellion. British History in Perspective Series*, edited by Jeremy Black. Houndmills, Basingstoke, Hampton, England: Palgrave, 2002.

Kinealy, Christine. *This Great Calamity: The Irish Famine 1845–1852*. Dublin: Gill and Macmillan, 1994.

Kirkland, Richard. "Questioning the Frame: Hybridity, Ireland and the Institution." In *Ireland and Cultural Theory: The Mechanics of Authenticity*, 210–228. London: Macmillian Press, 1999.

Kneale, James. "The Place of Drink: Temperance and the Public, 1856–1914." *Social and Cultural Geography* 2, no. 1 (2001): 43–59.

Koch, John T., and John Carey. *The Celtic Heroic Age: Literary Sources for Ancient Celtic Europe and Early Ireland and Wales*. Malden, Massachusetts: Celtic Studies Publications, 1995.

Kohl, Manfred Waldemar. *Congregationalism in America*. Oak Creek, Wisconsin: The Congregational Press, 1977.

Lebergott, Stanley. "Wage Trends, 1800–1900." In *Trends in the American Economy in the Nineteenth Century*. Princeton: Princeton University Press, 1960; accessed online 20 June 2016 at www.nber.org/chapters/c2486.pdf.

Lee, J.J., and Marion R. Casey. *Making the Irish American: History and Heritage of the Irish in the United States*. New York: New York University Press, 2006.

Levitt, Peggy, and Waters, Mary C., eds. *The Changing Face of Home: The Transnational Lives of the Second Generation*. New York: Russell Sage Foundation, 2002.

Lucey, S.J., and William Leo. *The Catholic Church in Maine*. Francestown, New Hampshire: Marshall Jones, 1957.

Lynch-Brennan, Margaret. *The Irish Bridget: Irish Immigrant Women in Domestic Service in America, 1840–1930*. Syracuse: Syracuse University Press, 2009.

MacDougal, Pauleena. *The Penobscot Dance of Resistance: Tradition in the*

History of a People. Durham, New Hampshire: University of New Hampshire Press, 2004.

MacLaughlin, Jim. "'Pestilence on their Backs, Famine in their Stomachs': The Racial Construction of Irishness and the Irish in Victorian Britain." In *Ireland and Cultural Theory: The Mechanics of Authenticity*, 50–76. London: Macmillian Press, 1999.

MacLysaght, Edward. *The Surnames of Ireland*, 3rd ed. Dublin: The Irish Academic Press, 1978.

MacSparran, Reverend James. "America Dissected, etc. in Sundry Letters from a Clergyman There: Letter 1: To the Hon. Col. Henry Cary, Esq." In *A History of the Episcopal Church in Narragansett, Rhode Island: Including a History of Other Episcopal Churches in the State*. Wilkins Updike, Boston: Merrymount Press, 1907.

Maine Catholic Historical Magazine.

McCarron, Edward T. "Facing the Atlantic: The Irish Merchant Community of Lincoln County, 1780–1820." In *They Change Their Sky: The Irish in Maine*, 61-96. Orono: University of Maine Press, 2004.

McCarron, Fidelma M. "Ireland along the Passamaquoddy: Rathlin Islanders in Washington County, Maine." In *They Change Their Sky: The Irish in Maine*, 97-120. Orono: University of Maine Press, 2004.

McCarthy, James, and Hague, Euan. "Race, Nation, and Nature: The Cultural Politics of 'Celtic' Identification in the American West." *Annals of the Association of American Geographers* 94, no. 2 (June 2004): 387–408.

McCarthy, Mark, ed. *Ireland's Heritages: Critical Perspectives on Memory and Identity*. Aldershot, England: Ashgate Publishing, 2005.

McGowan, Mark. "Contemporary Links Between Canadian and Irish Famine Commemoration." In *Global Legacies of the Great Irish Famine: Transnational and Interdisciplinary Perspectives*, edited by Marguerite Corporaal, et al., 267–283. New York: Peter Lang, 2014.

McKenna, Ellen. "The Visits to Ireland of John Hughes, Archbishop of New York, from 1840 to 1862." *Clogher Record* 20, no. 1 (2009): 19–38.

McMahon, Cian T. "Caricaturing Race and Nation in the Irish American Press, 1870-1880: A Transnational Perspective." *Journal of American Ethnic History* 33, no. 2 (Winter 2014): 33–56. JSTOR.

McMahon, Cian T. *The Global Dimensions of Irish Identity: Race, Nation, and the Popular Press, 1840-1880*. Chapel Hill: University of North Carolina Press, 2015.

McMahon, Cian T. "International Celebrities and Irish Identity in the United States and Beyond, 1840–1860." *American Nineteenth Century History* 15, no. 2 (2014): 147-168. DOI: 10.1080/14664658.2014.938951.

McMahon, Cian T. "Ireland and the Birth of the Irish-American Press, 1842–61." *American Periodicals* 19, no. 1 SPECIAL ISSUE: Immigrant Periodicals (2009): 5-20. https://www.jstor.org/stable/23025142.

McMahon, Sean. *A Short History of Ireland*. Chester Springs, PA: Dufour, 1996.

Marty, Martin E. *Pilgrims in Their Own Land: Five Hundred Years of Religion in America*. Boston: Little, Brown, and Company, 1984.

Matheson, Sir Robert E. *Special Report on Surnames in Ireland with Notes as to Numerical Strength, Derivation, Ethnology, and Distribution: Based on Information Extracted from the Indexes of the General Register Office*. Dublin: His Majesty's Stationery Office, 1909.

Meagher, Timothy J., ed. *From Paddy to Studs: Irish-American Communities in the Turn of the Century era, 1880–1920: Contributions in Ethnic Studies, No. 13.* Westport, Connecticut: Greenwood Press, 1986.

Meagher, Timothy J. *Inventing Irish America: Generation, Class, and Ethnic Identity in a New England City, 1880–1928.* Notre Dame: University Press, 2001.

Meagher, Timothy J. "Irish, American, Catholic: Irish-American Identity in Worcester, Massachusetts, 1880 to 1920." *From Paddy to Studs: Irish-American Communities in the Turn of the Century era, 1880-1920: Contributions in Ethnic Studies, No. 13,* edited by Timothy J. Meagher, 75–92. Westport, Connecticut: Greenwood Press, 1986.

Miller, Kerby A. *Emigrants and Exiles: Ireland and the Irish Exodus to North America.* Oxford: University Press, 1985.

Miller, Kerby A. *Ireland and Irish America: Culture, Class, and Transatlantic Migration.* Dublin: Field Day, 2008.

Miller, Kerby A. "Revd James MacSparran's 'America Dissected' (1753): Eighteenth-Century Emigration and Construction of 'Irishness'." *History Ireland* 11, no. 4 (2003): 17–22. Accessed 15 February 2021. http://www.jstor.org/stable/27725061.

Miller, Kerby A. "Ulster Presbyterians and the 'Two Traditions' in Ireland and America." In *Making the Irish American: History and Heritage of the Irish in the United States,* edited by J.J. Lee and Marion R. Casey, 255–270. New York: New York University Press, 2006.

Miller, Kerby A., Arnold Schrier, Bruce D. Boling, and David N. Doyle. *Irish Immigrants in the Land of Canaan: Letters and Memoirs from Colonial and Revolutionary America, 1675–1815.* Oxford: University Press, 2003.

Mitchell, Brian C. "'They Do Not Differ Greatly': The Pattern of Community Development among the Irish in Late Nineteenth Century Lowell, Massachusetts." In *From Paddy to Studs: Irish-American Communities in the Turn of the Century era, 1880–1920: Contributions in Ethnic Studies, No. 13,* edited by Timothy J. Meagher, 53–73. Westport, Connecticut: Greenwood Press, 1986.

Moloney, Deirdre. "Who's Irish? Ethnic Identity and Recent Trends in Irish American History." *Journal of American Ethnic History* 28, no. 4 (Summer 2009): 100–109.

Montgomery, Michael. "Presidential Address: Voices of My Ancestors: A Personal Search for the Language of the Scotch-Irish." *American Speech* 80, no. 4 (Winter 2005): 341–365.

Moody, T.W., and F.X. Martin. *The Course of Irish History,* revised and enlarged edition. Dublin: Radio Telefís Éireann, 1984.

Moran, William. *The Belles of New England.* New York: Thomas Dunne Books, 2002.

Morone, James A. *Hellfire Nation: The Politics of Sin in American History.* New Haven: Princeton University Press, 2003.

Moss, Kenneth. "St. Patrick's Day Celebration and the Formation of the Irish American Identity, 1845–1875." *Journal of Social History* 29, no. 9 (Fall 1995).

Mundy, James. *Hard Times, Hard Men*. Scarborough, ME: Harp Publications, 1990.

Nally, David P. *Human Encumbrances: Political Violence and the Great Irish Famine*. Notre Dame: University Press, 2011.

Nash, Catherine. *Of Irish Descent: Origin Stories, Genealogy, and the Politics of Belonging*. Syracuse, New York: New York University Press, 2008.

Nearing, Scott. "Wages in the United States." *Annals of the American Academy of Political and Social Science* 48 (July 1913): 42. JSTOR.

Negra, Diane, ed. *The Irish in Us: Irishness, Performativity, and Popular Culture*. Durham: Duke University Press, 2006.

Newby, Andrew G. "'Rather Peculiar Claims upon Our Sympathies': Britain and Famine in Finland, 1856–1868." In *Global Legacies of the Great Irish Famine: Transnational and Interdisciplinary Perspectives*, edited by Marguerite Corporaal, et al., 61–80. New York: Peter Lang, 2014.

Nolan, Janet. *Ourselves Alone: Women's Emigration from Ireland 1885–1920*. Lexington: University of Kentucky Press, 1989.

Nolan, Janet. "Woman's Place in the History of the Irish Diaspora: A Snapshot." *Journal of American Ethnic History* 28, no. 4 (Summer 2009): 76–81.

O'Grady, Joseph P. *How the Irish Became Americans*. New York: Twayne Publishers, 1973.

Ó hÓgáin, Dáithí. *The Celts: A History*. Cork: The Collins Press, 2002.

O'Neill, Jonathan. "A Nod is as Good as a Wink: Humor, Postcolonialism and the Case of Irish." *American Journal of Irish Studies* 13 (2016): 67–78.

O'Neill, Kevin. "'Man Overboard': Change and Stability in Post Famine Ireland." In *From Paddy to Studs: Irish-American Communities in the Turn of the Century era, 1880-1920: Contributions in Ethnic Studies, No. 13*, edited by Timothy J. Meagher, 27–51. Westport, Connecticut: Greenwood Press, 1986.

O'Sullivan, Patrick, "Introduction." In *The Irish in New Communities, Volume 2 in the Series, The Irish World Wide: History, Heritage, Identity*, 1–25. London: Leicester University Press, 1992.

Ó Tuathaigh, Gearóid. "The Role of Women in Ireland under the New English Order." In *Women in Irish Society: The Historical Dimension*, edited by Margaret MacCurtain and Donncha Ó Corráin. Westport, CT: Greenwood Press, 1979.

Okrent, Daniel. *Last Call: The Rise and Fall of Prohibition*. New York: Scribner, 2010.

Pease, Jane H., and William H. Pease. *Ladies, Women and Wenches: Choice and Constraint in Antebellum Charleston and Boston*. Chapel Hill: North Carolina Press, 1990.

Perry, the Rev. Arthur Latham. *Scotch-Irish in New England*. New York: Charles Scribner's Sons, 1896.

Pinette, Megan. "The Gardeners of Old Belfast." *Belfast Historical Society & Museum News* 5, no. 1 (Summer 2016).

Raftery, Barry. *Pagan Celtic Ireland: The Enigma of the Irish Iron Age*. London: Thames and Hudson, 1994.

Rains, Stephanie. "Irish Roots: Genealogy and the Performance of Irishness." In

The Irish in Us: Irishness, Performativity, and Popular Culture, edited by Diane Negra, 130–160. Durham: Duke University Press, 2006.

Reid, Anthony. "Lessons of Tambora Ignored, 200 Years on." https://www.eastasiaforum.org/2015/04/25/lessons-of-tambora-ignored-200-years-on/ accessed 16 March 2020.

Roediger, David R. *The Wages of Whiteness: Race and the Making of the American Working Class*. New York: Verso, 1991.

Rorabaugh, W.J. *The Alcoholic Republic: An American Tradition*. New York: Oxford University Press, 1979.

Rumbaut, Rubén. "Severed or Sustained Attachments?: Language, Identity, and Imagined Communities in post-Immigrant Generation." In *The Changing Face of Home: The Transnational Lives of the Second Generation*, edited by Peggy Levitt and Mary C. Waters, 43–95. New York: Russell Sage Foundation, 2002.

Sacks, Marie L. "The Two Faces of Ballstown: Religion, Governance, and Cultural Values on the Maine Frontier 1760–1820." *Maine History* 43 (January 2007).

Sarbaugh, Timothy. "Exiles of Confidence: The Irish-American Community of San Francisco, 1880–1920." In *From Paddy to Studs: Irish-American Communities in the Turn of the Century era, 1880–1920: Contributions in Ethnic Studies, No. 13*, edited by Timothy J. Meagher, 161–179. Westport, Connecticut: Greenwood Press, 1986.

Shannon, Catherine. "With Good Will Doing Service: The Charitable Irish Society of Boston." *Historical Journal of Massachusetts* 43, no. 1 (Winter 2015).

Skerrett, Ellen. "The Development of Catholic Identity among Irish Americans in Chicago, 1880 to 1920." In *From Paddy to Studs: Irish-American Communities in the Turn of the Century era, 1880–1920: Contributions in Ethnic Studies, No. 13*, edited by Timothy J. Meagher, 117–138. Westport, Connecticut: Greenwood Press, 1986.

Slomanson, Peter. "Cataclysm as Catalyst for Language Shift," *Global Legacies of the Great Irish Famine: Transnational and Interdisciplinary Perspectives*, edited by Marguerite Corporaal, et al. New York: Peter Lang, 2014: 81–99.

Smyth, Gerry. "Decolonizatin and Criticism: Towards a Theory of Irish Critical Discourse." In *Ireland and Cultural Theory: The Mechanics of Authenticity*, 29–49. London: Macmillian Press, 1999.

Spraker, Christopher M. "The Lost History of Slaves and Slave owners in Billerica." *Historical Journal of Massachusetts* 42, no. 1 (Winter 2014): 108–141.

Stampp, Kenneth M. *America in 1857: A Nation on the Brink*. Oxford University Press, 1992.

Stout, Geraldine. *Bend of the Boyne: An Archaeological Landscape*. Dublin: Country House, 1997.

Swift, Roger. "The Historiography of the Irish in Nineteenth-Century Britain." In *The Irish in New Communities, Volume 2 in the Series, The Irish World Wide: History, Heritage, Identity*, edited by Patrick O'Sullivan. London: Leicester University Press, 1992.

Taylor, Alan. "'Sprung up in a Day': Belfast, Maine, Emerges as a Market

Town." In *Early Histories of Belfast Maine: Annals of Belfast for Half a Century by William George Crosby, Sketches of the Early History of Belfast by John Lymburner Locke, History of Belfast by Herman Abbot, A History of Belfast with Introductory Remarks on Acadia by William White*, v-xiv. Camden, Maine: Picton Press, 1989.

"The Catholic Church in Belfast." *Maine Catholic Historical Magazine* 7, no. 3 (1917).

"The Gardeners of Old Belfast." *Belfast Historical Society & Museum News* 5, no. 1 (Summer 2016).

The Scots in Ulster: The First Scottish Migrations to Ulster, 1606-1641 Surname Map and Pocket History: Discover the Ulster-Scots, the Scots-Irish and the Scotch-Irish, published by Ulster-Scots Agency, Ulster Historical Foundation, Tourism Ireland. See www.ancestryireland.com/scotsinulster and www.maineulsterscots.com.

Towey, Martin G. "Kerry Patch Revisited: Irish Americans in St. Louis in the turn of the Century Era." In *From Paddy to Studs: Irish-American Communities in the Turn of the Century era, 1880–1920: Contributions in Ethnic Studies, No. 13*, edited by Timothy J. Meagher, 139–159. Westport, Connecticut: Greenwood Press, 1986.

Tyson, Lois. "Postcolonial Criticism." In *Critical Theory Today: A User Friendly Guide*, 3rd ed. Routledge, 2015.

Walker, Brian. "The Lost Tribes of Ireland: Diversity, Identity, and Loss among the Irish Diaspora." *Irish Studies Review* 15, no. 3 (2007): 267–282. https://www.tandfonline.com/loi/cisr20

Wallace, R. Stuart. "The Scotch-Irish of Provincial maine: Purpooduck, Merrymeeting Bay, and Georgia." In *They Change Their Sky: The Irish in Maine*, edited by Michael C. Connolly. Orono: University of Maine Press, 2004.

Walter, Bronwen. "Gendered Irishness in Britain: Changing Constructions." In *Ireland and Cultural Theory: The Mechanics of Authenticity*, 77–98. London: Macmillian Press, 1999.

Walters, Kerry S. *Benjamin Franklin and His Gods*. Urbana and Chicago: University of Illinois Press, 1999.

Waters, Mary C., and Eschbach, Karl. "Immigration and Ethnic and Racial Inequality in the United States." *Annual Review of Sociology* 21 (1995): 419-446.

Welter, Barbara. "The Cult of True Womanhood: 1820–1860." *American Quarterly* 18, no. 2 Part 1 (Summer 1966): 151–174. Downloaded from JSTOR, 10 June 2020.

Welsch, Roger. *Why I'm an Only Child and Other Slightly Naughty Plains Folktales*. Lincoln: University of Nebraska Press, 2016.

Wikipedia. http://en.wikipedia.org/wiki/List_of_countries_by_beer_consumption_per_capita

Wittke, Carl. *The Irish in America*. New York: Russell and Russell, 1970, reprinted. Copyright Louisiana State University Press, 1956.

Woodham-Smith, Cecil. *The Great Hunger: Ireland 1845–1849*. Originally published in 1962. New York: Penguin, 1991, reprinted.

Yancey, William A., Eugene P. Eriksen, and Richard N. Juliani. "Emergent Ethnicity: A Review and Reformulation." *American Sociological Review* 41 (June 1976): 391–403.

Index

White Indians of Greene Plantation *see* Greene Plantation
White, James P. 187
White, John W. 175
White, Robert 127
White, William: 43, 123; *A History of Belfast with Introductory Remarks on Acadia* 126, 128; Irishman 53
Whittier, Benjamin 149
Whittier, Thomas 145, 153
Whittier, Waitstill Bishop 145; gardening 153
Whittier's Tavern 103, 145
Williams College 86, 158
Williamson, Ada Hortense Peirce 182
Williamson, George 69
Williamson, Joseph, Jr.: Belfast historian 22, 62, 59, 86, 101, 187; on Civil War 174; on Crosby 39; disposition of children 182; on Herman Abbot 124; on Joseph Dolliff 103; photo of 23; on Revolutionary War loyalty oaths 128
Williamson, William 62
Wilson, John 39–42, 193; attempt to undo embargo 103; language use of 42, 47

Windham *see* New Hampshire
Wittke, Carl 5
women: Belfast gender norms 28, 145; boarders/boarding houses 30, 178; in business 24; child birth 162; clothing manufacture 101, 145, 146, 150–151, 153, 147, 178, 184; domestic service 12, 153; family economics 12; food preparation 153, 154, 157; in Ireland 12, 148; Irish immigrants 12, 145; keeping house 185; laundry 30, 163; omission from histories 23; othered 90; sphere 28; suffrage 88; teachers 159, 184; U.S. census records 178; urban 144, 149, 185; victims of violence 21, 23, 25–26; work 90, 145, 148, 149–150, 153, 178, 184
Wood, Abiel 38
Woodmason, Charles 80
Woodward, Moses 84
Worchester *see* Massachusetts

Yankee 16
Young Irelanders 6, 12